FROM THE PAGES OF PROJECT SUPERPOWERS:

the OWL®

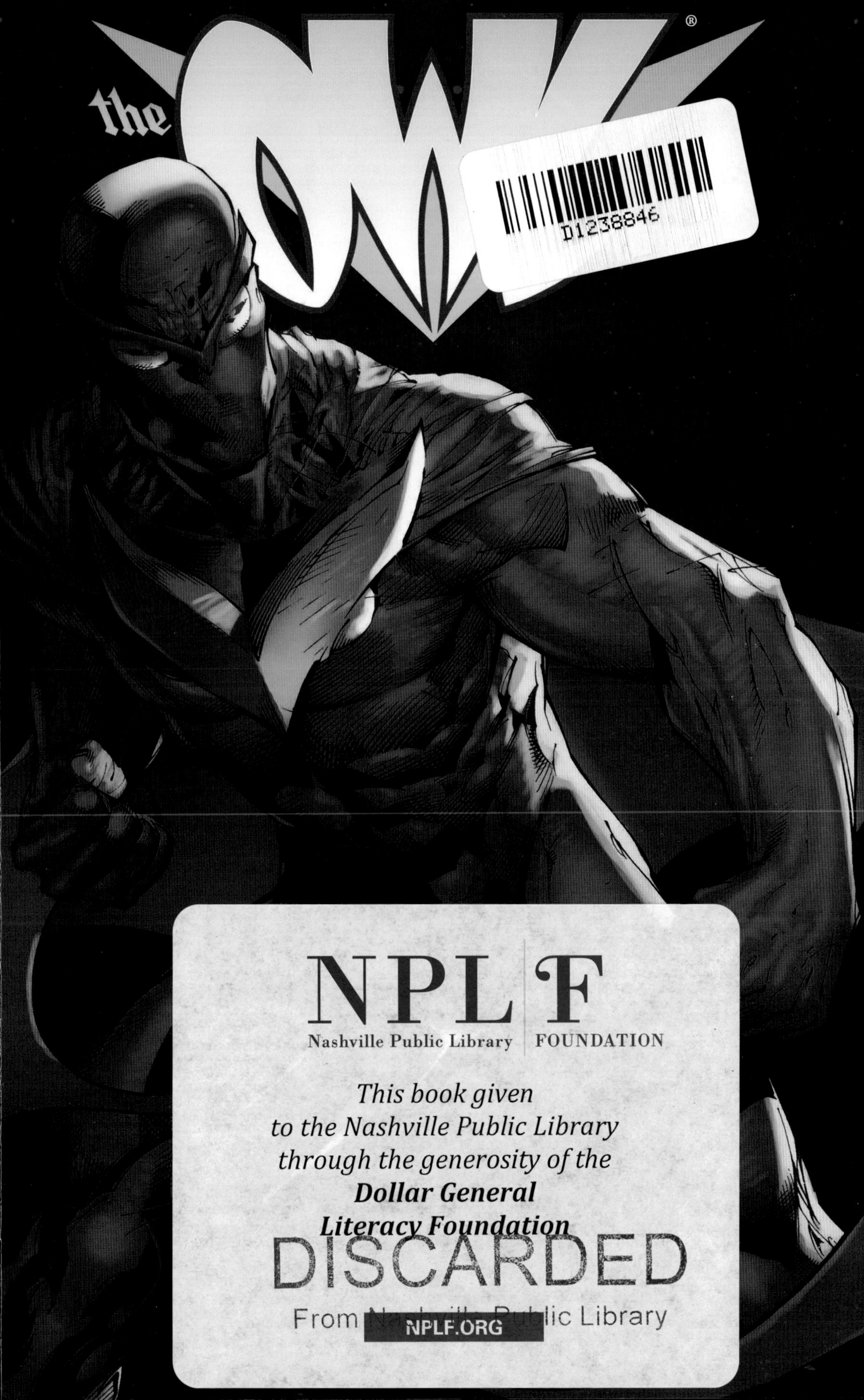

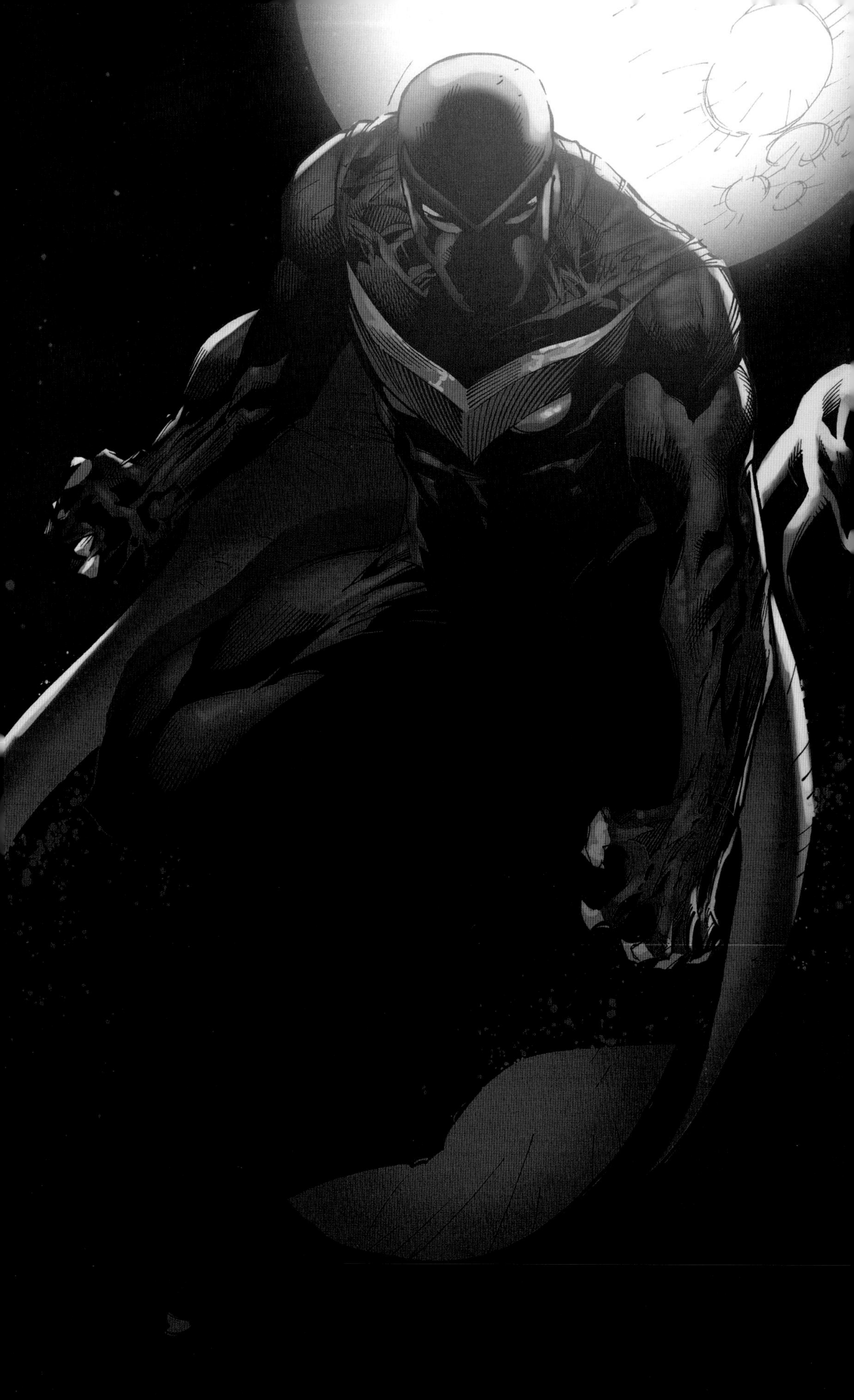

FROM THE PAGES OF PROJECT SUPERPOWERS:

WRITTEN BY
J. T. KRULL

ILLUSTRATED BY
HEUBERT KHAN MICHAEL

COLORED BY
VINICIUS ANDRADE

LETTERED BY
MARSHALL DILLON

COLLECTION COVER BY
ALEX ROSS

COLLECTION DESIGN BY
BILL TORTOLINI

This volume collections issues 1-4 of
The Owl from Dynamite Entertainment.

DYNAMITE f o t y You Tube

Online at www.DYNAMITE.com | On Facebook /Dynamitecomics
On Instagram @Dynamitecomics | On Tumblr dynamitecomics.tumblr.com
On Twitter @dynamitecomics | On YouTube /Dynamitecomics

ISBN13: 978-1-5241-0238-8   First printing 10 9 8 7 6 5 4 3 2 1   Printed in China

For information regarding press, media rights, foreign rights, licensing, promotions, and advertising e-mail:
marketing@dynamite.com

Nick Barrucci, CEO / Publisher
Juan Collado, President / COO

Joe Rybandt, Executive Editor
Matt Idelson, Senior Editor
Anthony Marques, Assistant Editor
Kevin Ketner, Editorial Assistant

Jason Ullmeyer, Art Director
Geoff Harkins, Senior Graphic Designer
Cathleen Heard, Graphic Designer
Alexis Persson, Production Artist

Chris Caniano, Digital Associate
Rachel Kilbury, Digital Assistant

Brandon Dante Primavera, V.P. of IT and Operations
Rich Young, Director of Business Development

Alan Payne, V.P. of Sales and Marketing
Keith Davidsen, Marketing Director
Pat O'Connell, Sales Manager

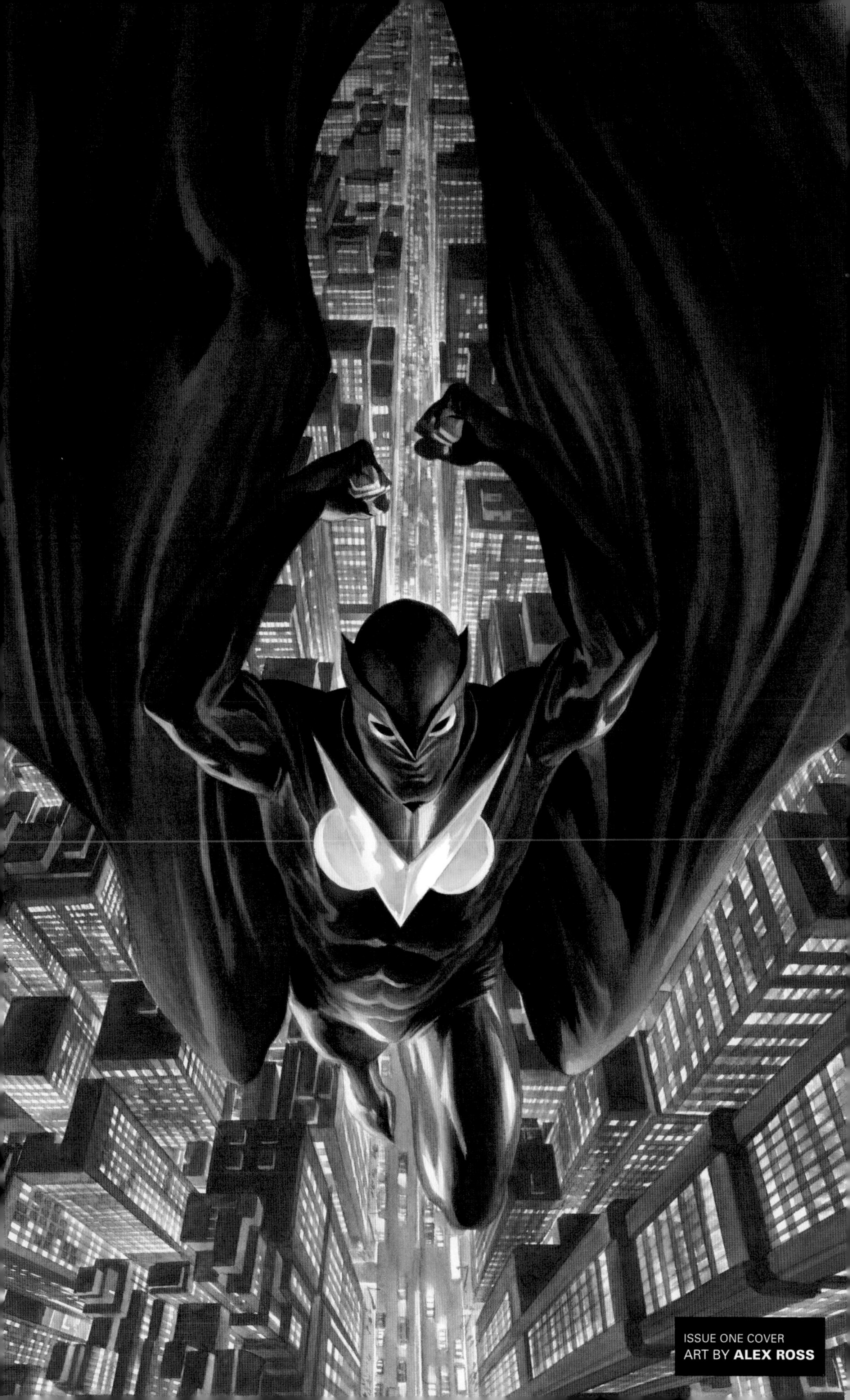

ISSUE ONE COVER
ART BY **ALEX ROSS**

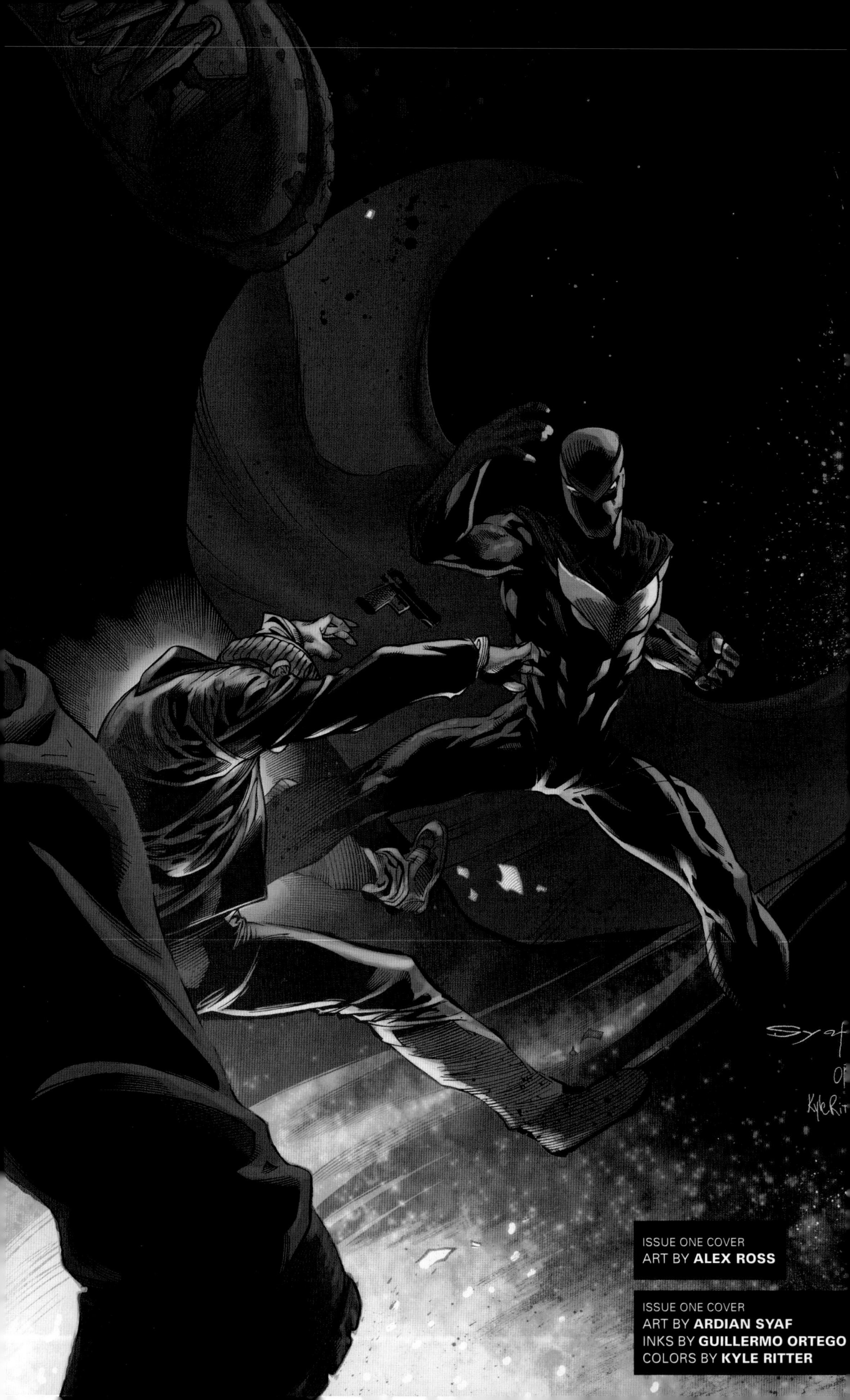

ISSUE ONE COVER
ART BY **ALEX ROSS**

ISSUE ONE COVER
ART BY **ARDIAN SYAF**
INKS BY **GUILLERMO ORTEGO**
COLORS BY **KYLE RITTER**

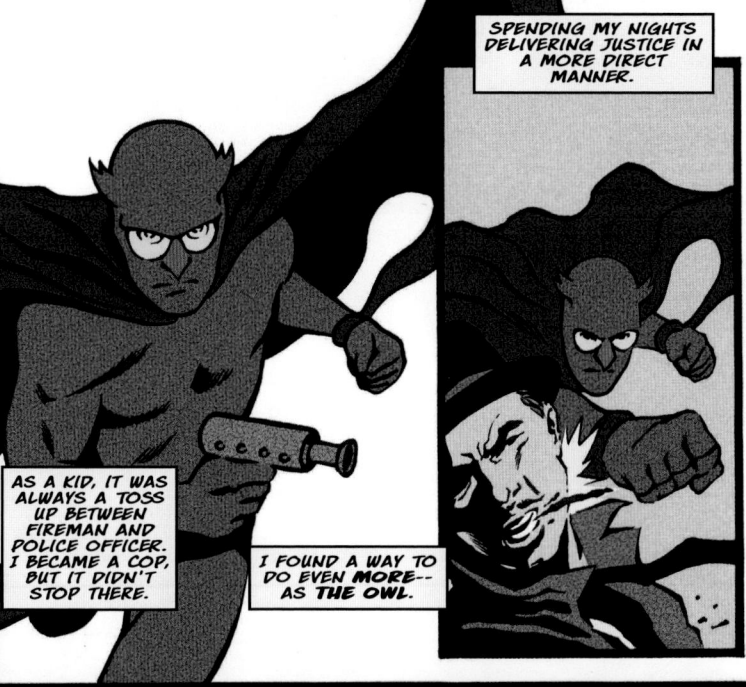

SPENDING MY NIGHTS DELIVERING JUSTICE IN A MORE DIRECT MANNER.

I DEVELOPED A HOST OF **GADGETS** TO TIP THE SCALE IN MY **FAVOR**--LIKE MY SIGNATURE **OWL** BOMBS.

AS A KID, IT WAS ALWAYS A TOSS UP BETWEEN FIREMAN AND POLICE OFFICER. I BECAME A COP, BUT IT DIDN'T STOP THERE.

I FOUND A WAY TO DO EVEN **MORE**-- AS **THE OWL**.

AND MY ULTIMATE CALLING CARD--THE OWL ROADSTER. IT ALWAYS GOT THEIR ATTENTION.

EVENTUALLY MY GIRLFRIEND **BELLE** GOT INTO THE ACT.

TOGETHER, WE KEPT THE CITY SAFE.

TOGETHER, THE OWL AND OWL GIRL WERE **UNBEATABLE**.

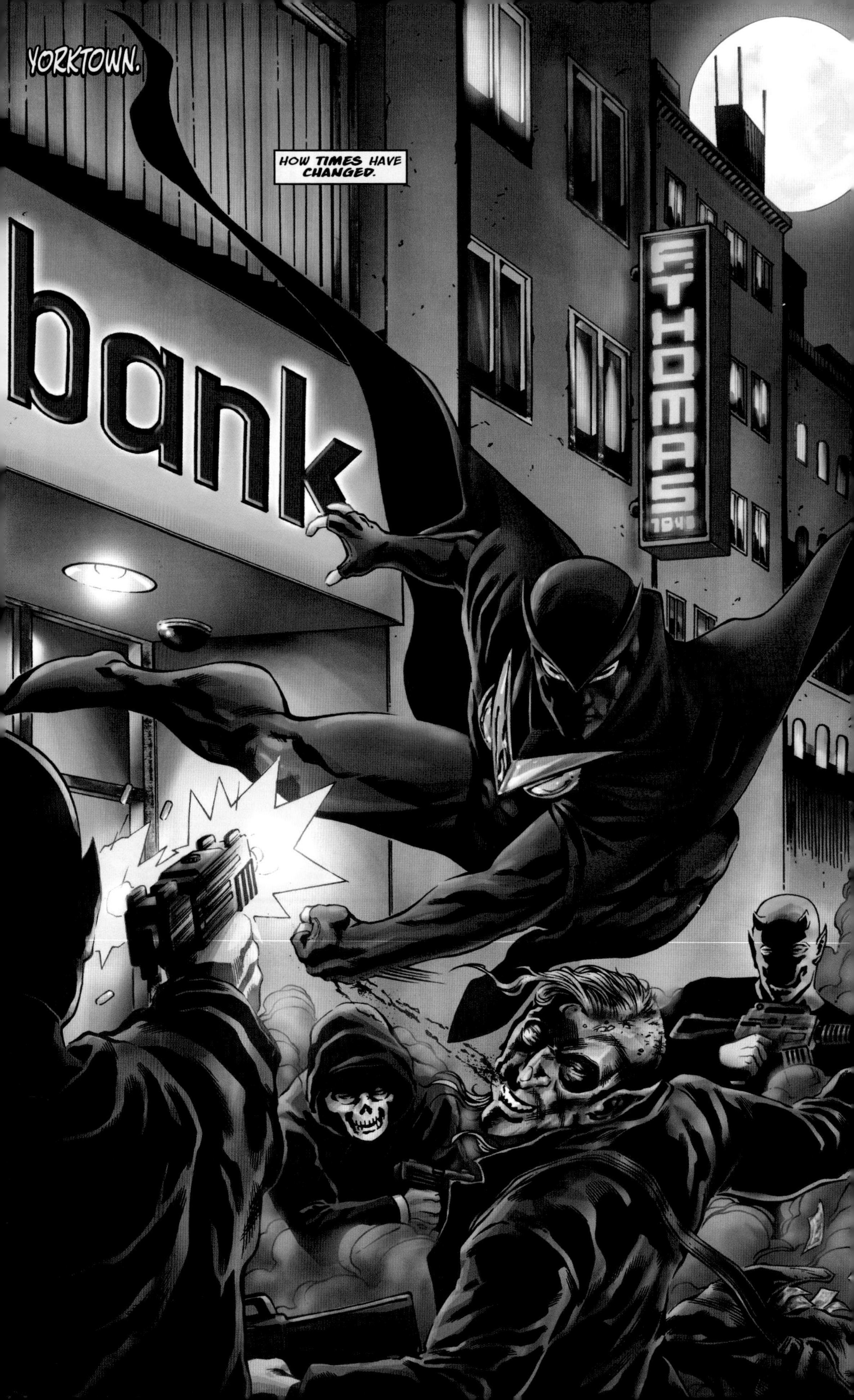
YORKTOWN.
HOW TIMES HAVE CHANGED.
bank
F. THOMAS 1941

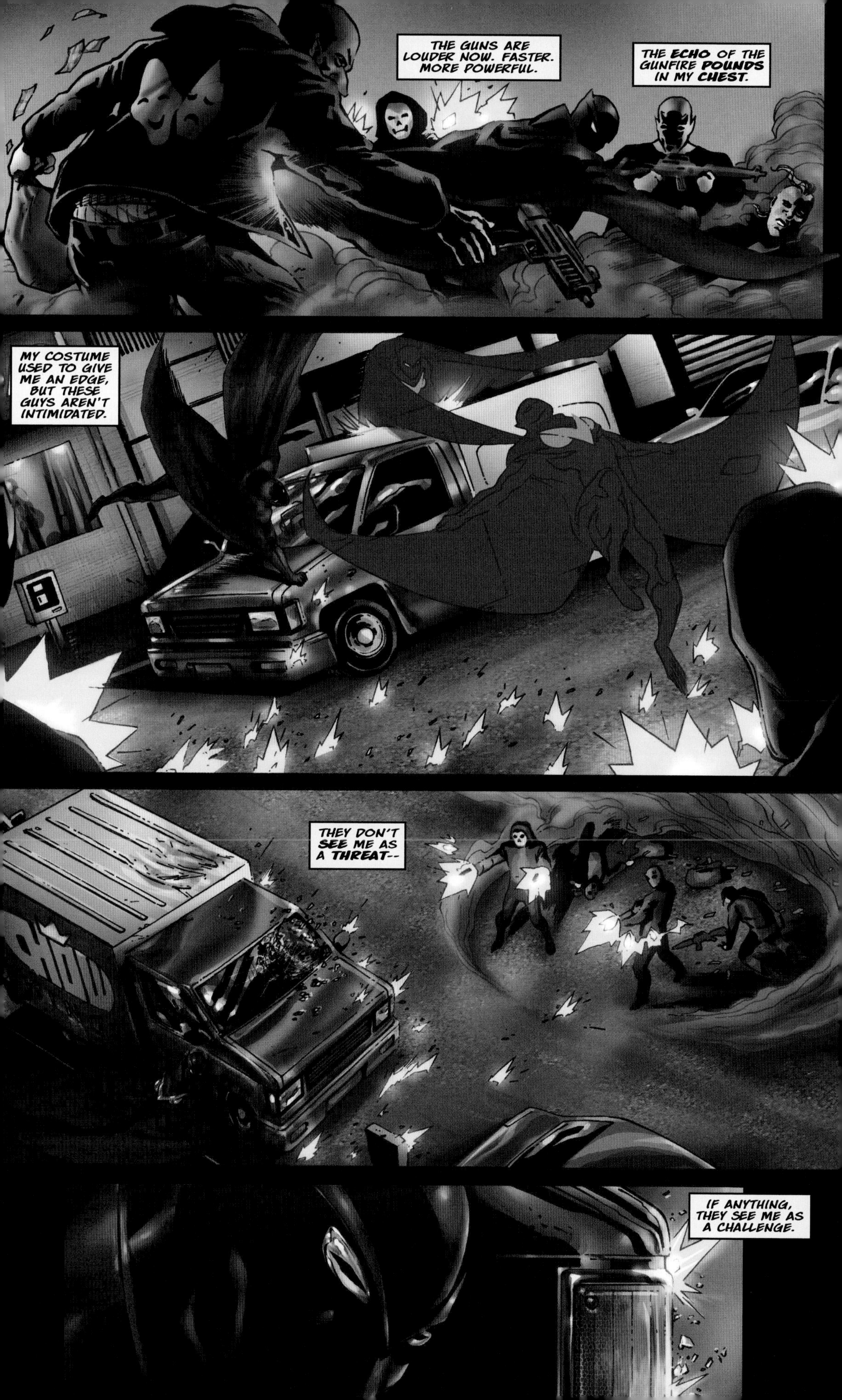
THE GUNS ARE LOUDER NOW. FASTER. MORE POWERFUL.
THE ECHO OF THE GUNFIRE POUNDS IN MY CHEST.
MY COSTUME USED TO GIVE ME AN EDGE, BUT THESE GUYS AREN'T INTIMIDATED.
THEY DON'T SEE ME AS A THREAT--
IF ANYTHING, THEY SEE ME AS A CHALLENGE.

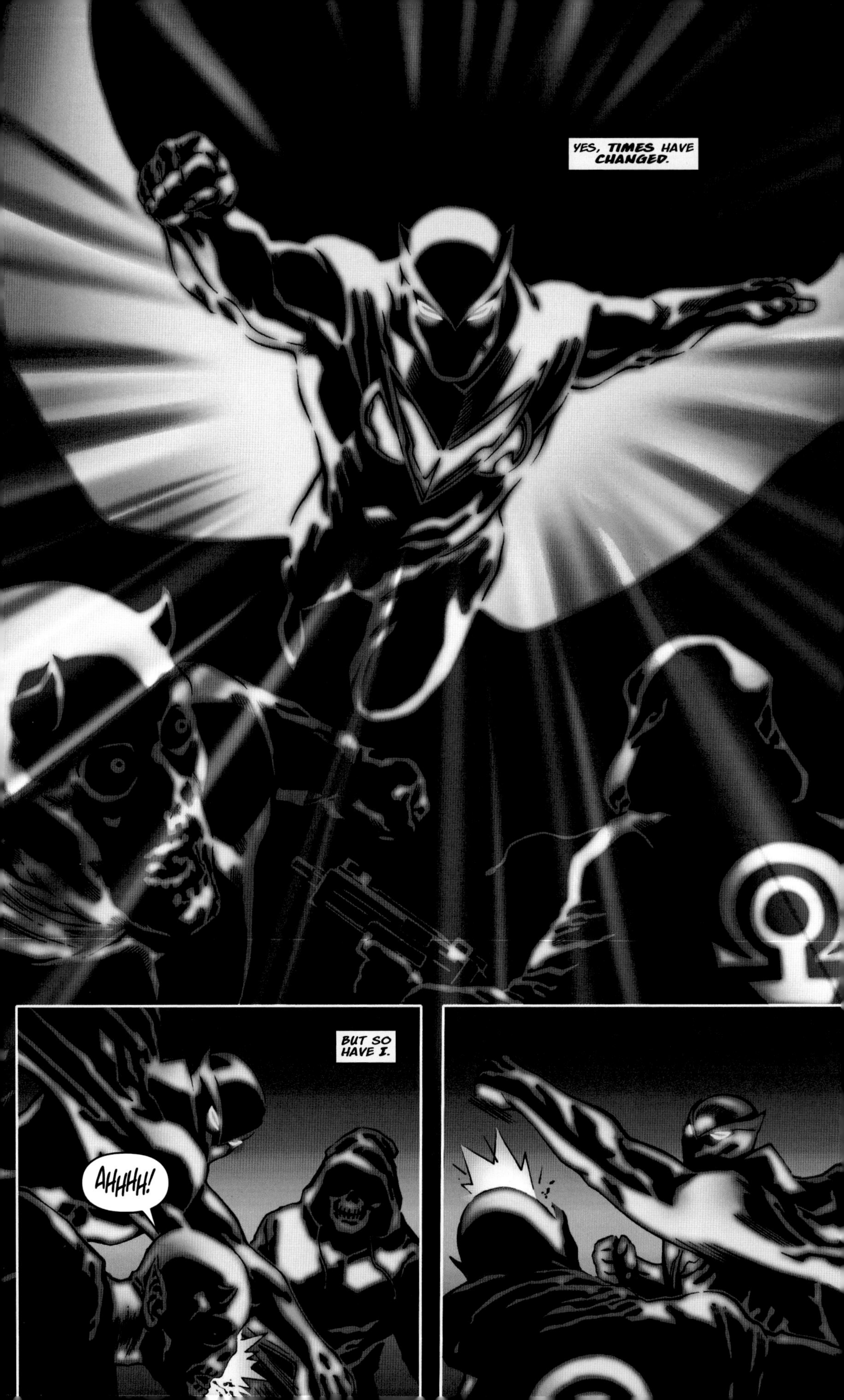
YES, TIMES HAVE CHANGED.
BUT SO HAVE I.
AHHHH!

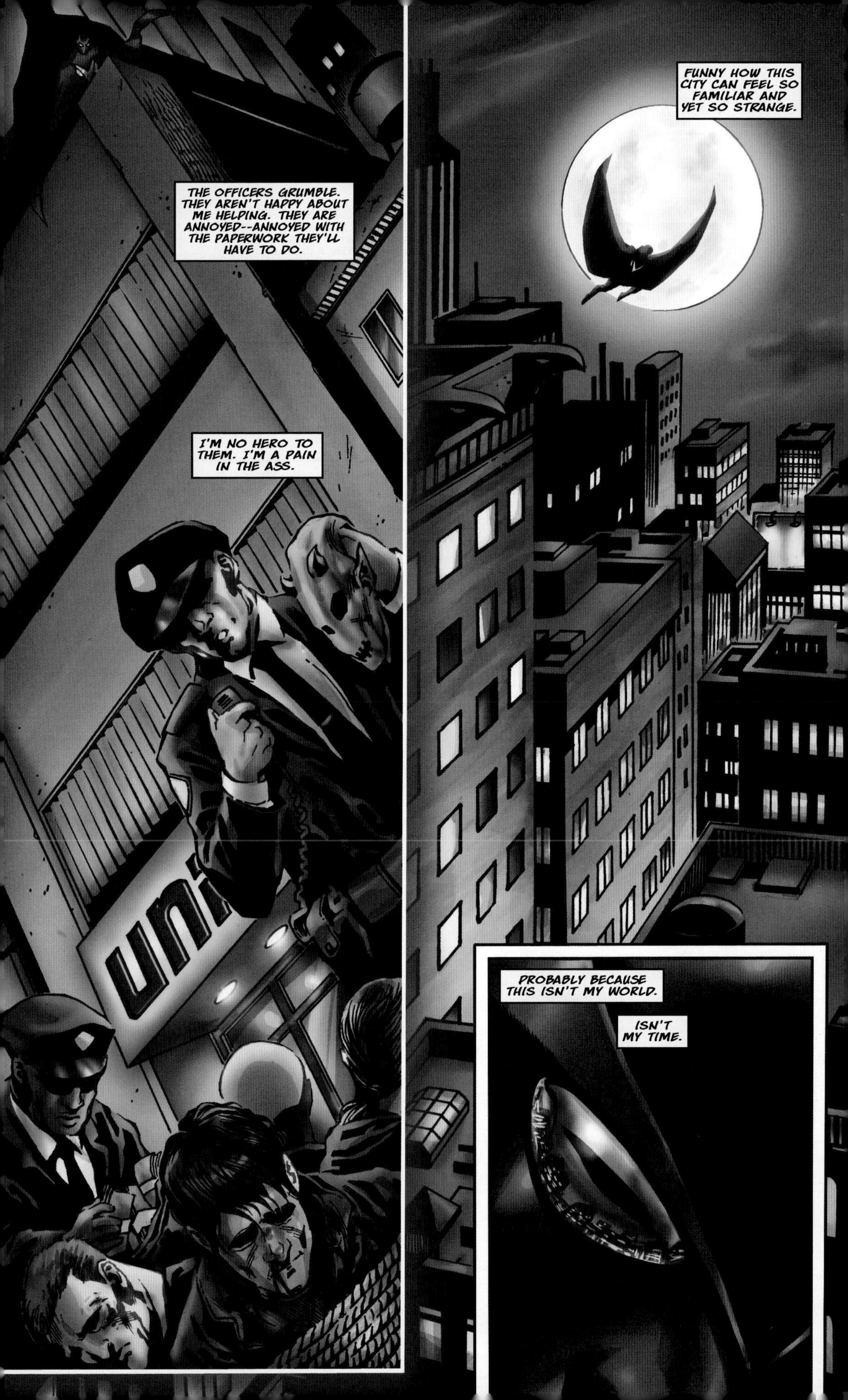
THE OFFICERS GRUMBLE. THEY AREN'T HAPPY ABOUT ME HELPING. THEY ARE ANNOYED--ANNOYED WITH THE PAPERWORK THEY'LL HAVE TO DO.
I'M NO HERO TO THEM. I'M A PAIN IN THE ASS.
FUNNY HOW THIS CITY CAN FEEL SO FAMILIAR AND YET SO STRANGE.
PROBABLY BECAUSE THIS ISN'T MY WORLD.
ISN'T MY TIME.

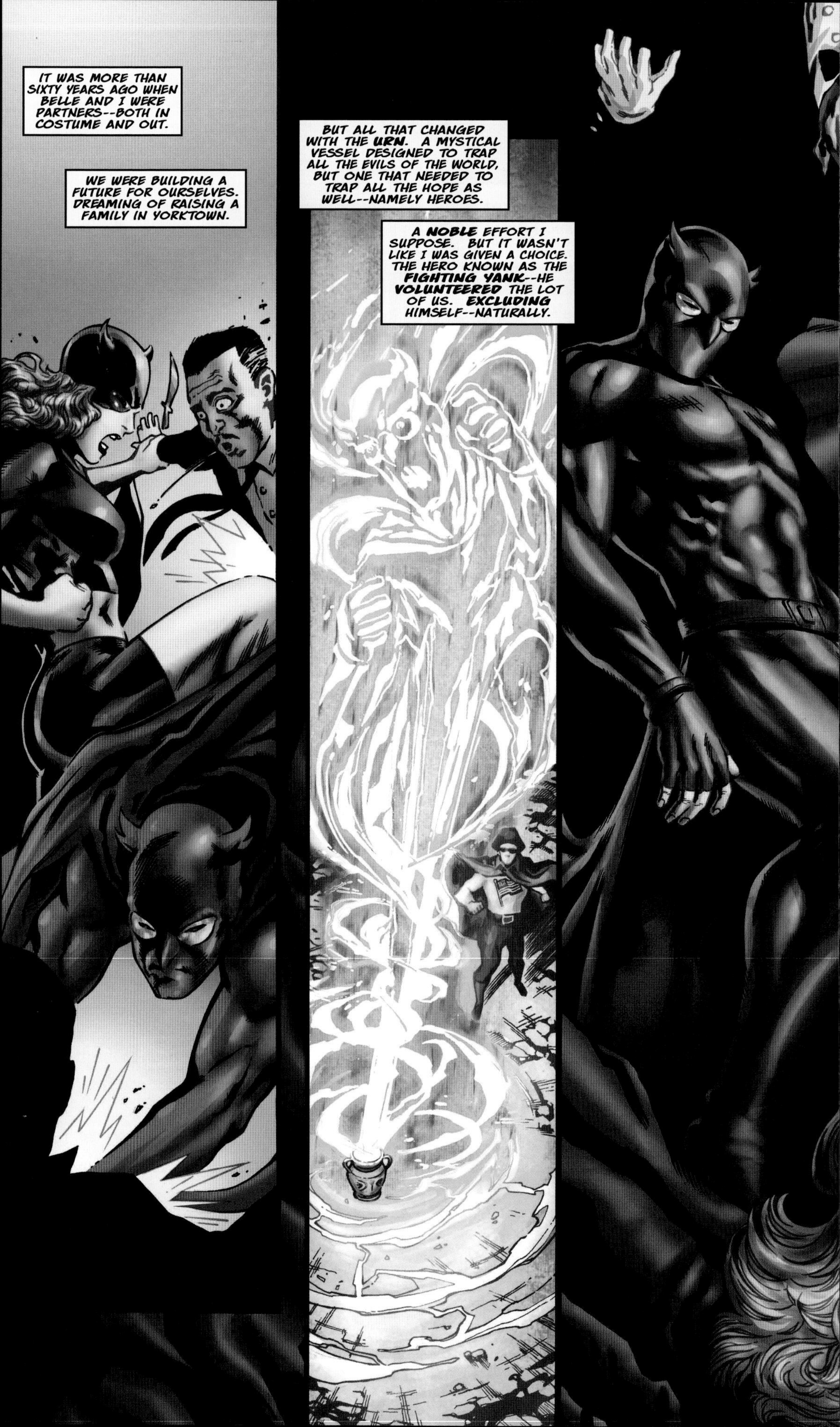
IT WAS MORE THAN SIXTY YEARS AGO WHEN BELLE AND I WERE PARTNERS--BOTH IN COSTUME AND OUT.
WE WERE BUILDING A FUTURE FOR OURSELVES. DREAMING OF RAISING A FAMILY IN YORKTOWN.
BUT ALL THAT CHANGED WITH THE URN. A MYSTICAL VESSEL DESIGNED TO TRAP ALL THE EVILS OF THE WORLD, BUT ONE THAT NEEDED TO TRAP ALL THE HOPE AS WELL--NAMELY HEROES.
A NOBLE EFFORT I SUPPOSE. BUT IT WASN'T LIKE I WAS GIVEN A CHOICE. THE HERO KNOWN AS THE FIGHTING YANK--HE VOLUNTEERED THE LOT OF US. EXCLUDING HIMSELF--NATURALLY.

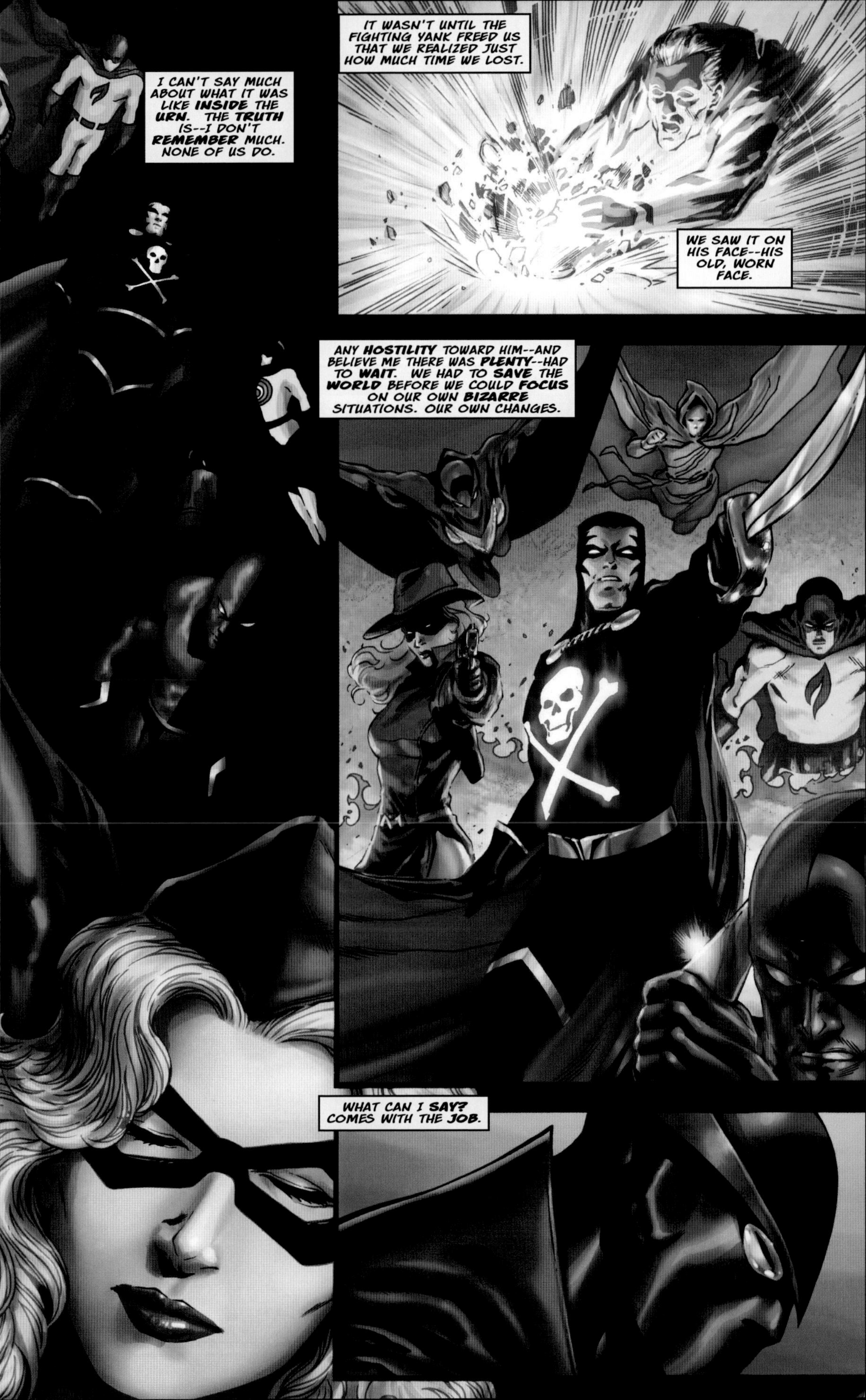
I CAN'T SAY MUCH ABOUT WHAT IT WAS LIKE INSIDE THE URN. THE TRUTH IS--I DON'T REMEMBER MUCH. NONE OF US DO.
IT WASN'T UNTIL THE FIGHTING YANK FREED US THAT WE REALIZED JUST HOW MUCH TIME WE LOST.
WE SAW IT ON HIS FACE--HIS OLD, WORN FACE.
ANY HOSTILITY TOWARD HIM--AND BELIEVE ME THERE WAS PLENTY--HAD TO WAIT. WE HAD TO SAVE THE WORLD BEFORE WE COULD FOCUS ON OUR OWN BIZARRE SITUATIONS. OUR OWN CHANGES.
WHAT CAN I SAY? COMES WITH THE JOB.

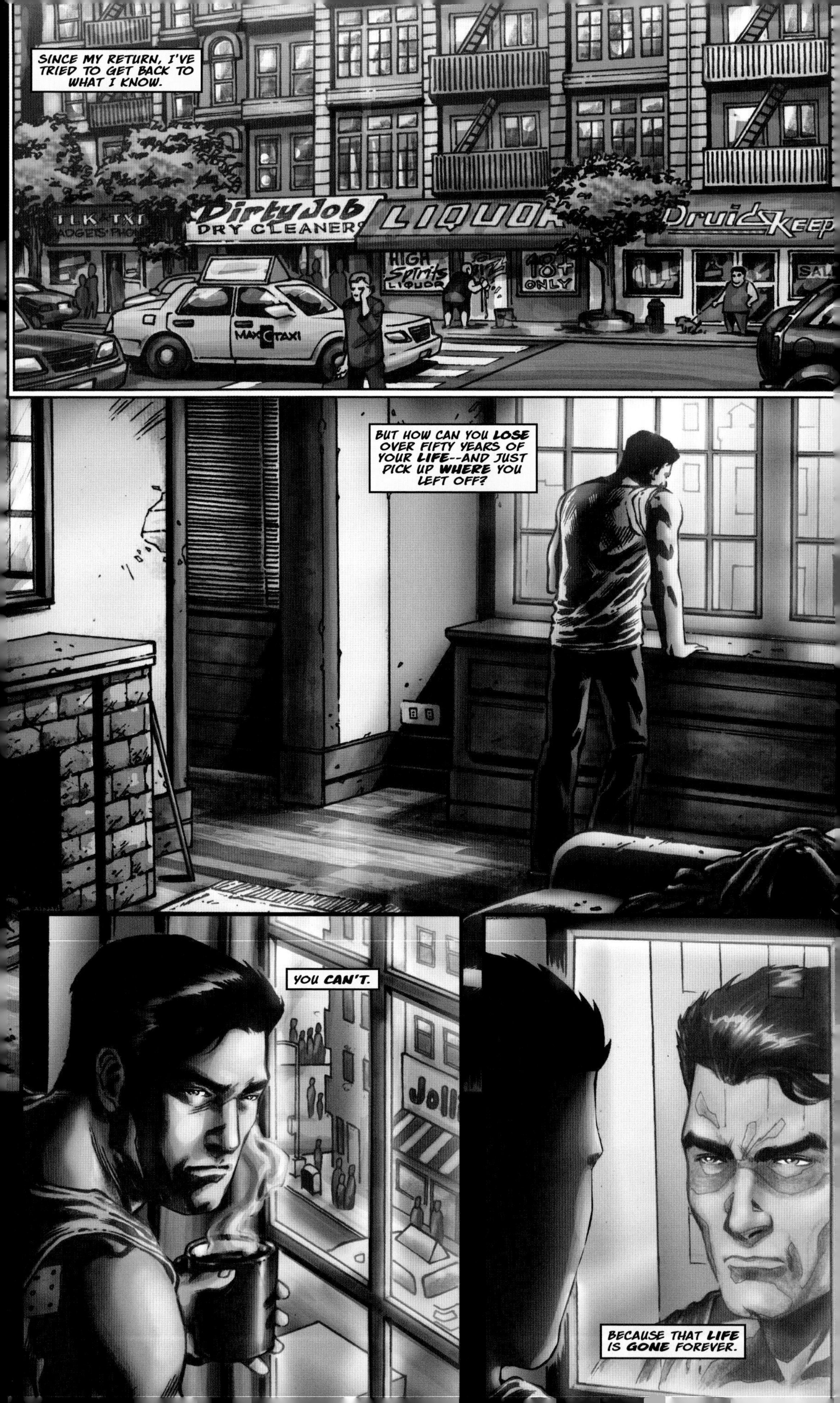
SINCE MY RETURN, I'VE TRIED TO GET BACK TO WHAT I KNOW.
Dirty Job
DRY CLEANERS
LIQUOR
Druids Keep
HIGH Spirits LIQUOR
18+ ONLY
MAX TAXI
BUT HOW CAN YOU LOSE OVER FIFTY YEARS OF YOUR LIFE--AND JUST PICK UP WHERE YOU LEFT OFF?
YOU CAN'T.
BECAUSE THAT LIFE IS GONE FOREVER.

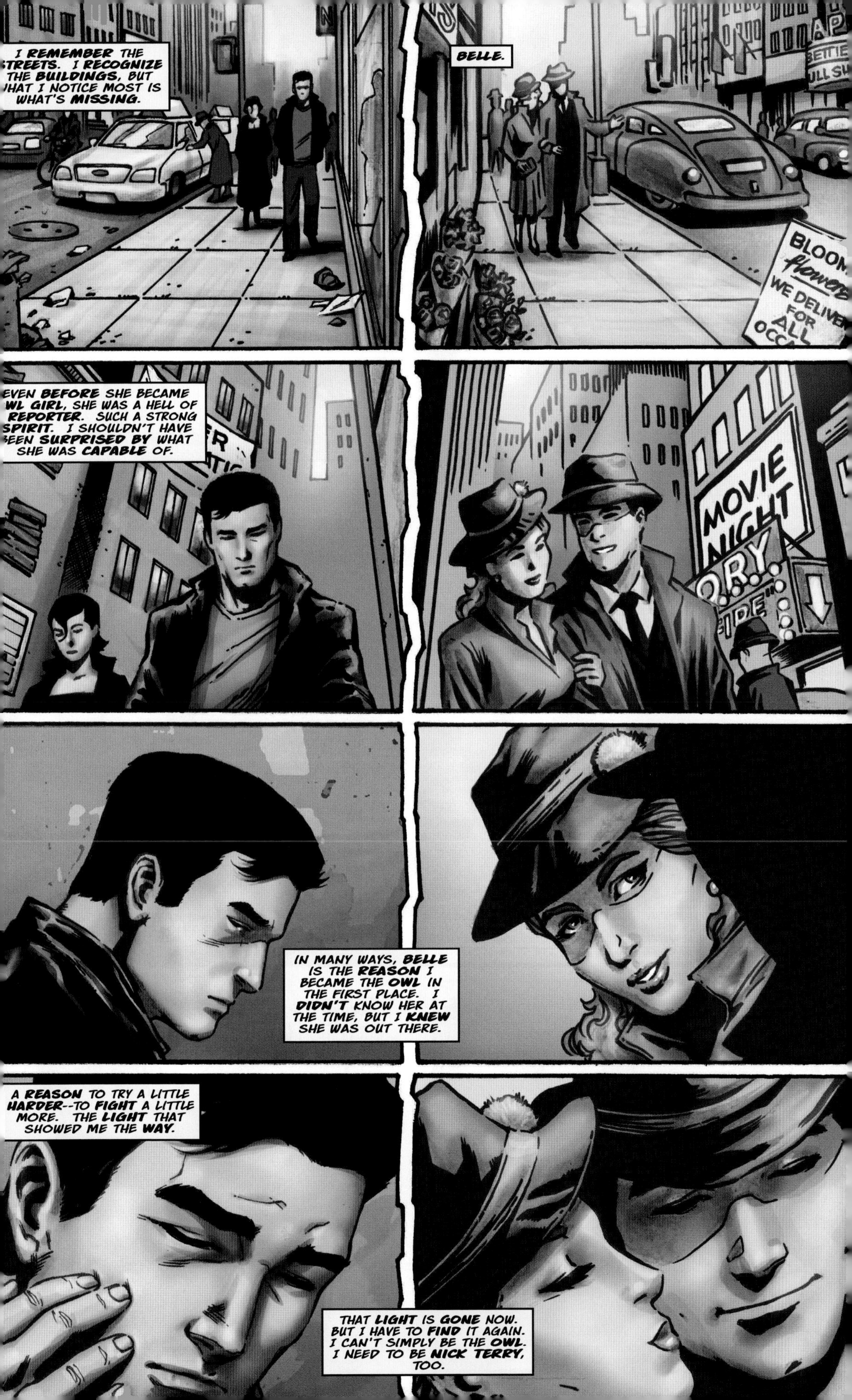
I REMEMBER THE STREETS. I RECOGNIZE THE BUILDINGS, BUT WHAT I NOTICE MOST IS WHAT'S MISSING.
BELLE.
BLOOM Flowers WE DELIVER FOR ALL OCCA
EVEN BEFORE SHE BECAME OWL GIRL, SHE WAS A HELL OF REPORTER. SUCH A STRONG SPIRIT. I SHOULDN'T HAVE BEEN SURPRISED BY WHAT SHE WAS CAPABLE OF.
MOVIE NIGHT
IN MANY WAYS, BELLE IS THE REASON I BECAME THE OWL IN THE FIRST PLACE. I DIDN'T KNOW HER AT THE TIME, BUT I KNEW SHE WAS OUT THERE.
A REASON TO TRY A LITTLE HARDER--TO FIGHT A LITTLE MORE. THE LIGHT THAT SHOWED ME THE WAY.
THAT LIGHT IS GONE NOW. BUT I HAVE TO FIND IT AGAIN. I CAN'T SIMPLY BE THE OWL. I NEED TO BE NICK TERRY, TOO.

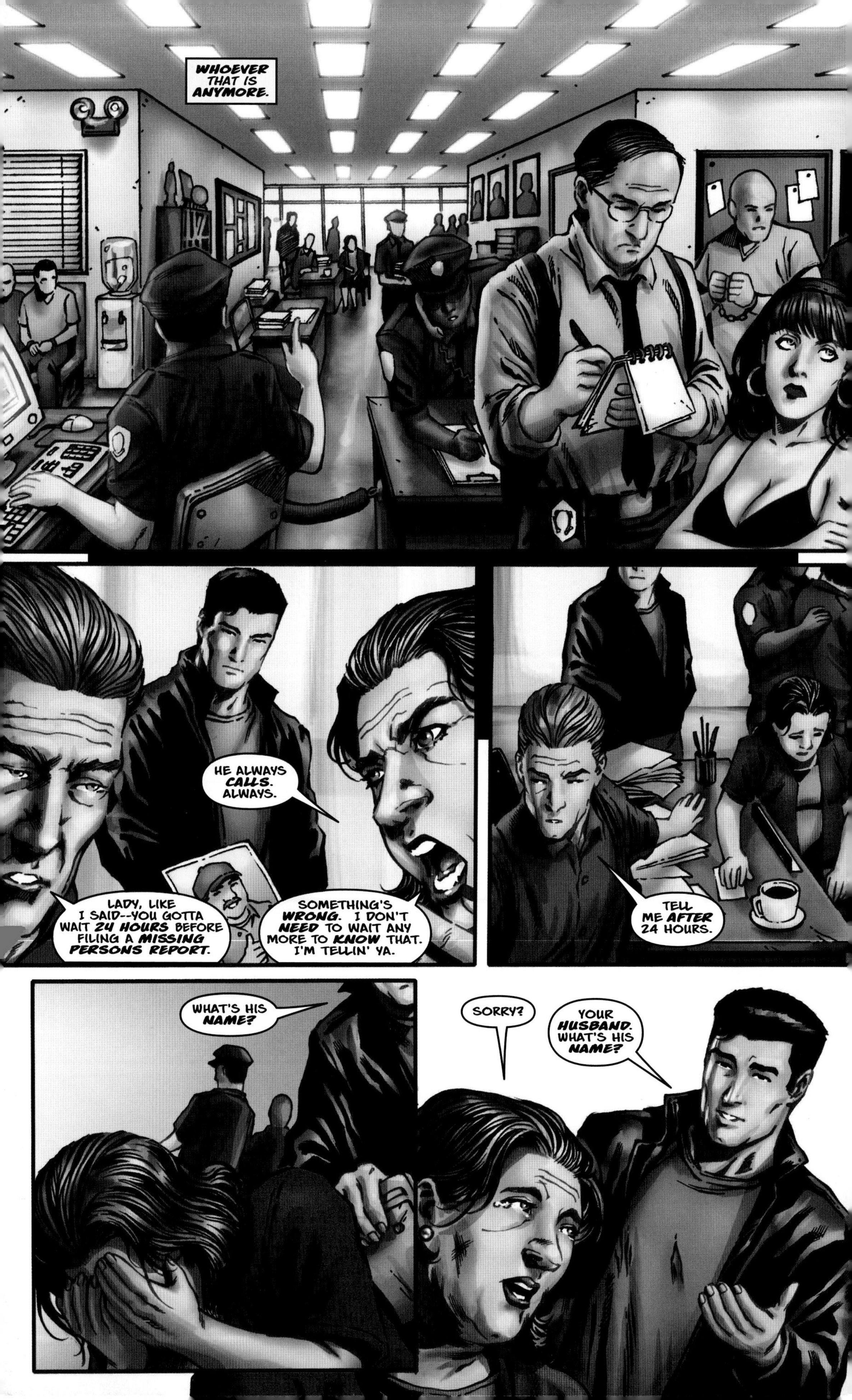
WHOEVER THAT IS ANYMORE.
HE ALWAYS CALLS. ALWAYS.
LADY, LIKE I SAID--YOU GOTTA WAIT 24 HOURS BEFORE FILING A MISSING PERSONS REPORT.
SOMETHING'S WRONG. I DON'T NEED TO WAIT ANY MORE TO KNOW THAT. I'M TELLIN' YA.
TELL ME AFTER 24 HOURS.
WHAT'S HIS NAME?
SORRY?
YOUR HUSBAND. WHAT'S HIS NAME?

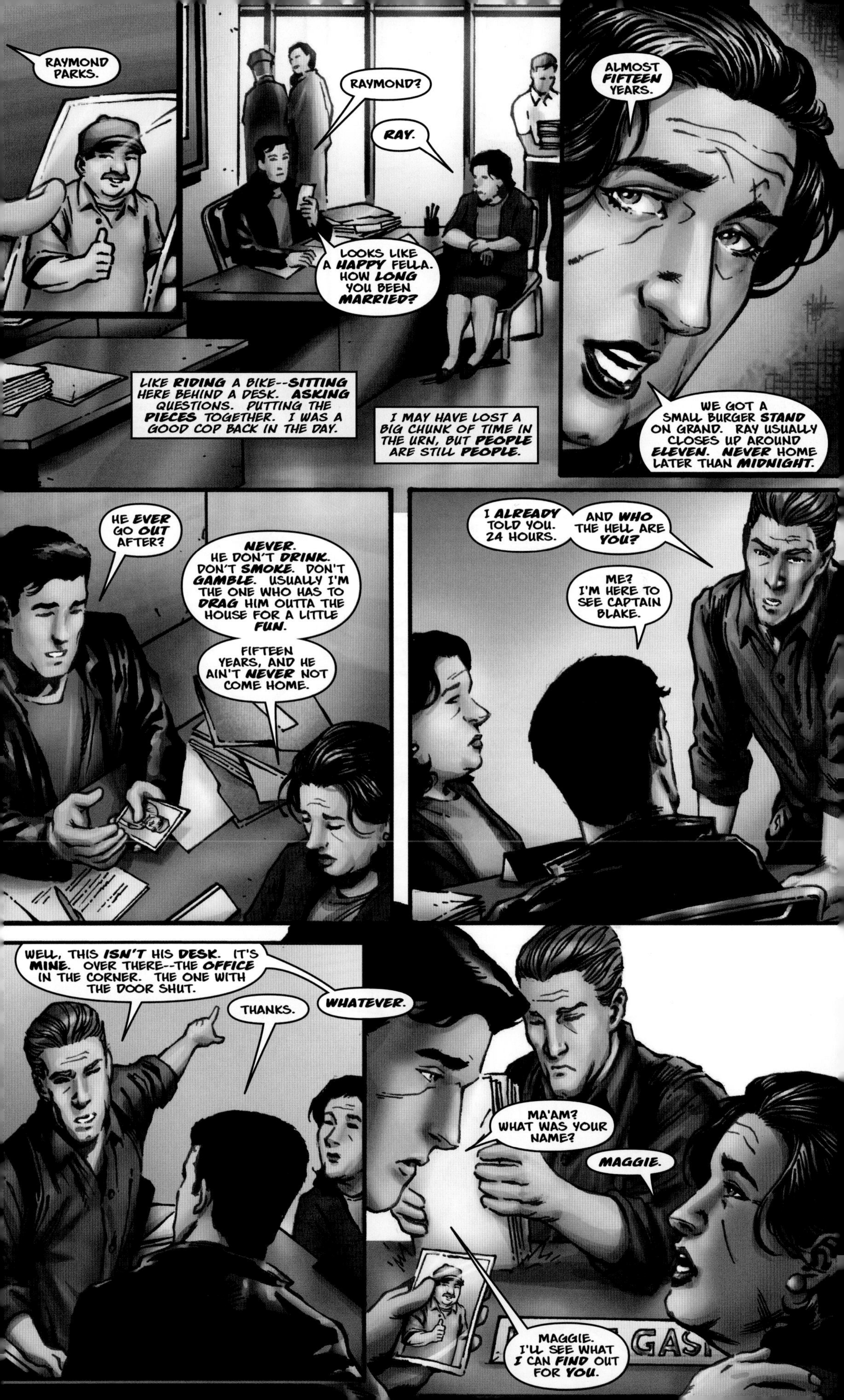
RAYMOND PARKS.
RAYMOND?
RAY.
LOOKS LIKE A HAPPY FELLA. HOW LONG YOU BEEN MARRIED?
ALMOST FIFTEEN YEARS.
LIKE RIDING A BIKE--SITTING HERE BEHIND A DESK. ASKING QUESTIONS. PUTTING THE PIECES TOGETHER. I WAS A GOOD COP BACK IN THE DAY.
I MAY HAVE LOST A BIG CHUNK OF TIME IN THE URN, BUT PEOPLE ARE STILL PEOPLE.
WE GOT A SMALL BURGER STAND ON GRAND. RAY USUALLY CLOSES UP AROUND ELEVEN. NEVER HOME LATER THAN MIDNIGHT.
HE EVER GO OUT AFTER?
NEVER. HE DON'T DRINK. DON'T SMOKE. DON'T GAMBLE. USUALLY I'M THE ONE WHO HAS TO DRAG HIM OUTTA THE HOUSE FOR A LITTLE FUN.
FIFTEEN YEARS, AND HE AIN'T NEVER NOT COME HOME.
I ALREADY TOLD YOU. 24 HOURS.
AND WHO THE HELL ARE YOU?
ME? I'M HERE TO SEE CAPTAIN BLAKE.
WELL, THIS ISN'T HIS DESK. IT'S MINE. OVER THERE--THE OFFICE IN THE CORNER. THE ONE WITH THE DOOR SHUT.
THANKS.
WHATEVER.
MA'AM? WHAT WAS YOUR NAME?
MAGGIE.
MAGGIE. I'LL SEE WHAT I CAN FIND OUT FOR YOU.
GAS

DETECTIVE TERRY, HUH?
YOU GOT IMPRESSIVE CREDENTIALS, I'LL GIVE YOU THAT.
CAPT. BLAKE
THANKS.
THEY SHOULD BE. I MADE THEM UP THIS MORNING.
NOW WOULD NORMALLY BE THE TIME WHERE I ASK YOU WHY YOU SOUGHT OUT OUR LITTLE CORNER OF HELL. BUT IT DON'T REALLY MATTER.
IF IT WERE IN MY POWER, I'D HIRE YOU ON THE SPOT. AND ABOUT TEN OTHER GUYS TO GO WITH YOU. EVEN THEN, WE'D STILL BE SHORT FROM WHERE WE WERE LAST YEAR.
CRAPPY ECONOMY MEANS CRAPPY BUDGET. CRAPPY BUDGET MEANS LESS COPS. ESPECIALLY DETECTIVES.
GOD FORBID WE ACTUALLY HAVE THE MANPOWER TO WORK YORKTOWN PROPER.
SOUNDS LIKE YOUR HANDS ARE TIED.
MY HANDS, MY FEET, AND MY BALLS. IN THAT ORDER.
WELL, I APPRECIATE YOU TAKING THE TIME WITH ME, CAPTAIN.
IF ANYTHING CHANGES, LET ME KNOW.
CAPT. BLAKE
BELIEVE ME, I WILL

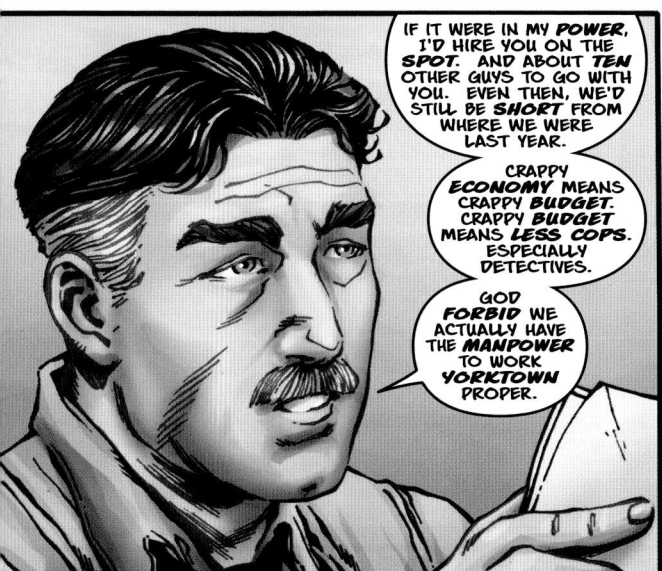

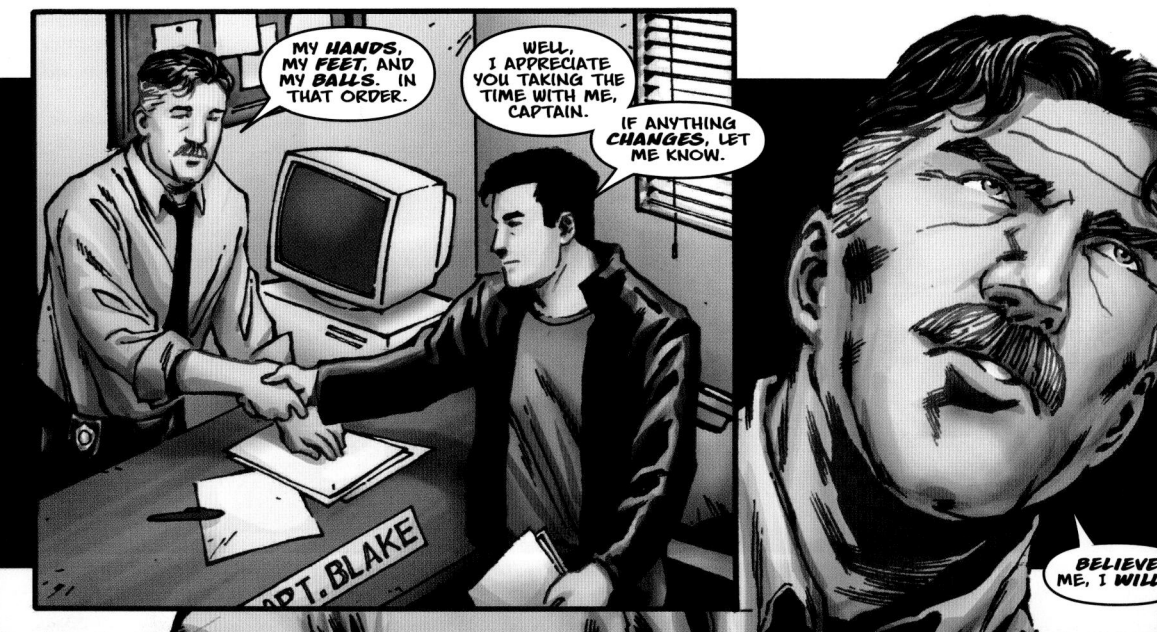

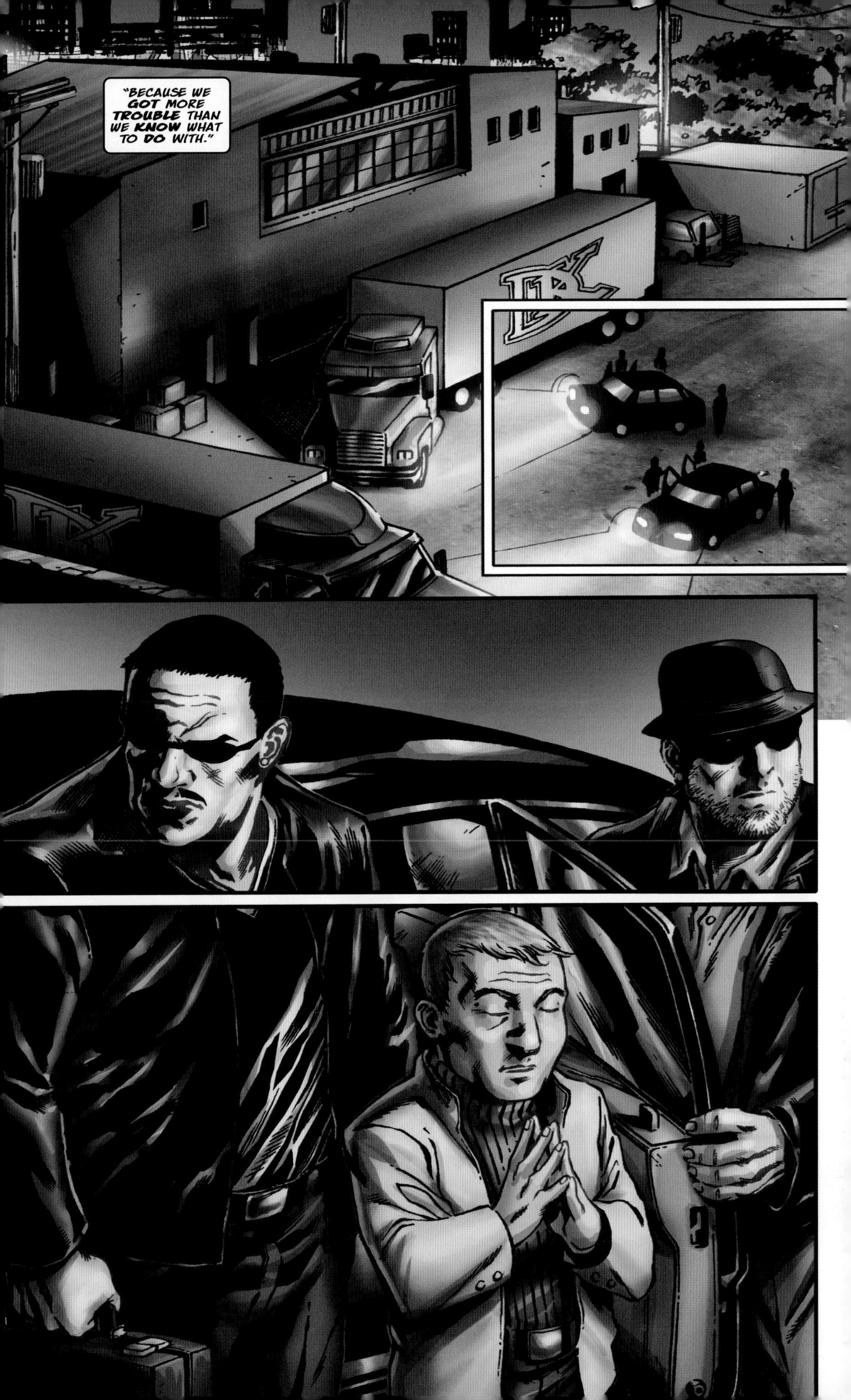
"BECAUSE WE GOT MORE TROUBLE THAN WE KNOW WHAT TO DO WITH."

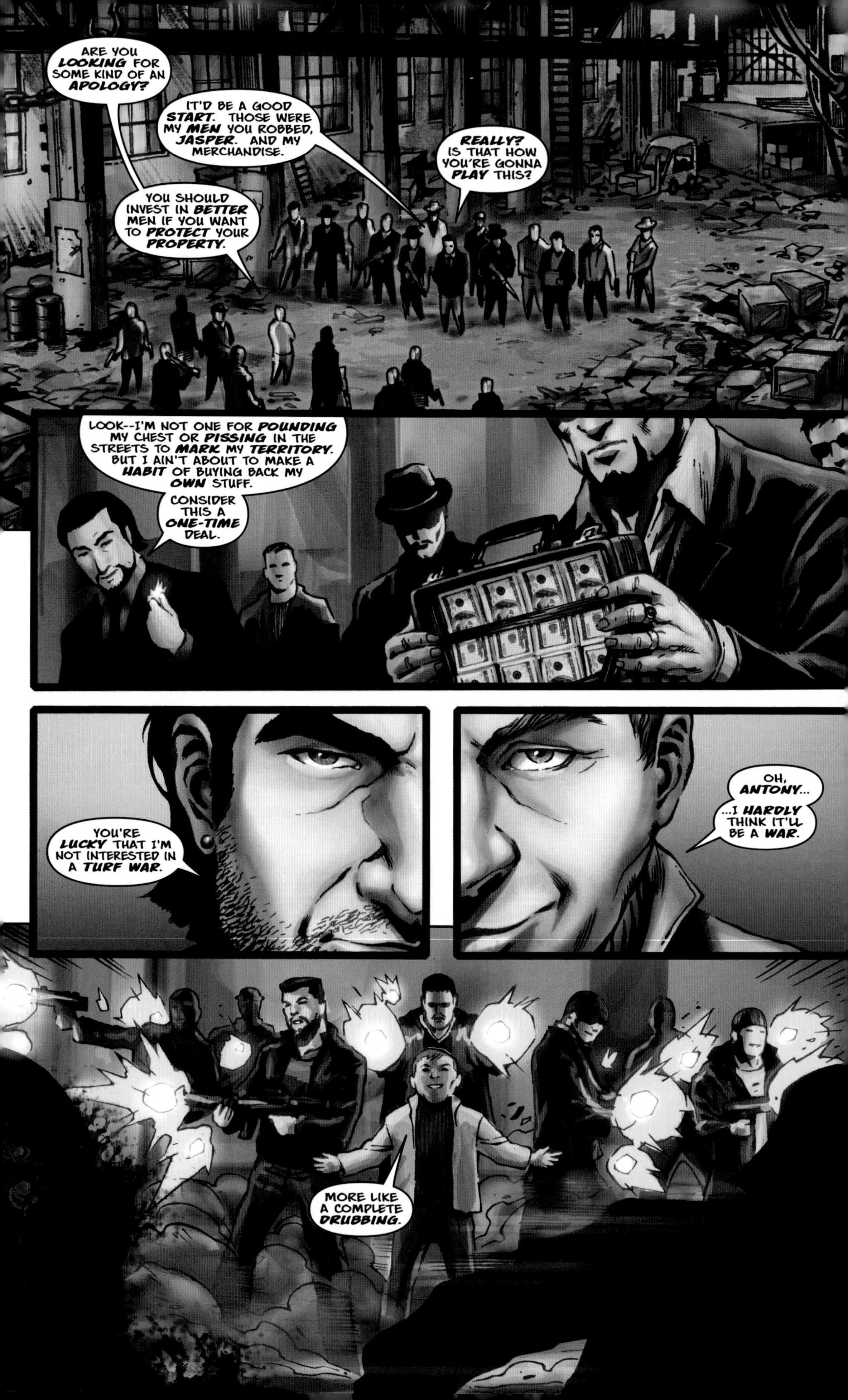
ARE YOU LOOKING FOR SOME KIND OF AN APOLOGY?
IT'D BE A GOOD START. THOSE WERE MY MEN YOU ROBBED, JASPER. AND MY MERCHANDISE.
REALLY? IS THAT HOW YOU'RE GONNA PLAY THIS?
YOU SHOULD INVEST IN BETTER MEN IF YOU WANT TO PROTECT YOUR PROPERTY.
LOOK--I'M NOT ONE FOR POUNDING MY CHEST OR PISSING IN THE STREETS TO MARK MY TERRITORY. BUT I AIN'T ABOUT TO MAKE A HABIT OF BUYING BACK MY OWN STUFF.
CONSIDER THIS A ONE-TIME DEAL.
YOU'RE LUCKY THAT I'M NOT INTERESTED IN A TURF WAR.
OH, ANTONY...
...I HARDLY THINK IT'LL BE A WAR.
MORE LIKE A COMPLETE DRUBBING.

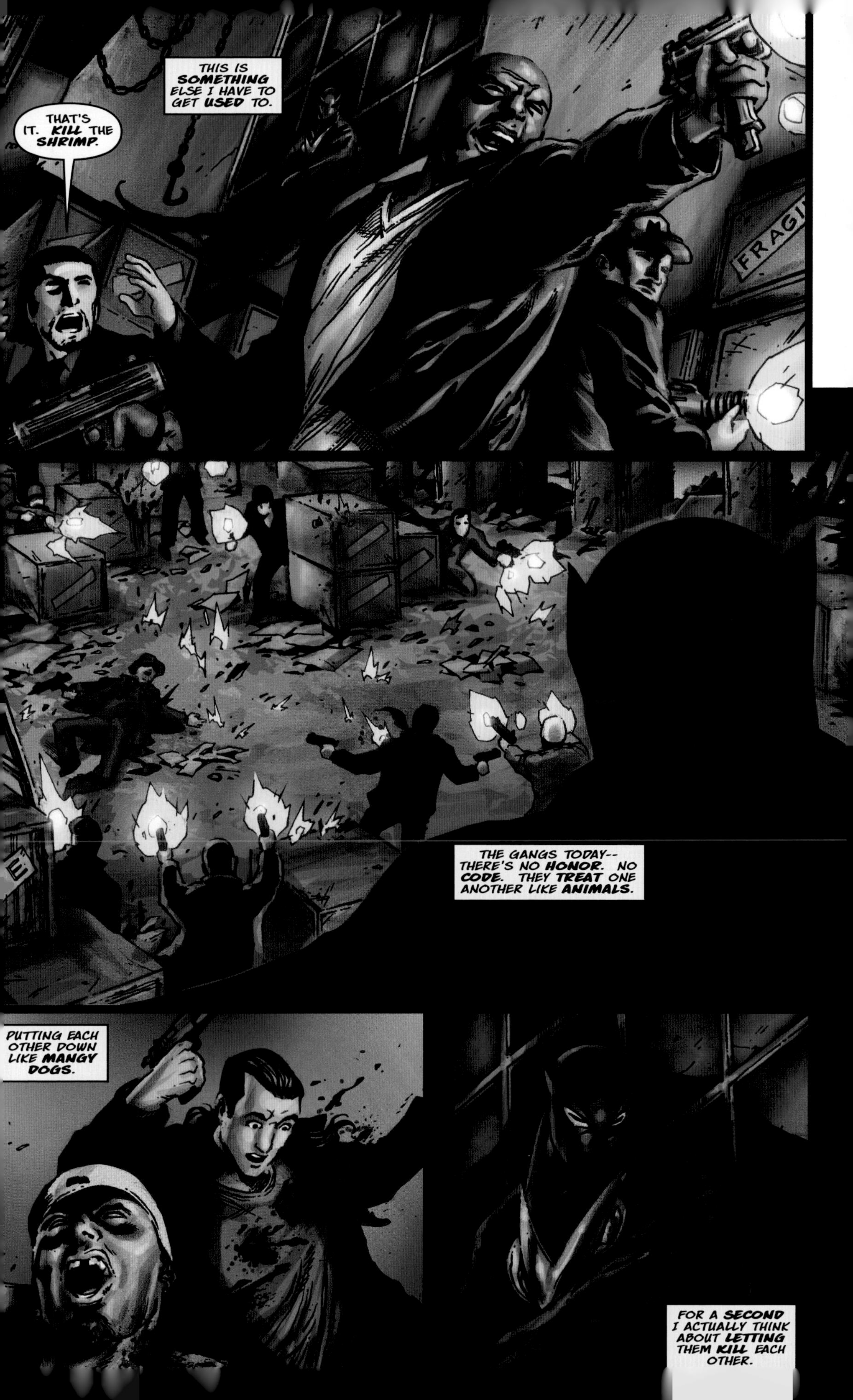
THIS IS SOMETHING ELSE I HAVE TO GET USED TO.
THAT'S IT. KILL THE SHRIMP.
FRAGI
THE GANGS TODAY-- THERE'S NO HONOR. NO CODE. THEY TREAT ONE ANOTHER LIKE ANIMALS.
PUTTING EACH OTHER DOWN LIKE MANGY DOGS.
FOR A SECOND I ACTUALLY THINK ABOUT LETTING THEM KILL EACH OTHER.

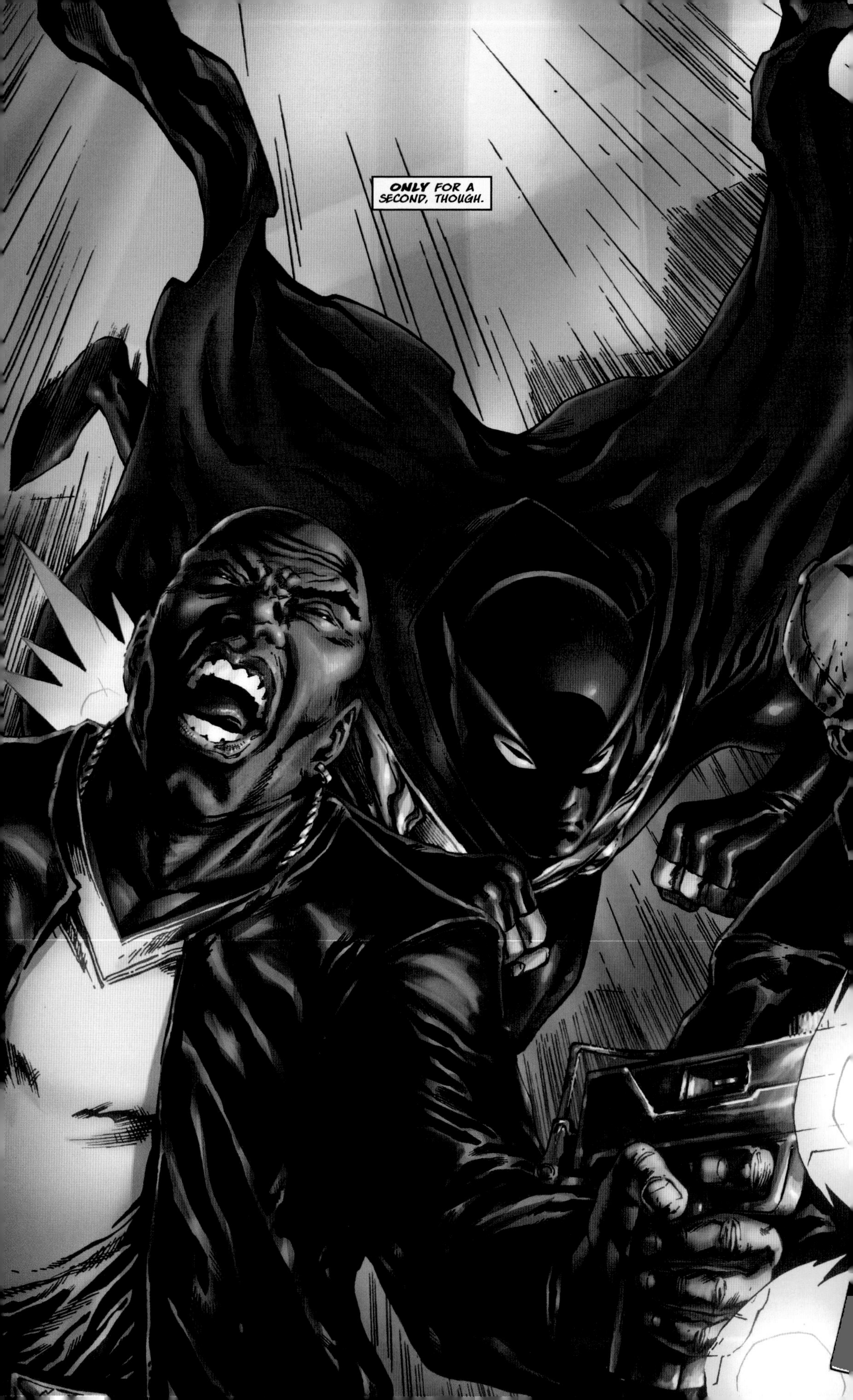
ONLY FOR A SECOND, THOUGH.

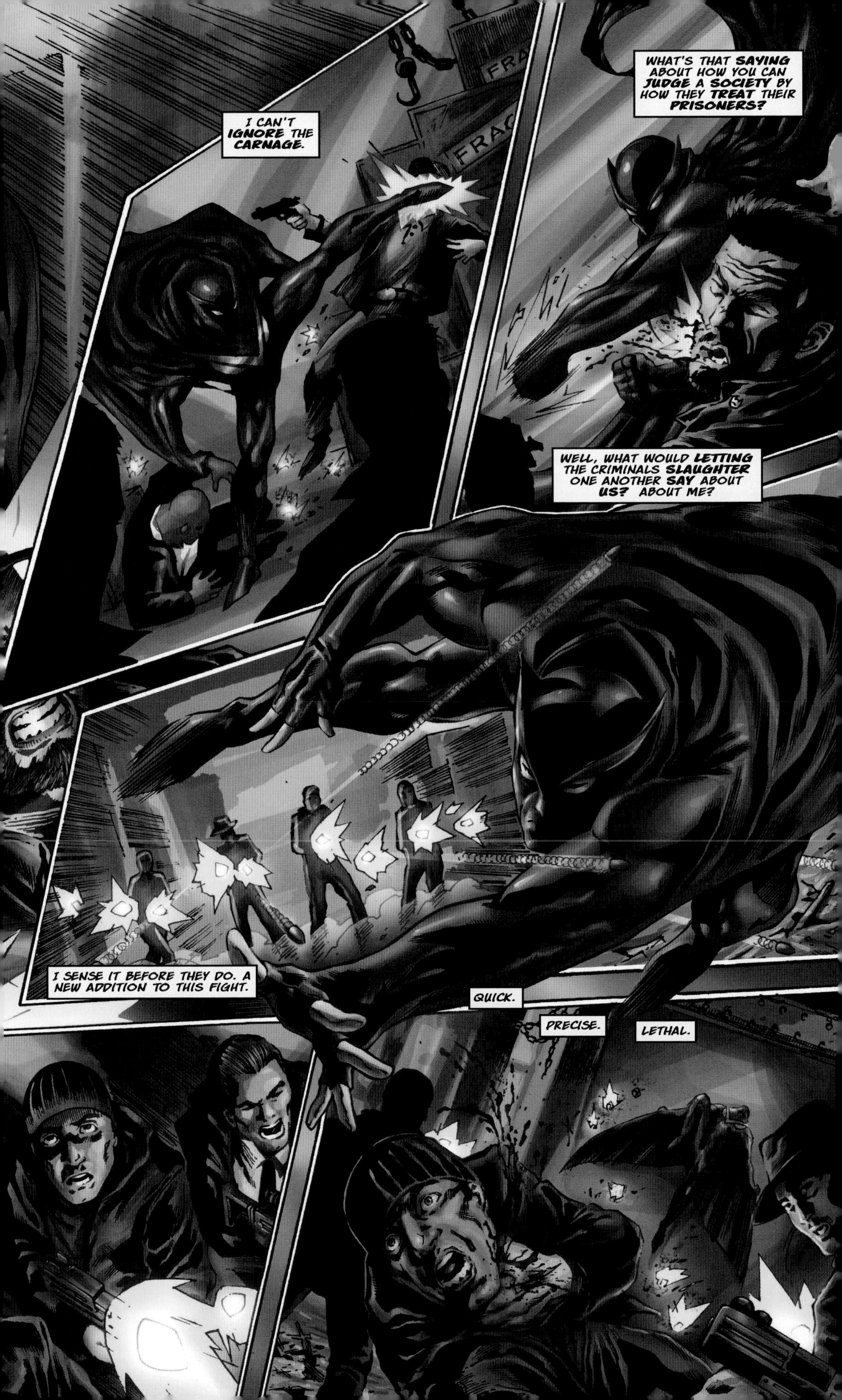
I CAN'T IGNORE THE CARNAGE.
WHAT'S THAT SAYING ABOUT HOW YOU CAN JUDGE A SOCIETY BY HOW THEY TREAT THEIR PRISONERS?
WELL, WHAT WOULD LETTING THE CRIMINALS SLAUGHTER ONE ANOTHER SAY ABOUT US? ABOUT ME?
I SENSE IT BEFORE THEY DO. A NEW ADDITION TO THIS FIGHT.
QUICK.
PRECISE.
LETHAL.

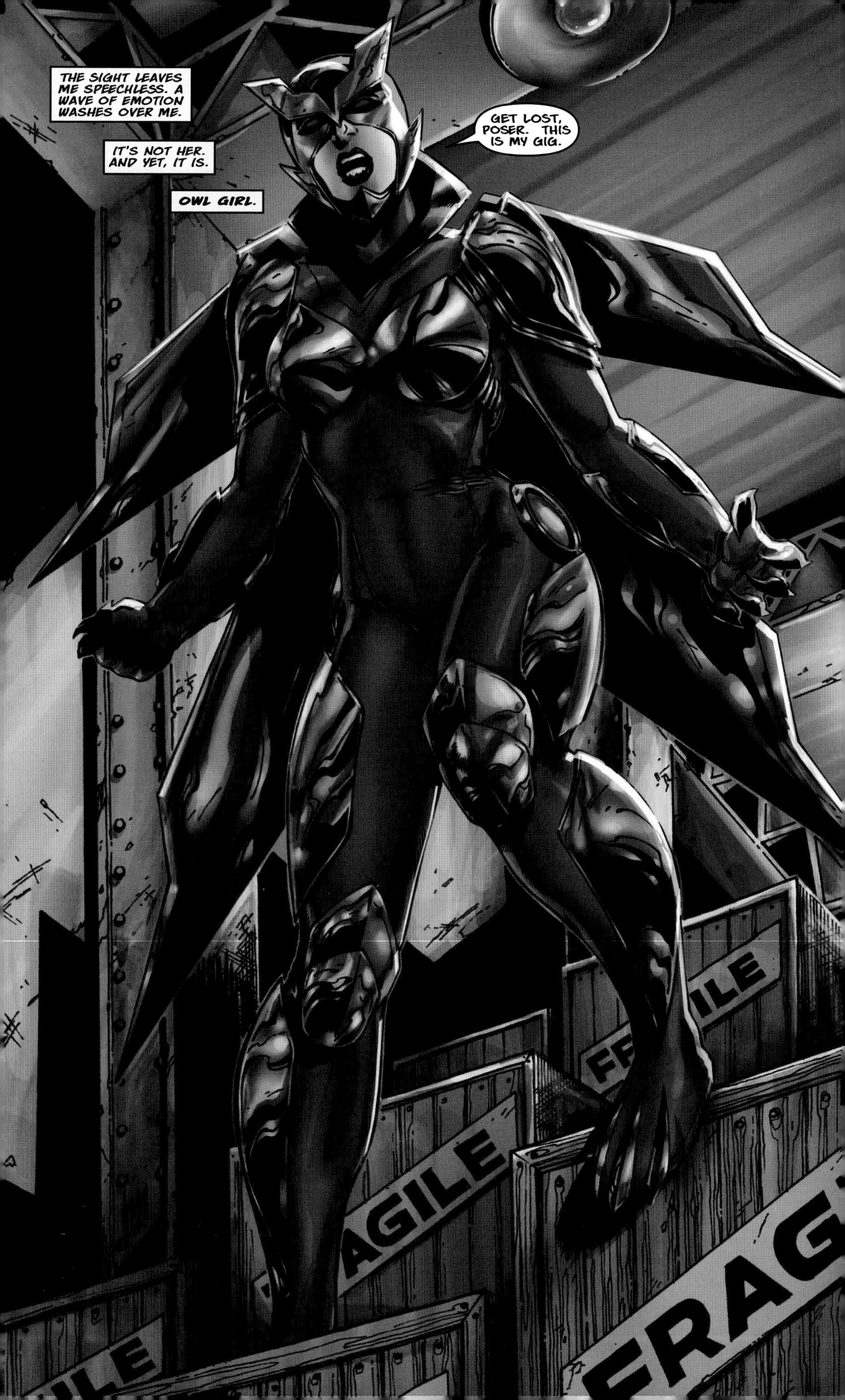
THE SIGHT LEAVES ME SPEECHLESS. A WAVE OF EMOTION WASHES OVER ME.
IT'S NOT HER. AND YET, IT IS.
OWL GIRL.
GET LOST, POSER. THIS IS MY GIG.
FRAGILE
AGILE
FRAG
ILE

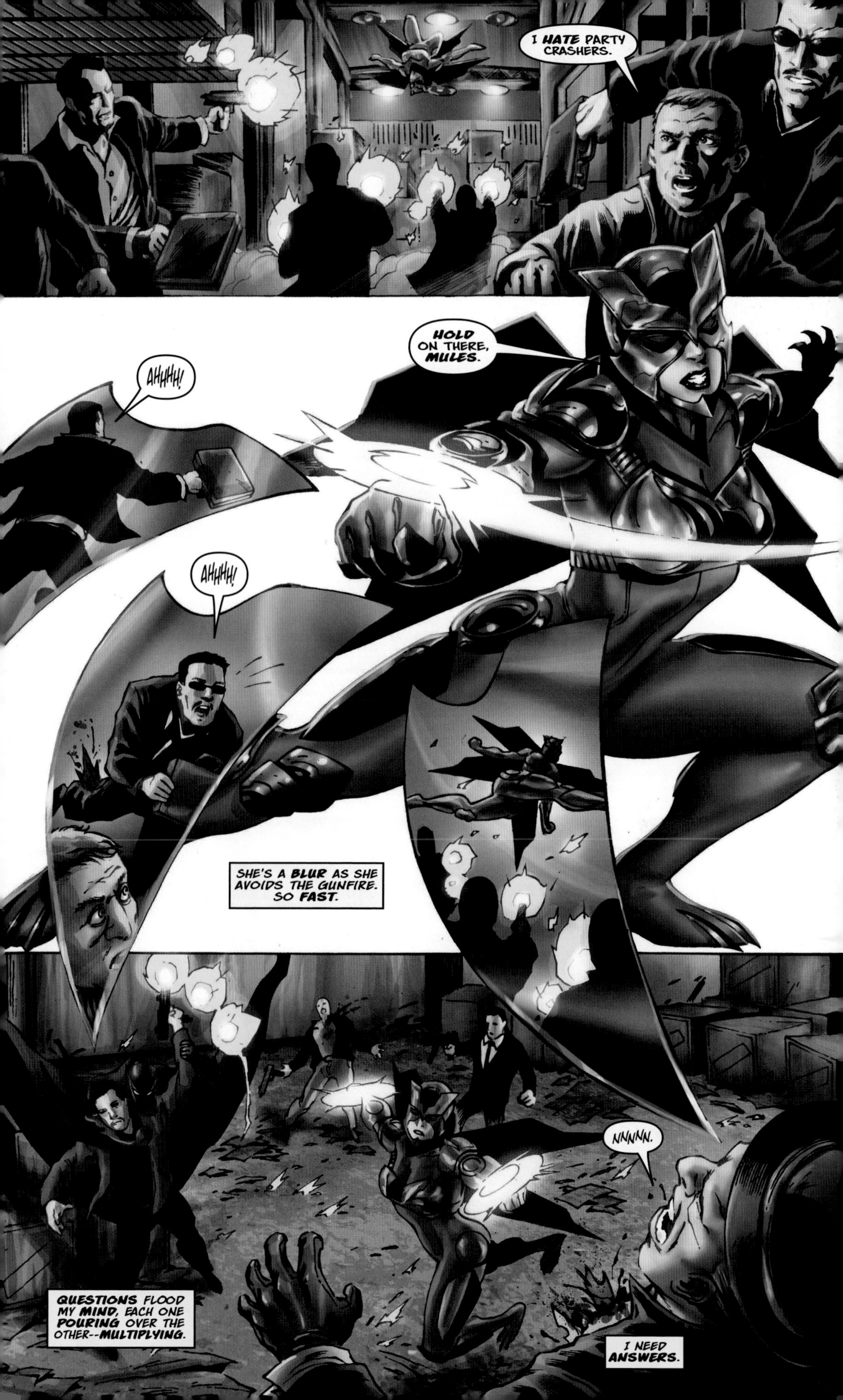

I **HATE** PARTY CRASHERS.
HOLD ON THERE, **MULES**.
AHHHH!
AHHHH!
SHE'S A **BLUR** AS SHE AVOIDS THE GUNFIRE. SO **FAST**.
NNNNN.
QUESTIONS FLOOD MY **MIND**, EACH ONE **POURING** OVER THE OTHER--**MULTIPLYING**.
I NEED **ANSWERS**.

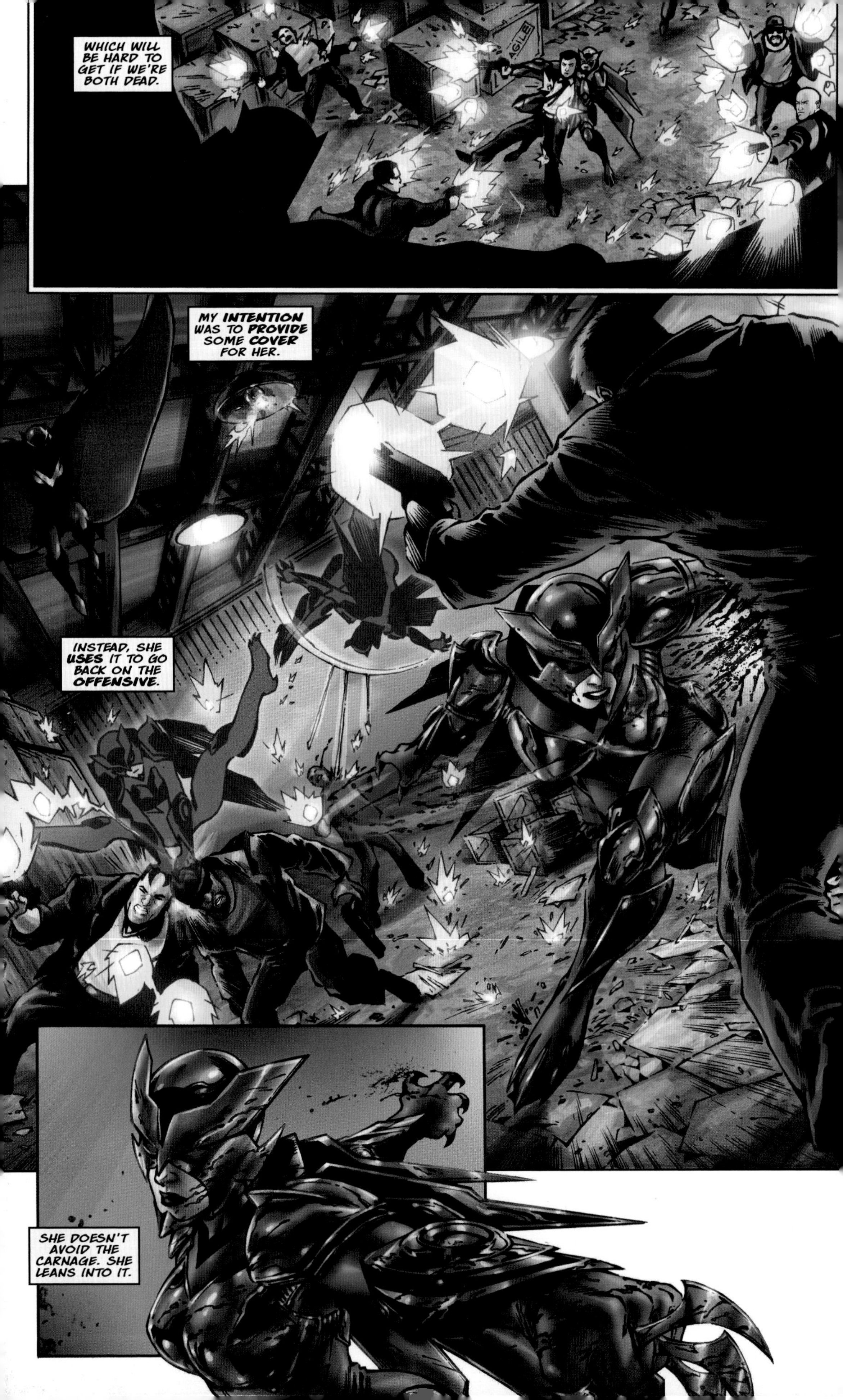
WHICH WILL BE HARD TO GET IF WE'RE BOTH DEAD.
MY INTENTION WAS TO PROVIDE SOME COVER FOR HER.
INSTEAD, SHE USES IT TO GO BACK ON THE OFFENSIVE.
SHE DOESN'T AVOID THE CARNAGE. SHE LEANS INTO IT.

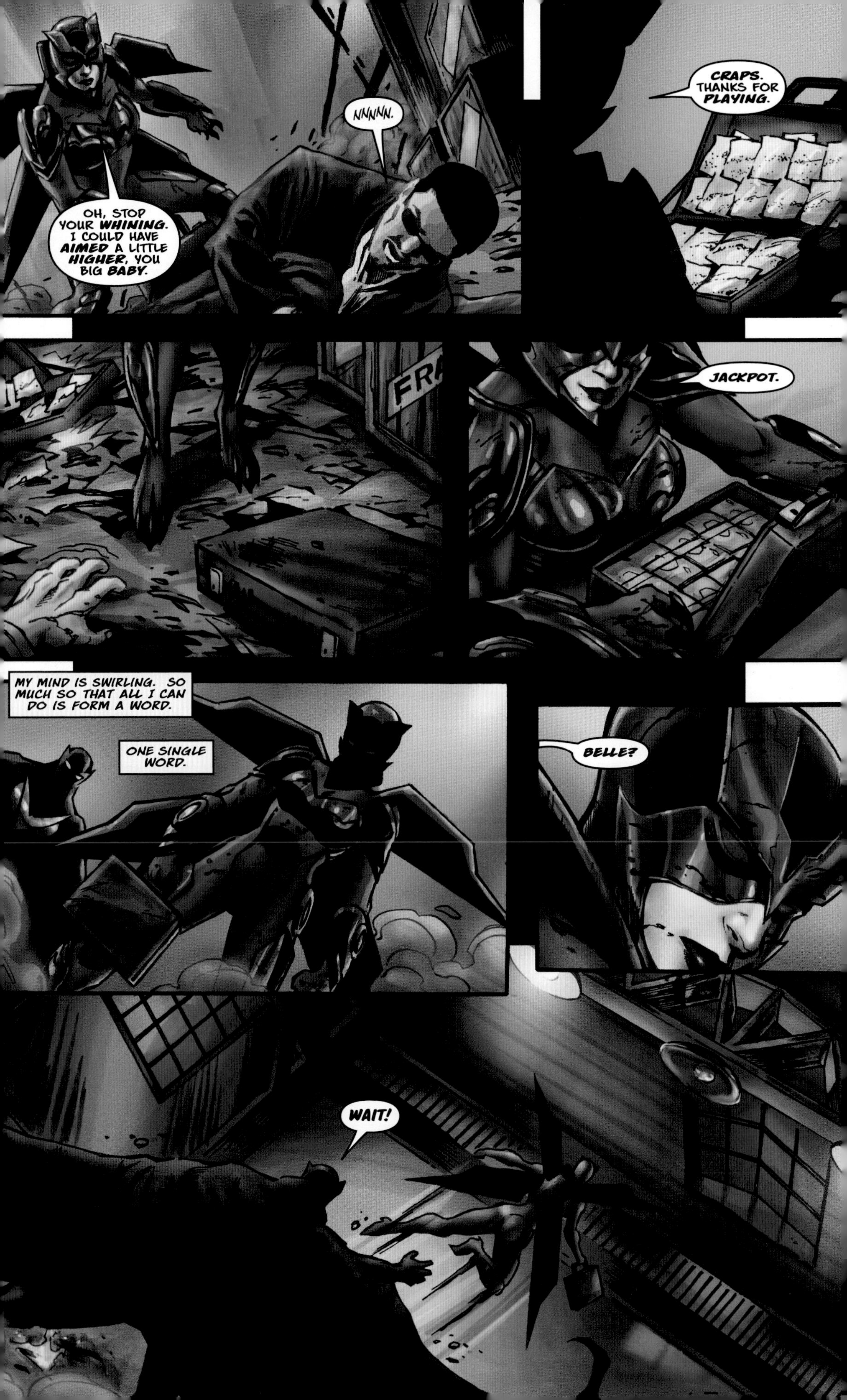
NNNNN.
OH, STOP YOUR WHINING. I COULD HAVE AIMED A LITTLE HIGHER, YOU BIG BABY.
CRAPS. THANKS FOR PLAYING.
JACKPOT.
MY MIND IS SWIRLING. SO MUCH SO THAT ALL I CAN DO IS FORM A WORD.
ONE SINGLE WORD.
BELLE?
WAIT!

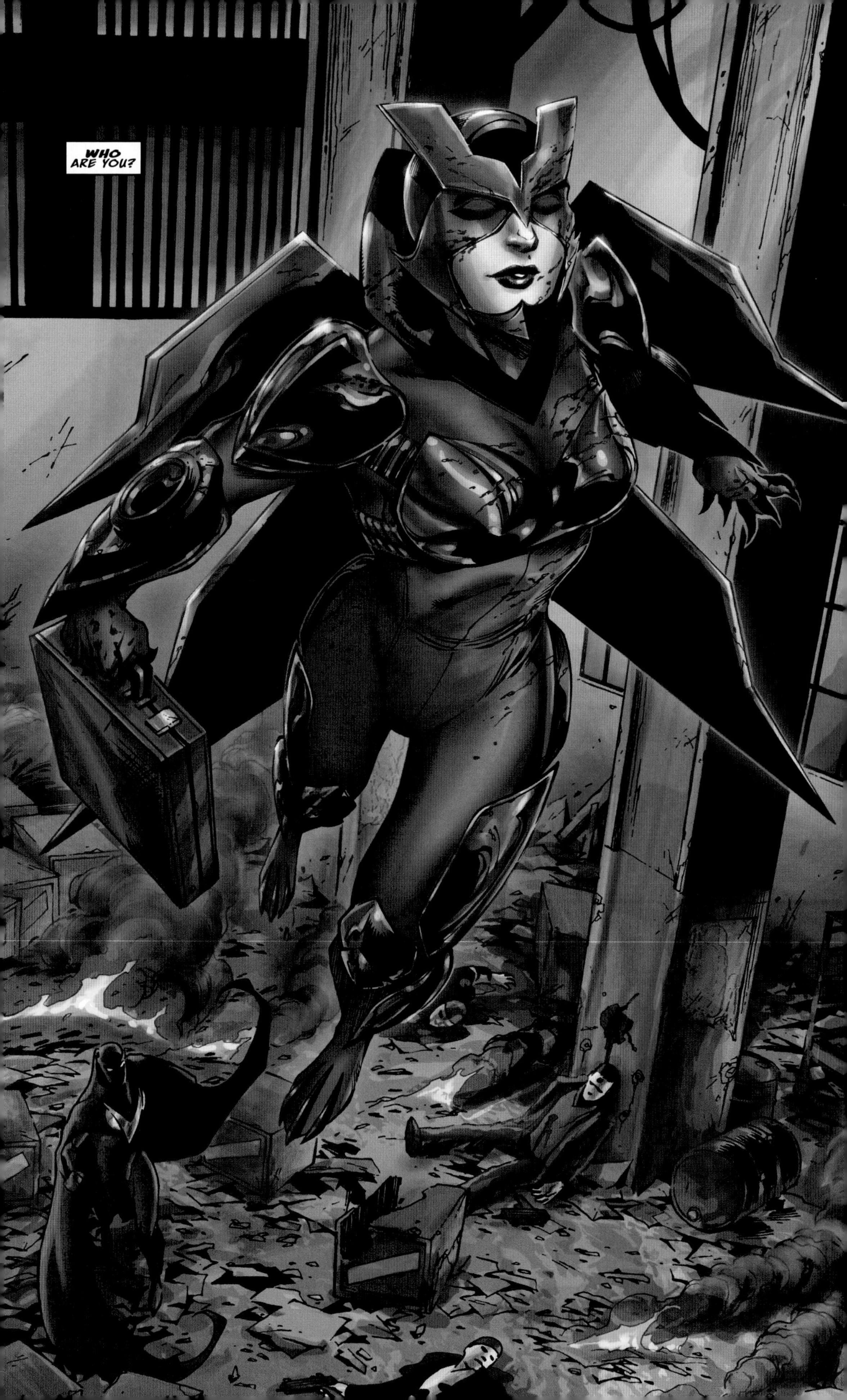
WHO ARE YOU?

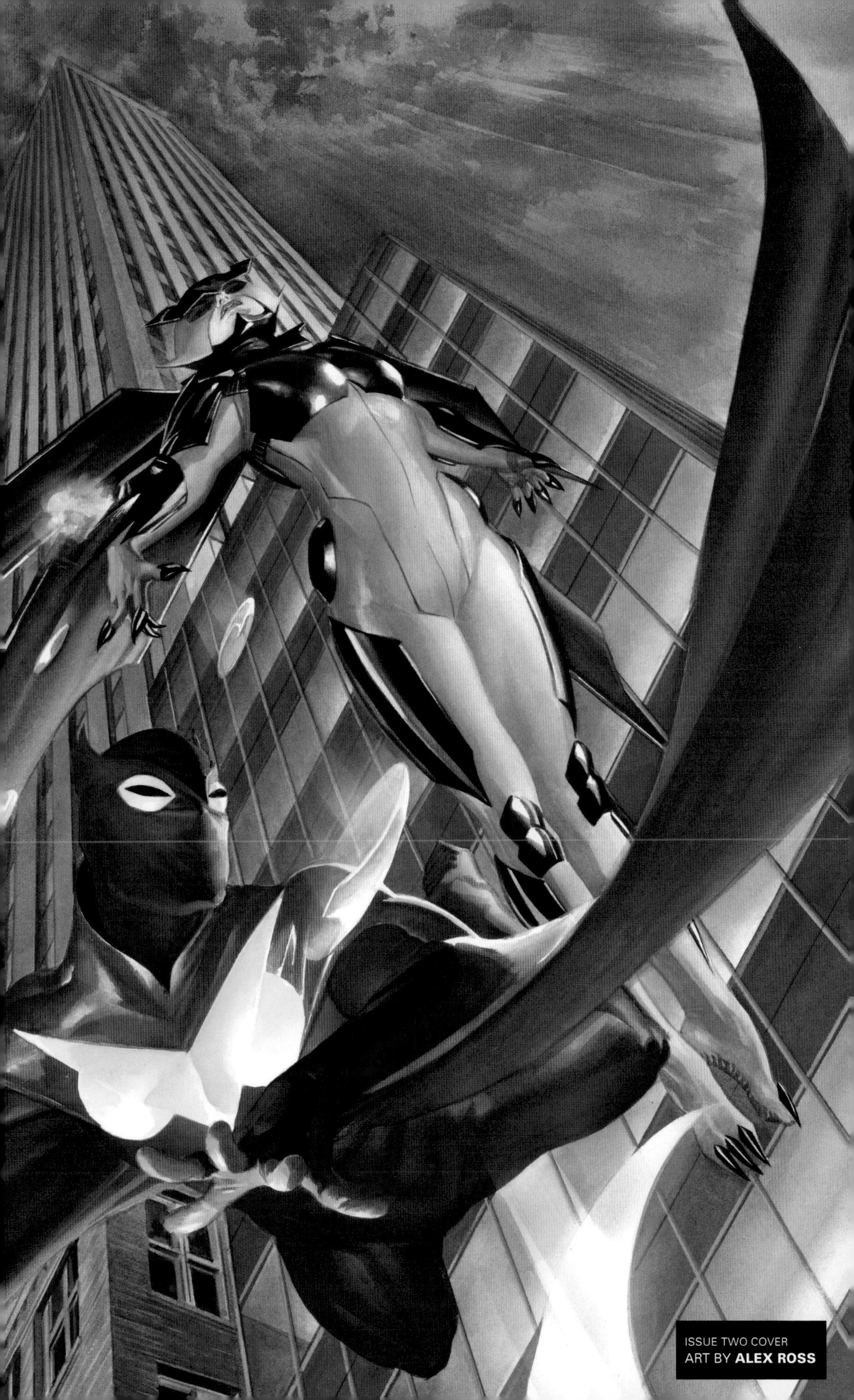

ISSUE TWO COVER
ART BY **ALEX ROSS**

ISSUE TWO COVER
ART BY **ARDIAN SYAF**
INKS BY **GUILLERMO ORTEGO**
COLORS BY **KYLE RITTER**

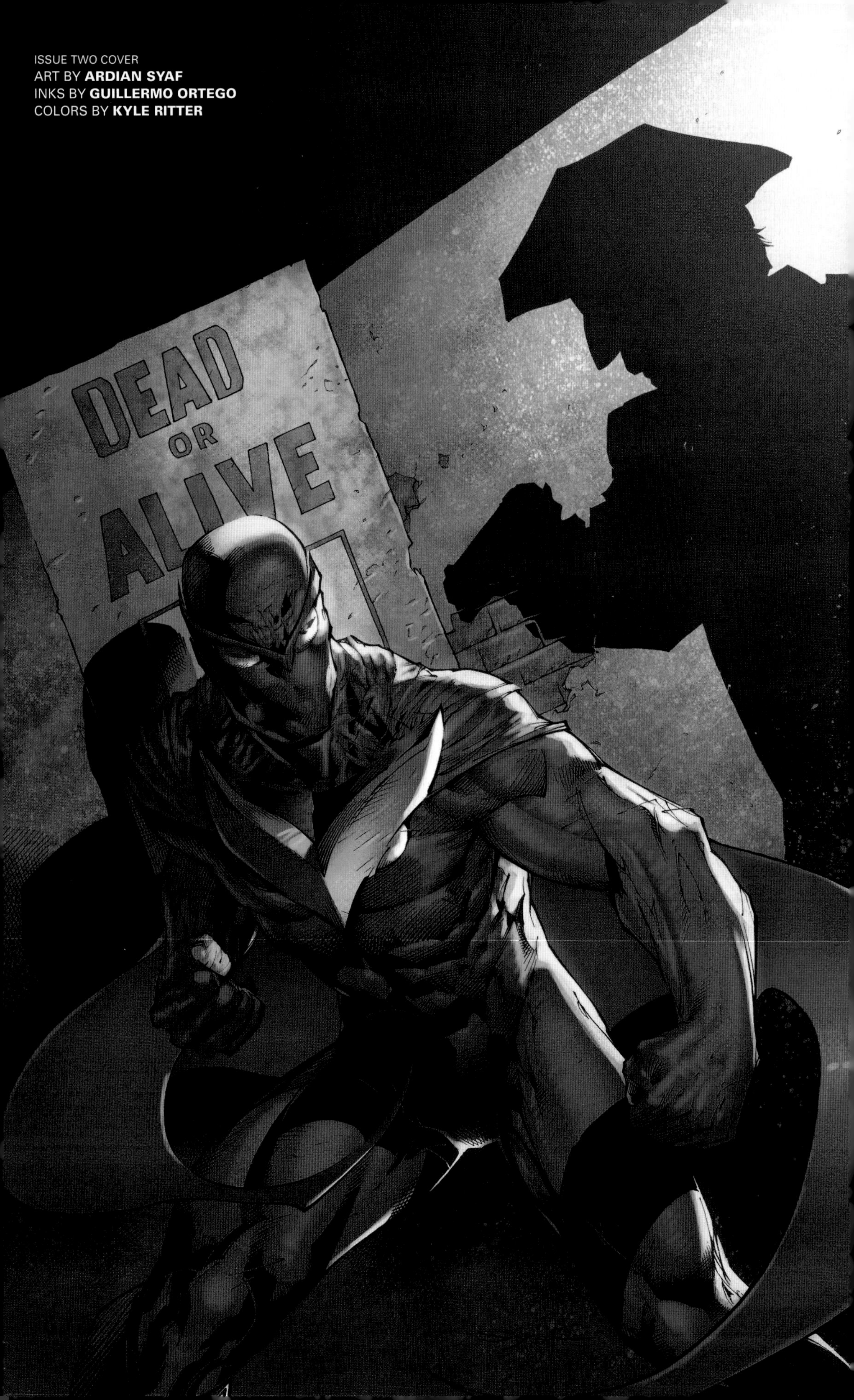
DEAD OR ALIVE

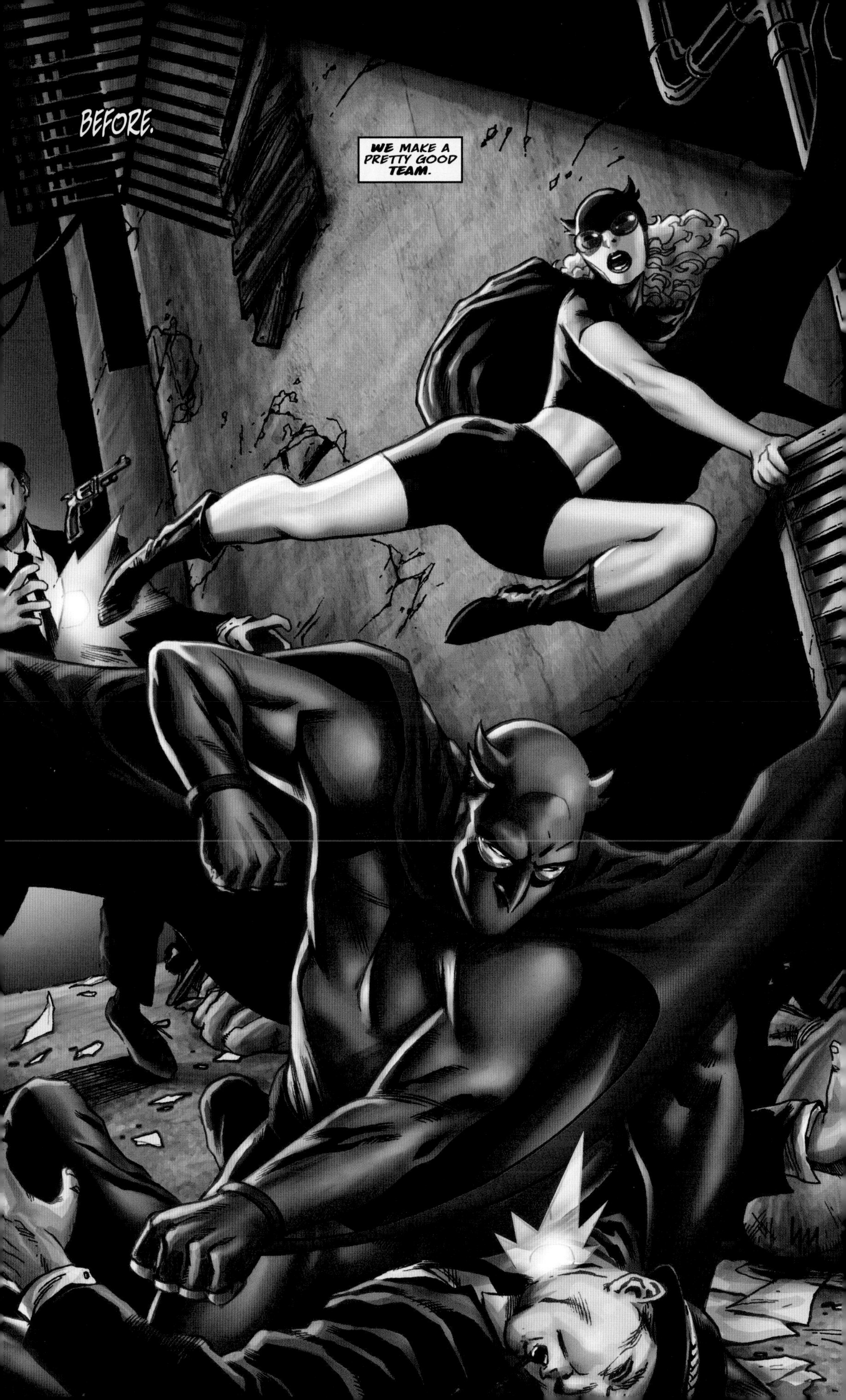
BEFORE.
WE MAKE A PRETTY GOOD TEAM.

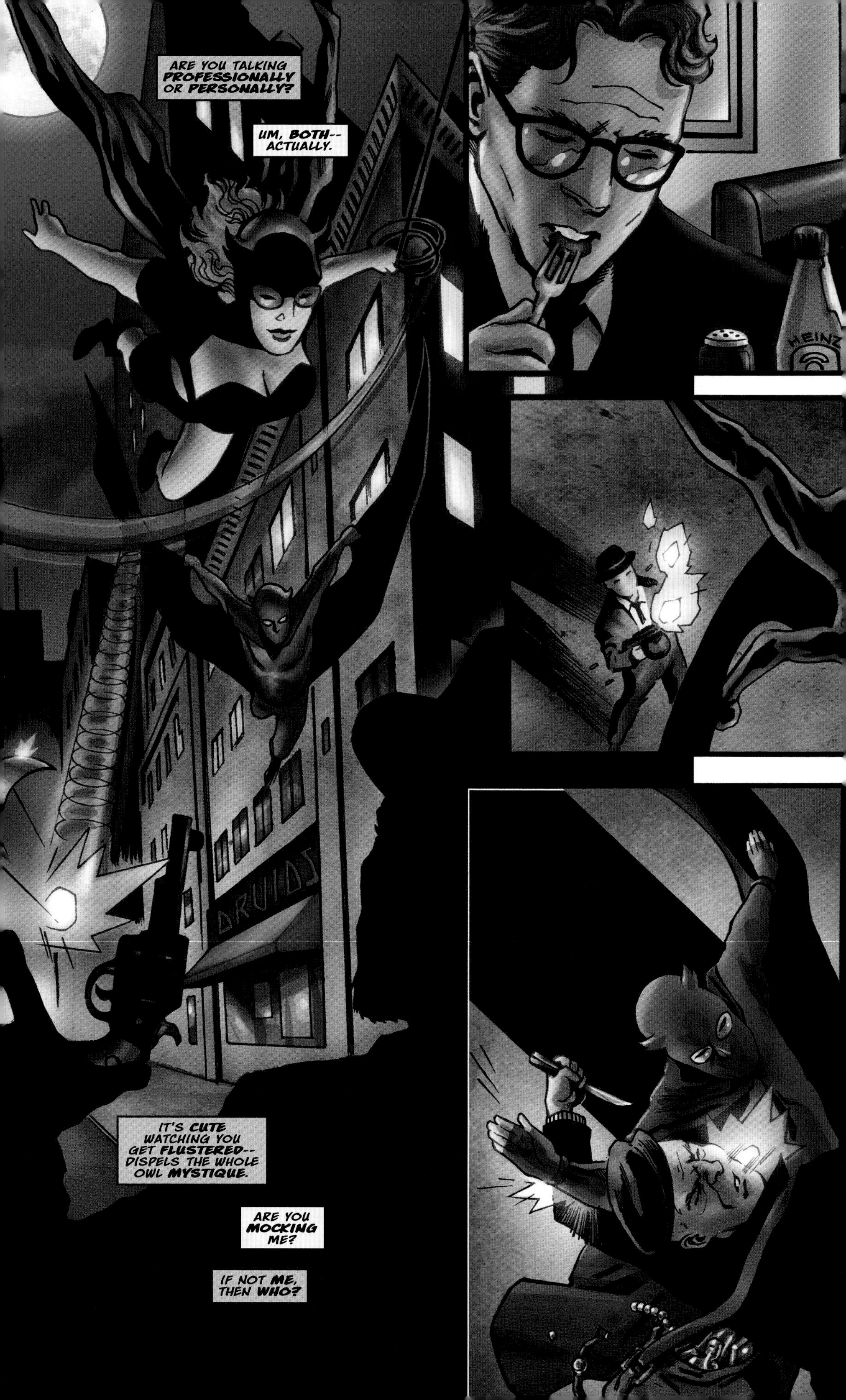
ARE YOU TALKING PROFESSIONALLY OR PERSONALLY?
UM, BOTH-- ACTUALLY.
HEINZ
DRUIDS
IT'S CUTE WATCHING YOU GET FLUSTERED-- DISPELS THE WHOLE OWL MYSTIQUE.
ARE YOU MOCKING ME?
IF NOT ME, THEN WHO?

I ADMIT-- I WAS MORE THAN A LITTLE WORRIED ABOUT YOU TAKING UP THE FIGHT--JOINING ME OUT THERE AS OWL GIRL.

NO MORE WORRIED THAN I WAS WATCHING YOU HEAD OFF TO THE ROOFTOPS EVERY NIGHT.

NEVER THOUGHT I'D HAVE A PARTNER WHO SAW THE WORLD EXACTLY AS I DID.

GREAT MINDS THINK ALIKE. AND YOU'D BETTER GET USED TO IT. I'M NOT GOING ANYWHERE.

SOMETHING TELLS ME WE MAY HAVE TO MAKE THIS PARTNERSHIP PERMANENT ONE OF THESE DAYS.

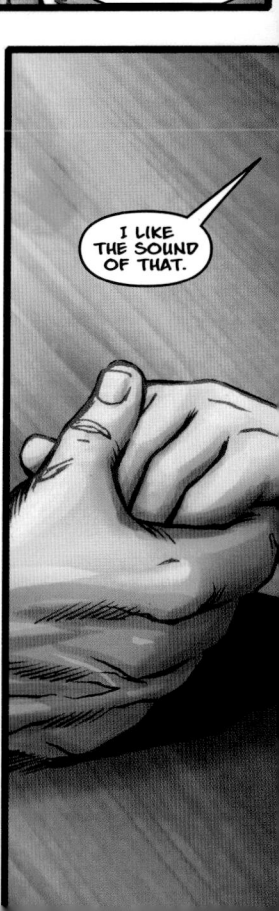

I LIKE THE SOUND OF THAT.

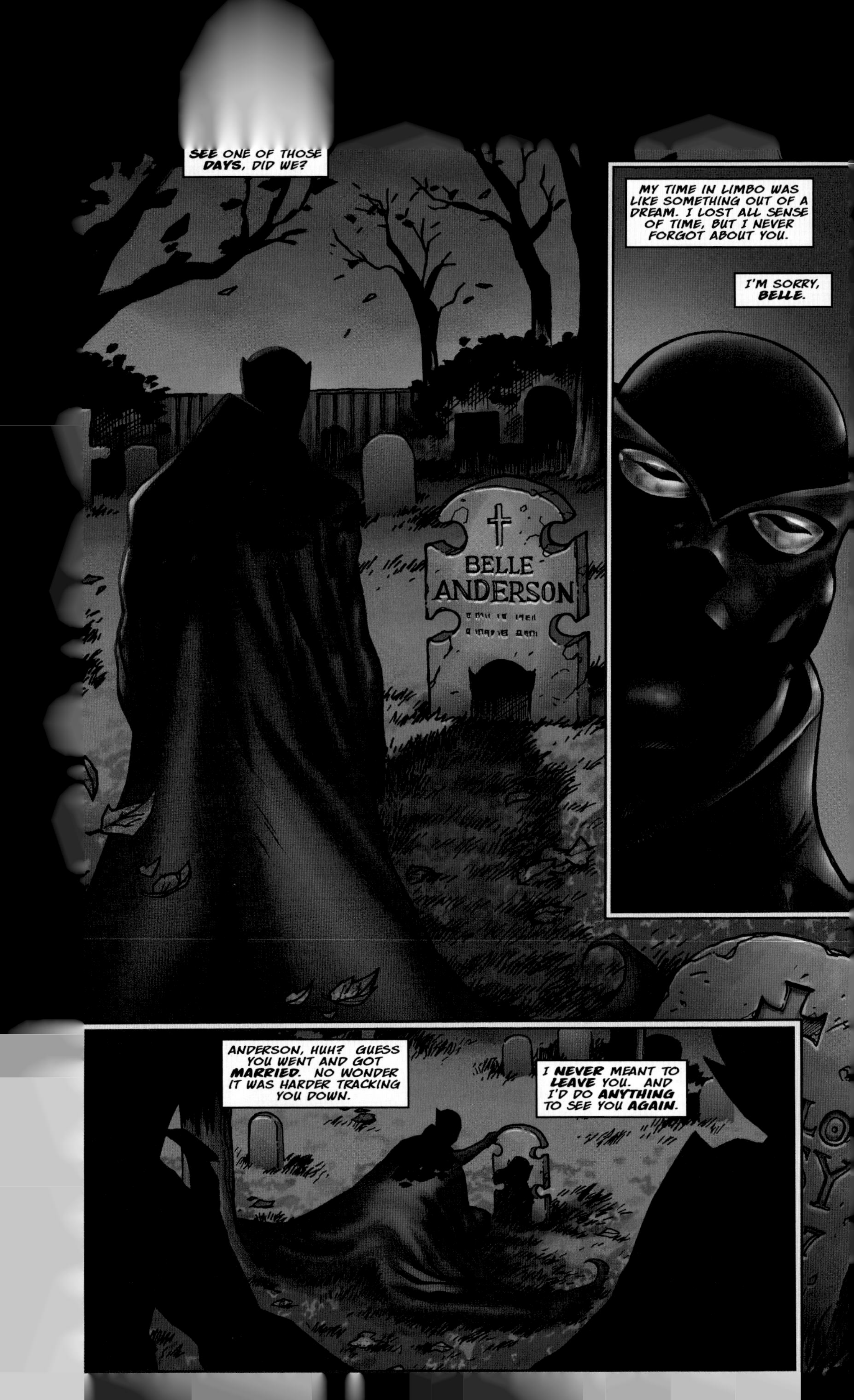
SEE ONE OF THOSE DAYS, DID WE?
MY TIME IN LIMBO WAS LIKE SOMETHING OUT OF A DREAM. I LOST ALL SENSE OF TIME, BUT I NEVER FORGOT ABOUT YOU.
I'M SORRY, BELLE.
BELLE ANDERSON
ANDERSON, HUH? GUESS YOU WENT AND GOT MARRIED. NO WONDER IT WAS HARDER TRACKING YOU DOWN.
I NEVER MEANT TO LEAVE YOU. AND I'D DO ANYTHING TO SEE YOU AGAIN.

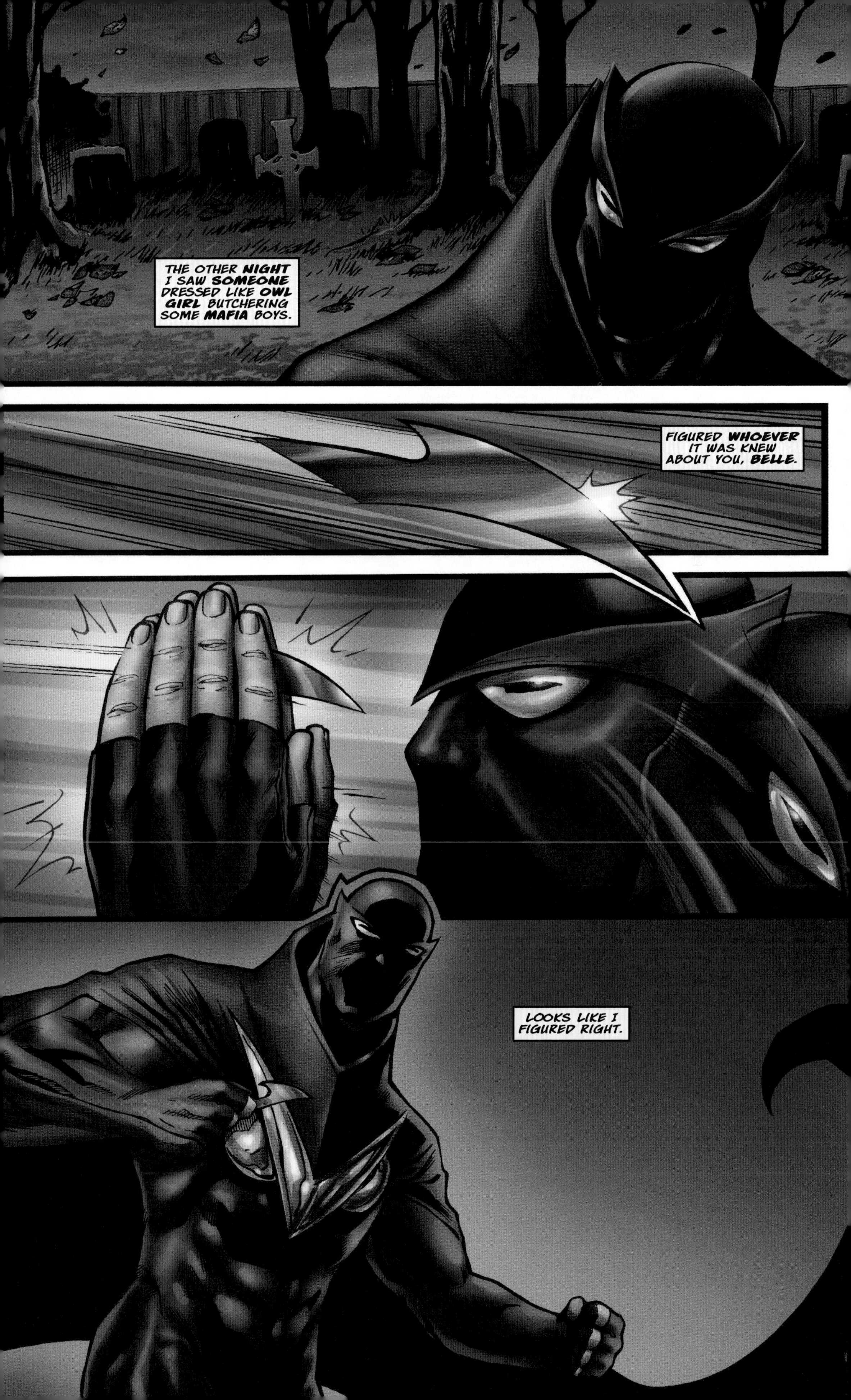
THE OTHER NIGHT I SAW SOMEONE DRESSED LIKE OWL GIRL BUTCHERING SOME MAFIA BOYS.
FIGURED WHOEVER IT WAS KNEW ABOUT YOU, BELLE.
LOOKS LIKE I FIGURED RIGHT.

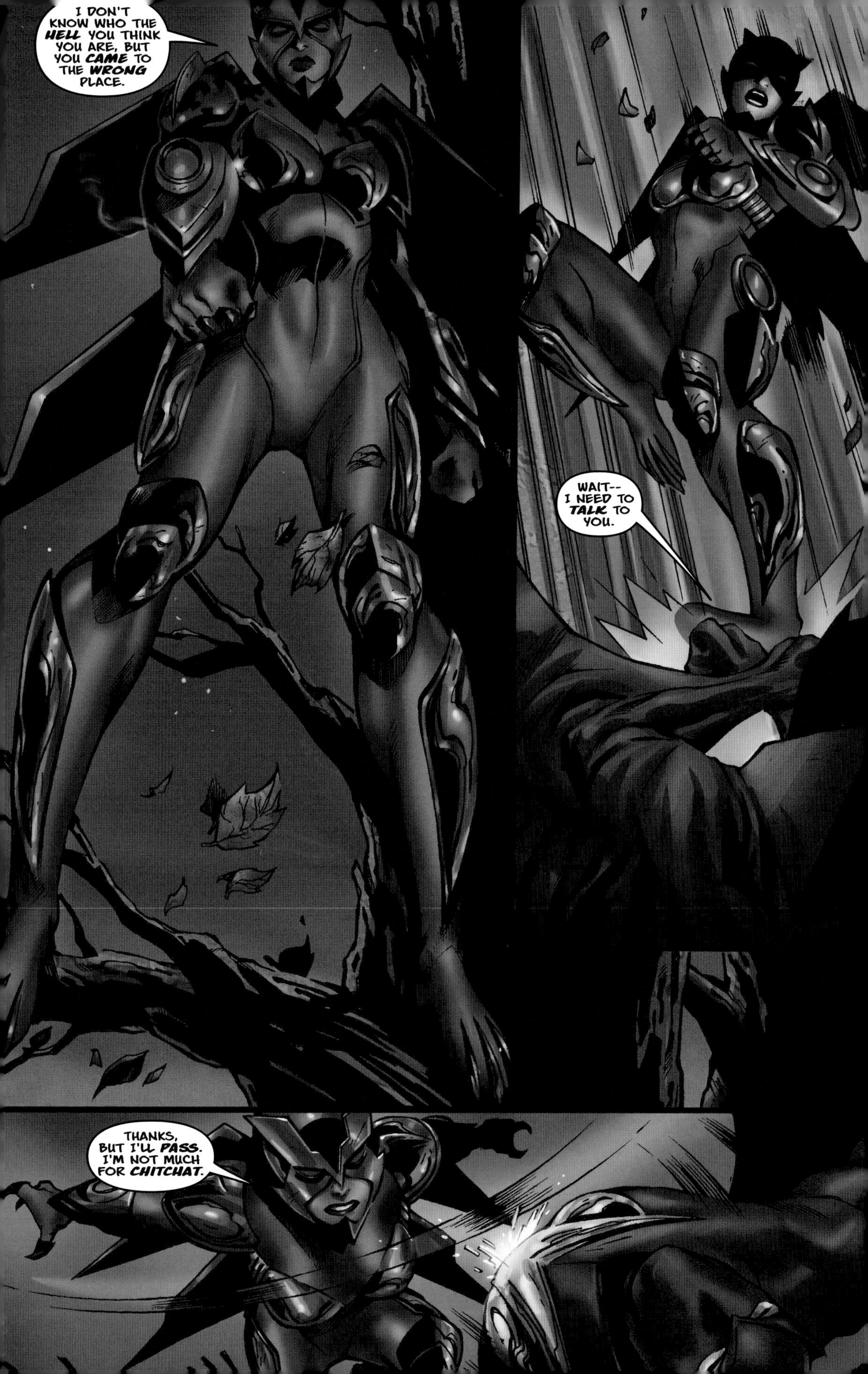
I DON'T KNOW WHO THE HELL YOU THINK YOU ARE, BUT YOU CAME TO THE WRONG PLACE.
WAIT-- I NEED TO TALK TO YOU.
THANKS, BUT I'LL PASS. I'M NOT MUCH FOR CHITCHAT.

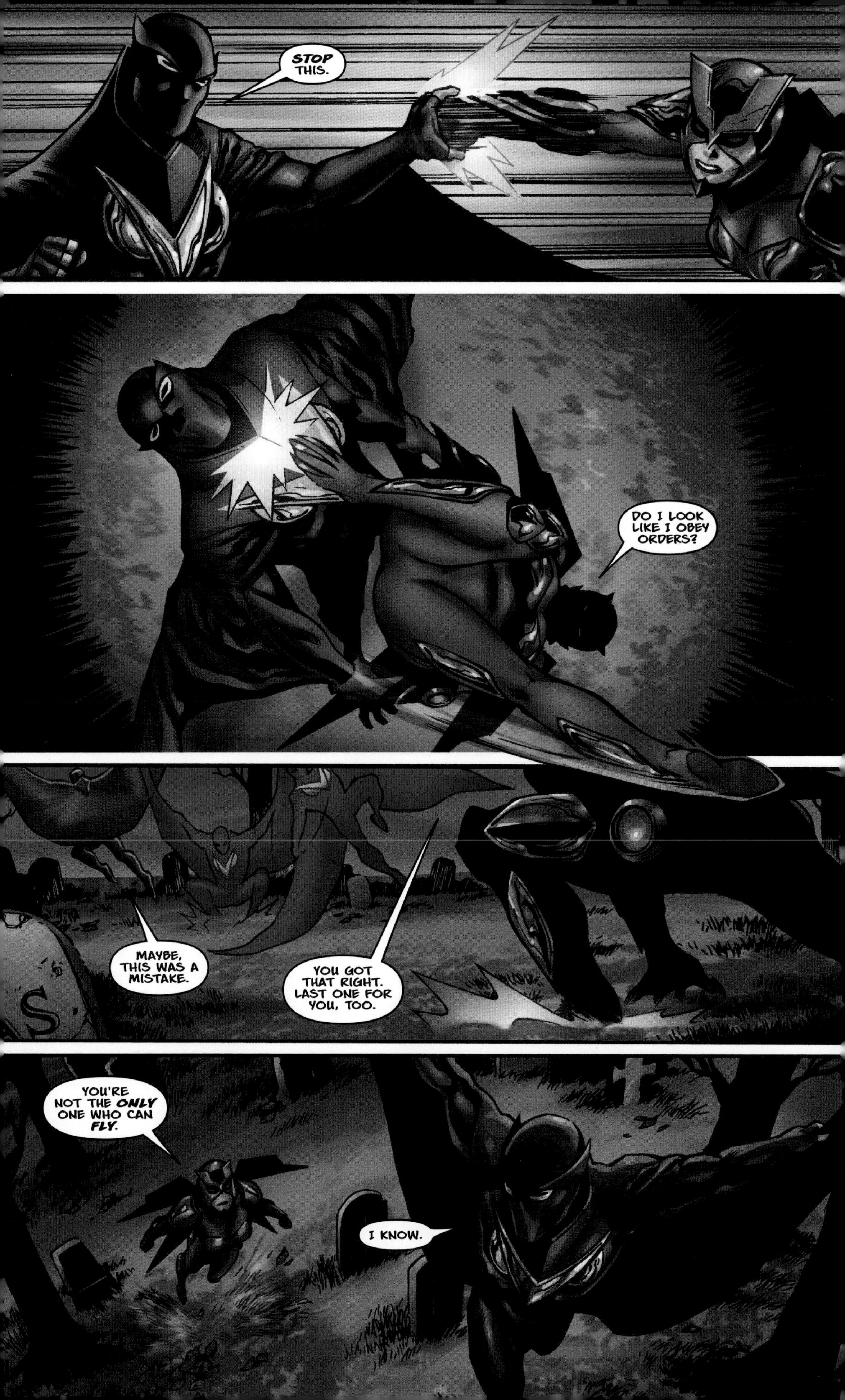
STOP THIS.
DO I LOOK LIKE I OBEY ORDERS?
MAYBE, THIS WAS A MISTAKE.
YOU GOT THAT RIGHT. LAST ONE FOR YOU, TOO.
YOU'RE NOT THE ONLY ONE WHO CAN FLY.
I KNOW.

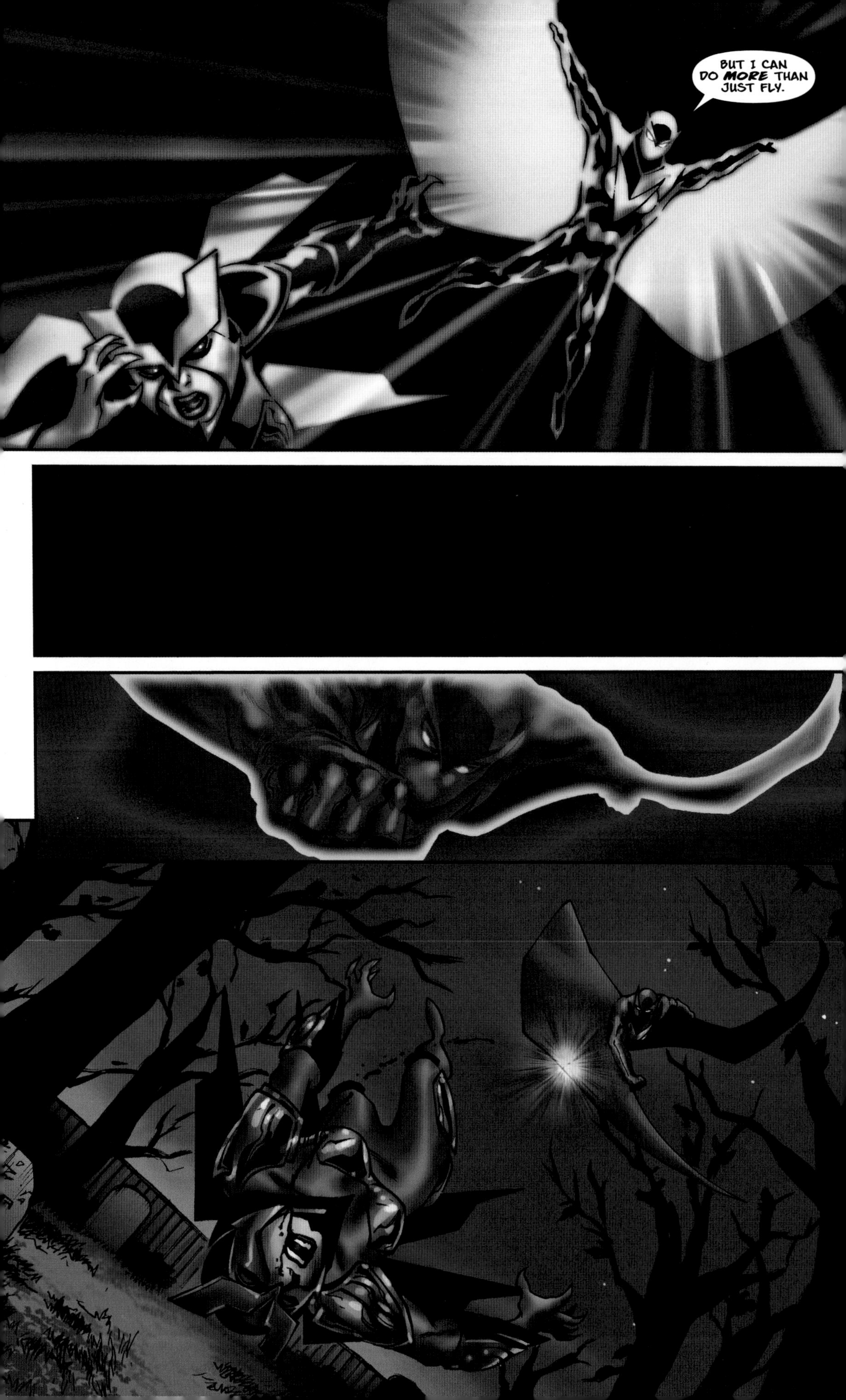
BUT I CAN DO **MORE** THAN JUST FLY.

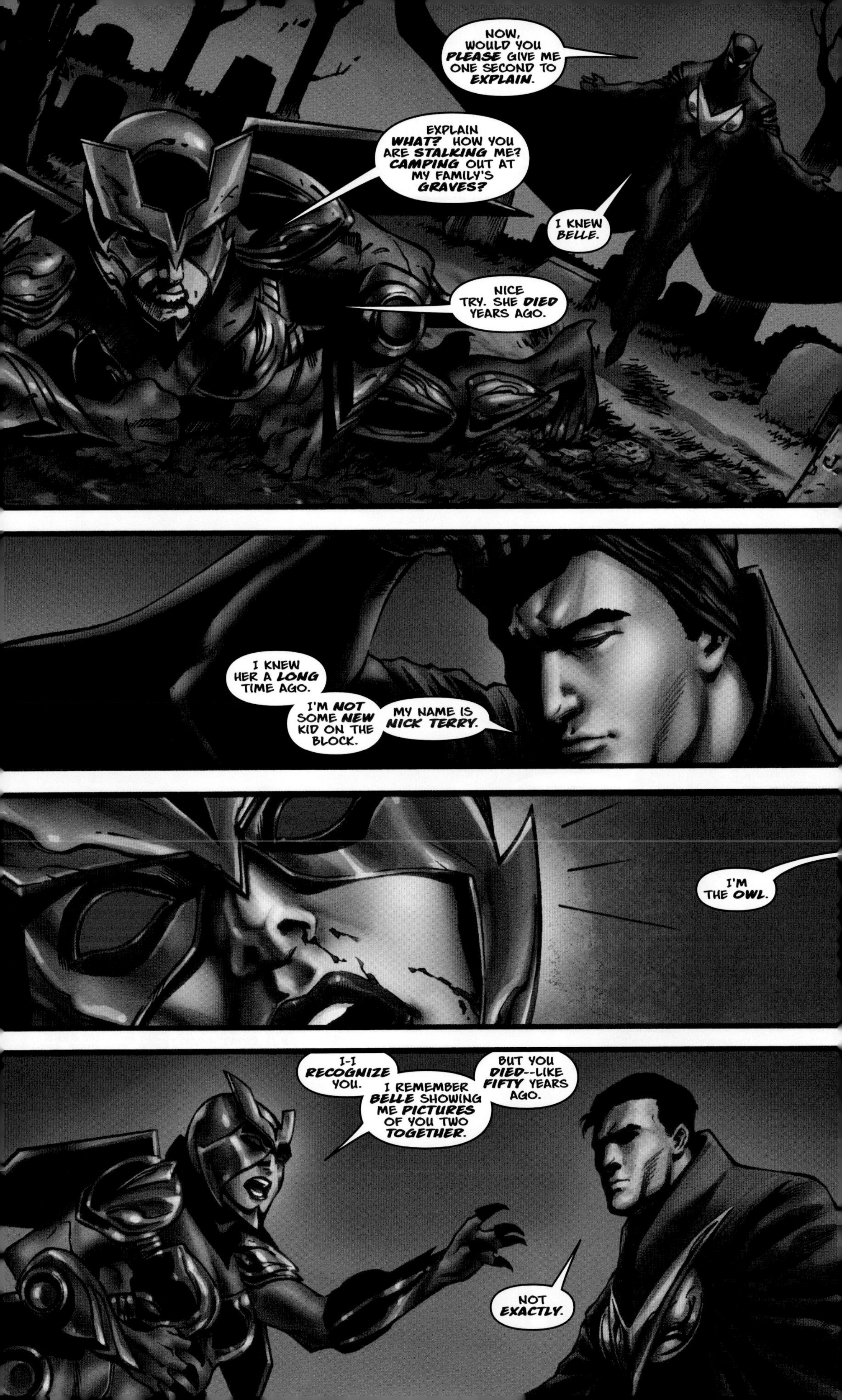
NOW, WOULD YOU PLEASE GIVE ME ONE SECOND TO EXPLAIN.
EXPLAIN WHAT? HOW YOU ARE STALKING ME? CAMPING OUT AT MY FAMILY'S GRAVES?
I KNEW BELLE.
NICE TRY. SHE DIED YEARS AGO.
I KNEW HER A LONG TIME AGO.
I'M NOT SOME NEW KID ON THE BLOCK.
MY NAME IS NICK TERRY.
I'M THE OWL.
I-I RECOGNIZE YOU.
I REMEMBER BELLE SHOWING ME PICTURES OF YOU TWO TOGETHER.
BUT YOU DIED--LIKE FIFTY YEARS AGO.
NOT EXACTLY.

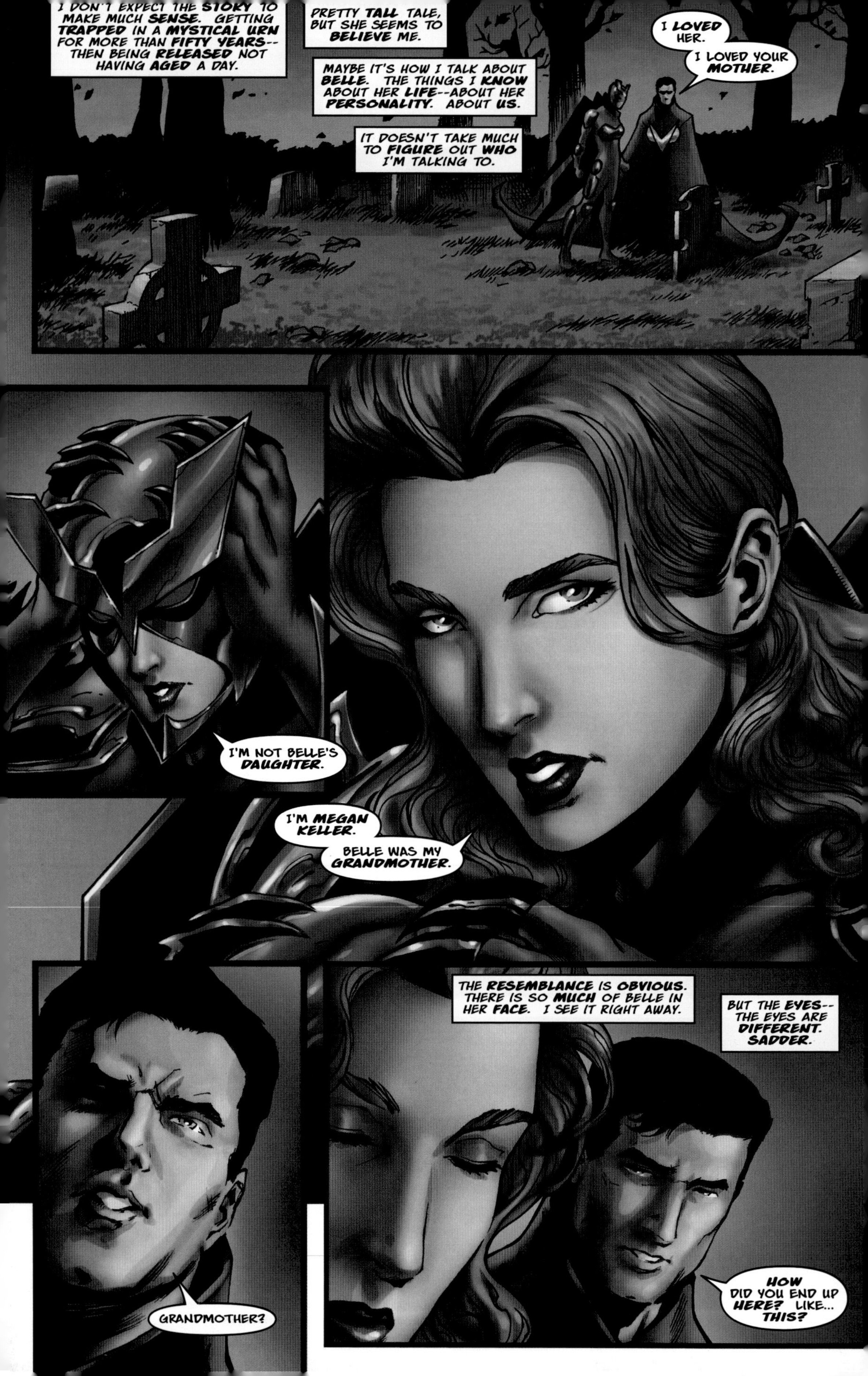
I DON'T EXPECT THE STORY TO MAKE MUCH SENSE. GETTING TRAPPED IN A MYSTICAL URN FOR MORE THAN FIFTY YEARS-- THEN BEING RELEASED NOT HAVING AGED A DAY.
PRETTY TALL TALE, BUT SHE SEEMS TO BELIEVE ME.
MAYBE IT'S HOW I TALK ABOUT BELLE. THE THINGS I KNOW ABOUT HER LIFE--ABOUT HER PERSONALITY. ABOUT US.
IT DOESN'T TAKE MUCH TO FIGURE OUT WHO I'M TALKING TO.
I LOVED HER.
I LOVED YOUR MOTHER.
I'M NOT BELLE'S DAUGHTER.
I'M MEGAN KELLER.
BELLE WAS MY GRANDMOTHER.
GRANDMOTHER?
THE RESEMBLANCE IS OBVIOUS. THERE IS SO MUCH OF BELLE IN HER FACE. I SEE IT RIGHT AWAY.
BUT THE EYES-- THE EYES ARE DIFFERENT. SADDER.
HOW DID YOU END UP HERE? LIKE... THIS?

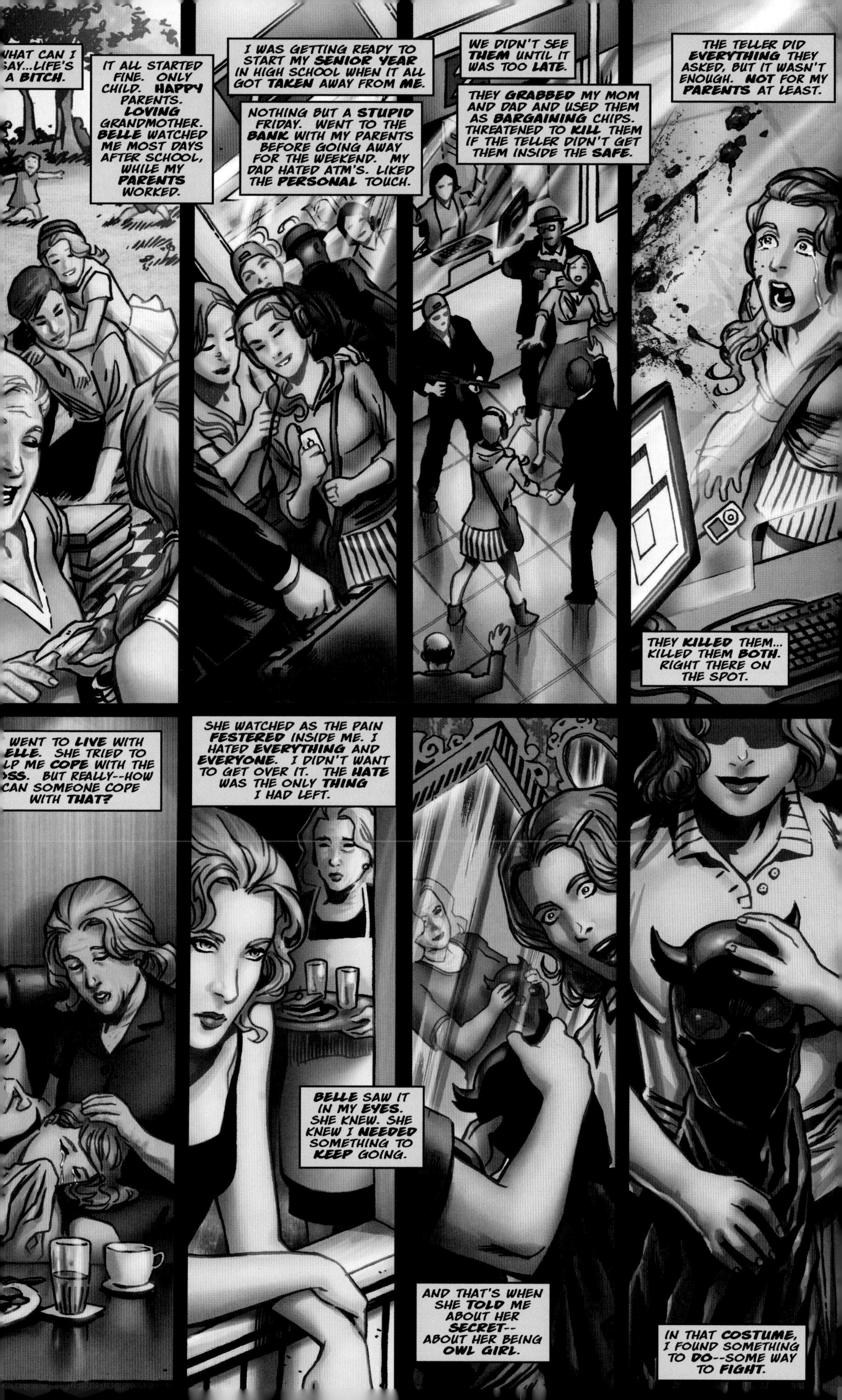

WHAT CAN I SAY...LIFE'S A BITCH.
IT ALL STARTED FINE. ONLY CHILD. HAPPY PARENTS. LOVING GRANDMOTHER. BELLE WATCHED ME MOST DAYS AFTER SCHOOL, WHILE MY PARENTS WORKED.
I WAS GETTING READY TO START MY SENIOR YEAR IN HIGH SCHOOL WHEN IT ALL GOT TAKEN AWAY FROM ME.
NOTHING BUT A STUPID FRIDAY. WENT TO THE BANK WITH MY PARENTS BEFORE GOING AWAY FOR THE WEEKEND. MY DAD HATED ATM'S. LIKED THE PERSONAL TOUCH.
WE DIDN'T SEE THEM UNTIL IT WAS TOO LATE.
THEY GRABBED MY MOM AND DAD AND USED THEM AS BARGAINING CHIPS. THREATENED TO KILL THEM IF THE TELLER DIDN'T GET THEM INSIDE THE SAFE.
THE TELLER DID EVERYTHING THEY ASKED, BUT IT WASN'T ENOUGH. NOT FOR MY PARENTS AT LEAST.
THEY KILLED THEM... KILLED THEM BOTH. RIGHT THERE ON THE SPOT.
WENT TO LIVE WITH BELLE. SHE TRIED TO HELP ME COPE WITH THE LOSS. BUT REALLY--HOW CAN SOMEONE COPE WITH THAT?
SHE WATCHED AS THE PAIN FESTERED INSIDE ME. I HATED EVERYTHING AND EVERYONE. I DIDN'T WANT TO GET OVER IT. THE HATE WAS THE ONLY THING I HAD LEFT.
BELLE SAW IT IN MY EYES. SHE KNEW. SHE KNEW I NEEDED SOMETHING TO KEEP GOING.
AND THAT'S WHEN SHE TOLD ME ABOUT HER SECRET-- ABOUT HER BEING OWL GIRL.
IN THAT COSTUME, I FOUND SOMETHING TO DO--SOME WAY TO FIGHT.

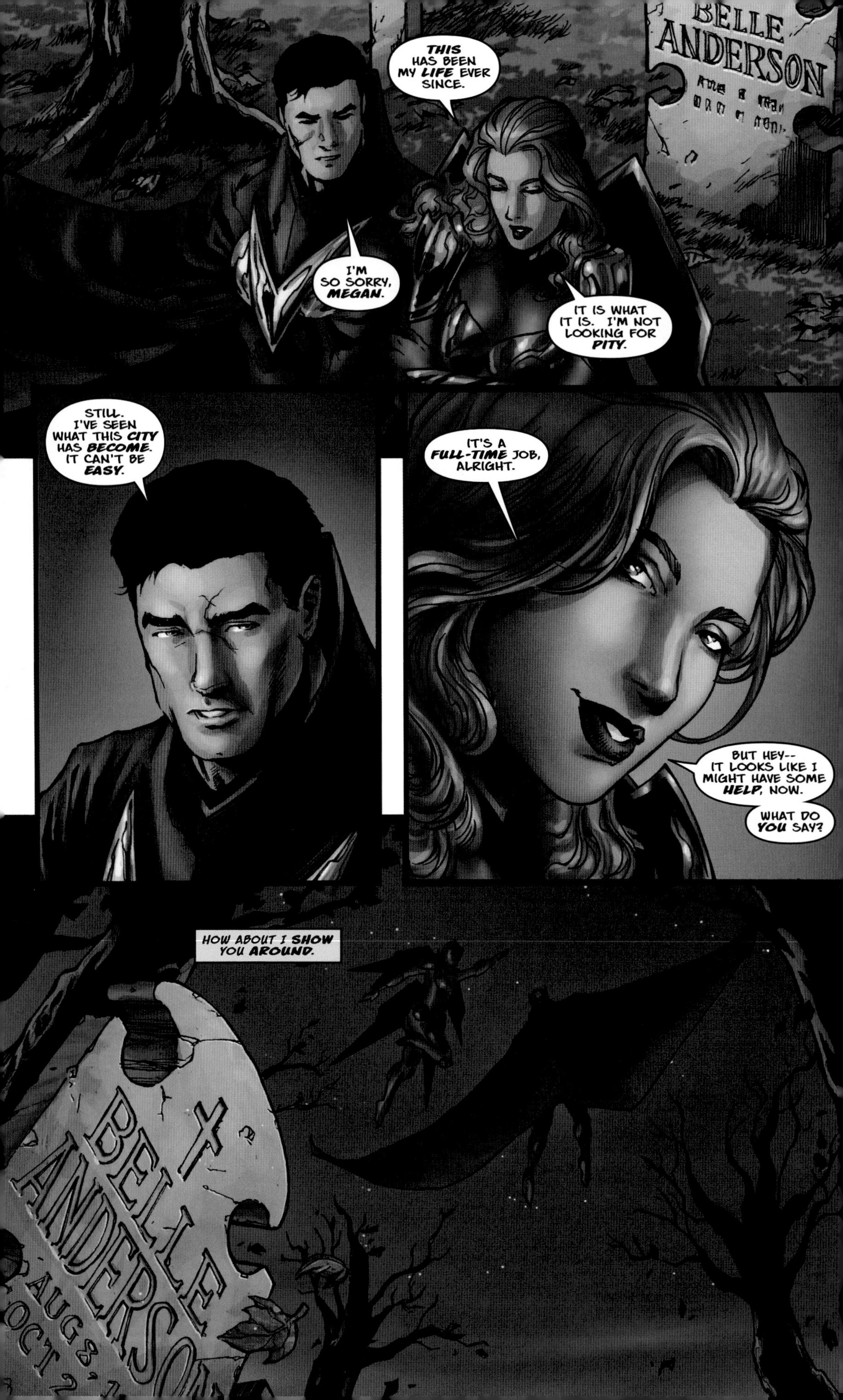
BELLE ANDERSON
THIS HAS BEEN MY LIFE EVER SINCE.
I'M SO SORRY, MEGAN.
IT IS WHAT IT IS. I'M NOT LOOKING FOR PITY.
STILL. I'VE SEEN WHAT THIS CITY HAS BECOME. IT CAN'T BE EASY.
IT'S A FULL-TIME JOB, ALRIGHT.
BUT HEY-- IT LOOKS LIKE I MIGHT HAVE SOME HELP, NOW.
WHAT DO YOU SAY?
HOW ABOUT I SHOW YOU AROUND.
BELLE ANDERSON

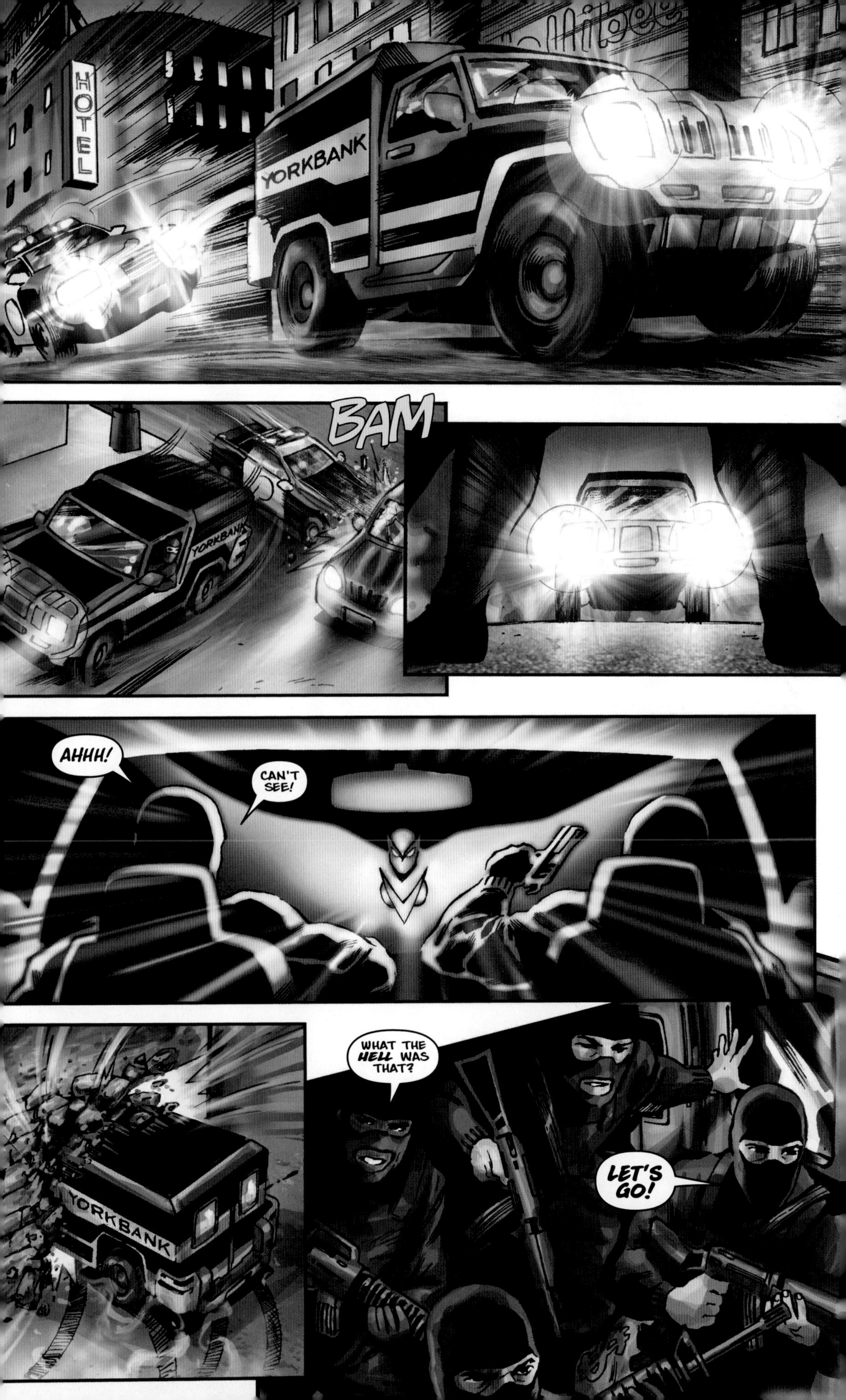
HOTEL
YORKBANK
YORKBANK
BAM
YORKBANK
AHHH!
CAN'T SEE!
YORKBANK
WHAT THE HELL WAS THAT?
LET'S GO!

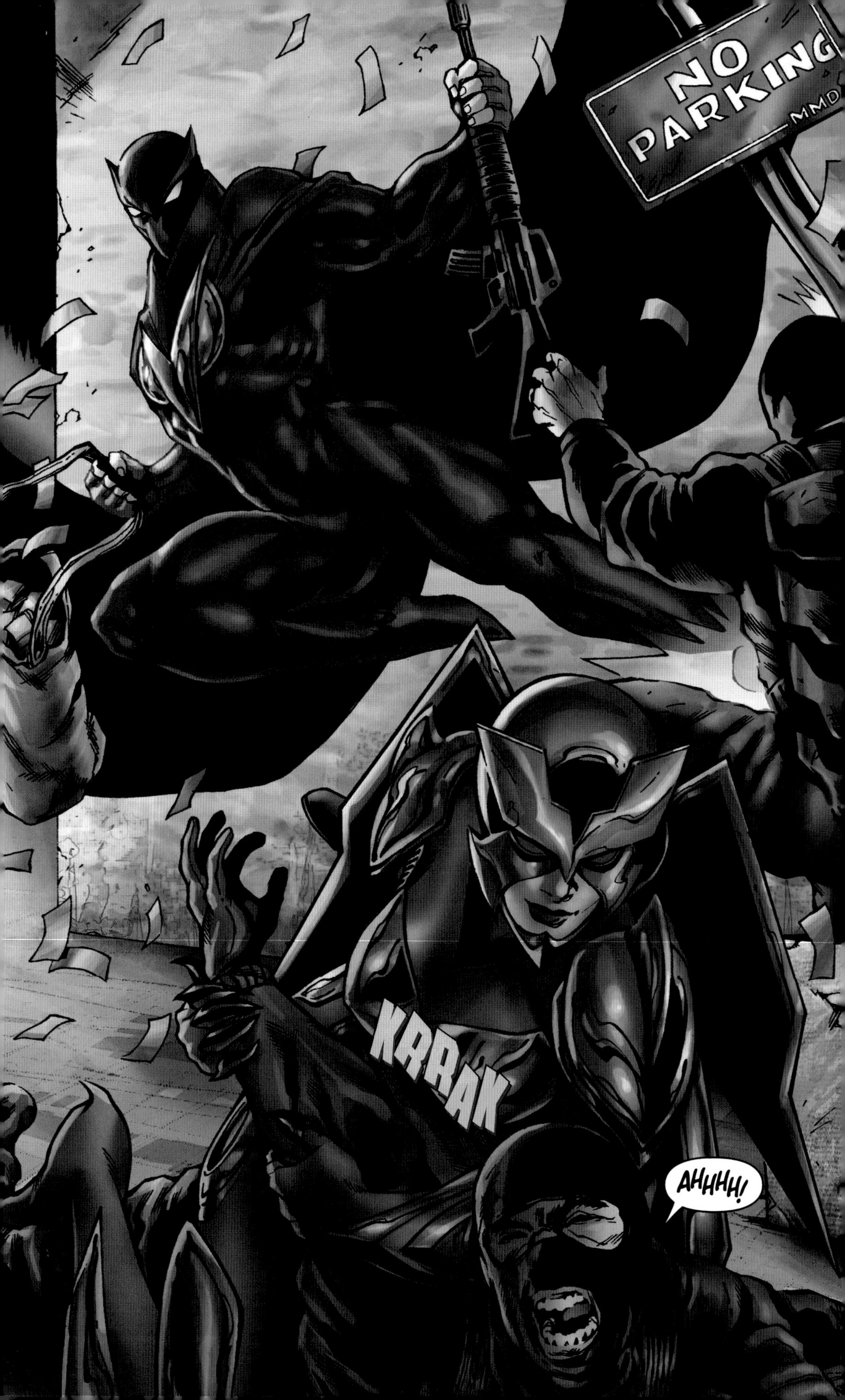
NO PARKING
MMD
KRRAK
AHHHH!

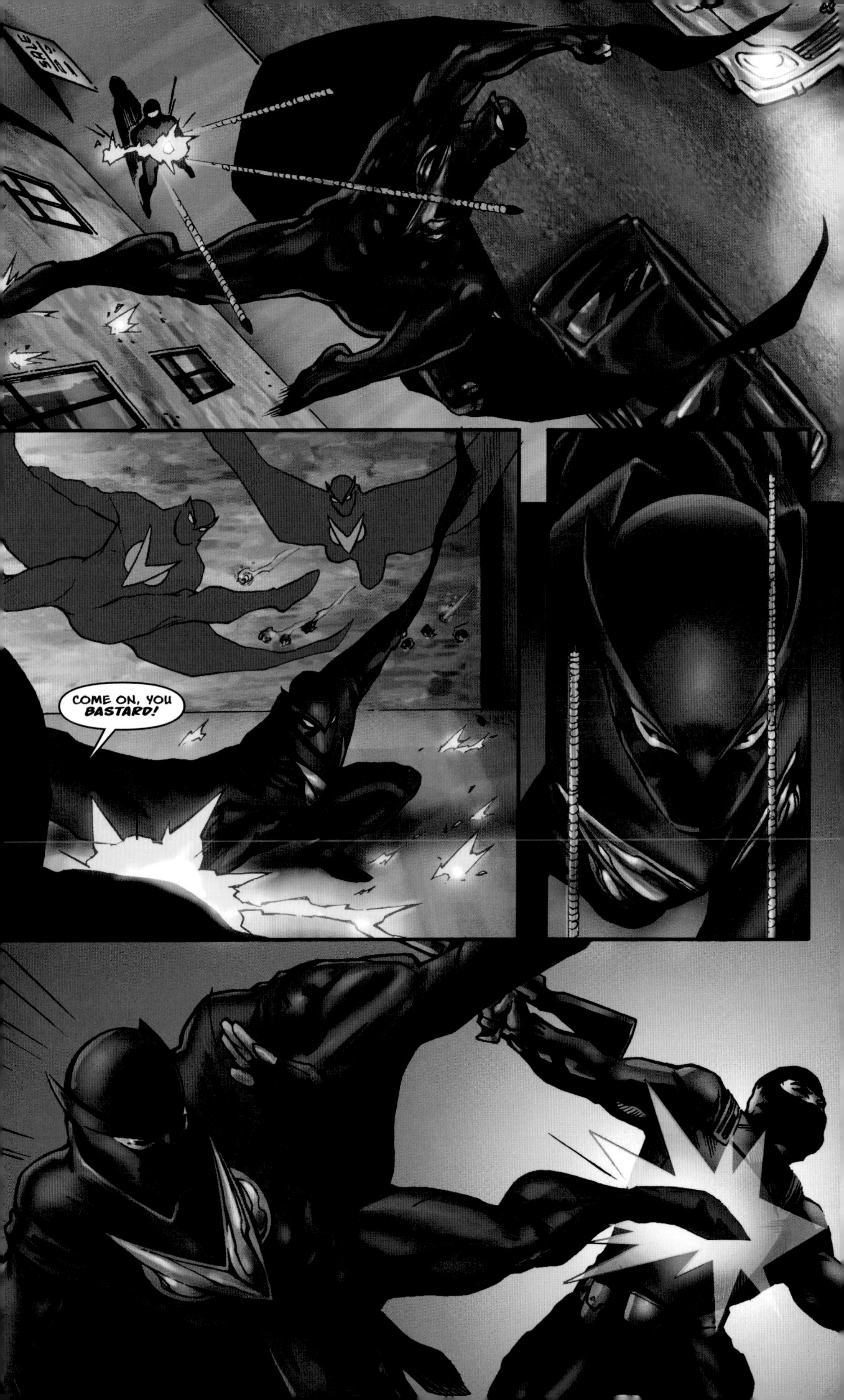
COME ON, YOU BASTARD!

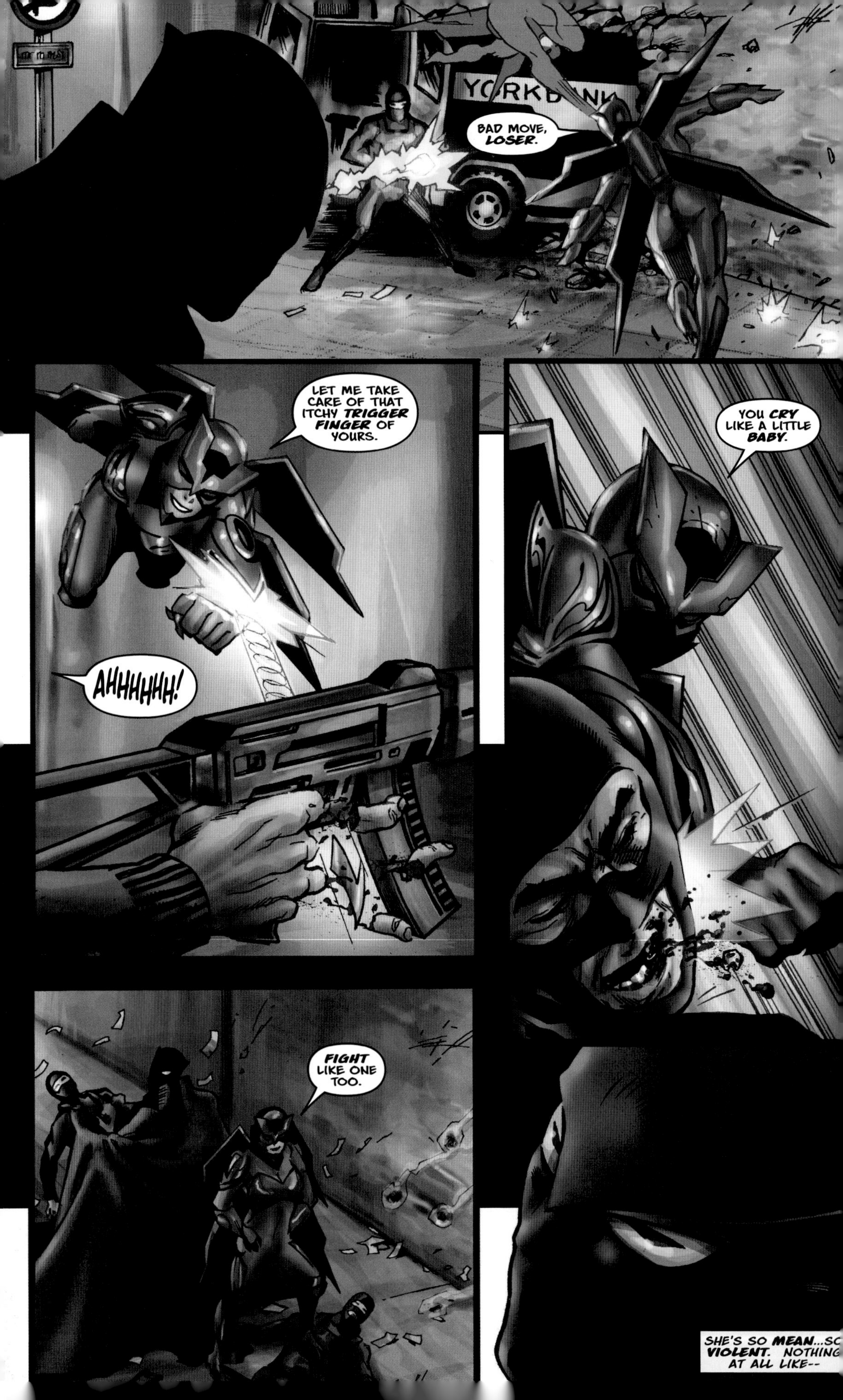
YORKBANK
BAD MOVE, LOSER.
LET ME TAKE CARE OF THAT ITCHY TRIGGER FINGER OF YOURS.
AHHHHHH!
YOU CRY LIKE A LITTLE BABY.
FIGHT LIKE ONE TOO.
SHE'S SO MEAN...SO VIOLENT. NOTHING AT ALL LIKE--

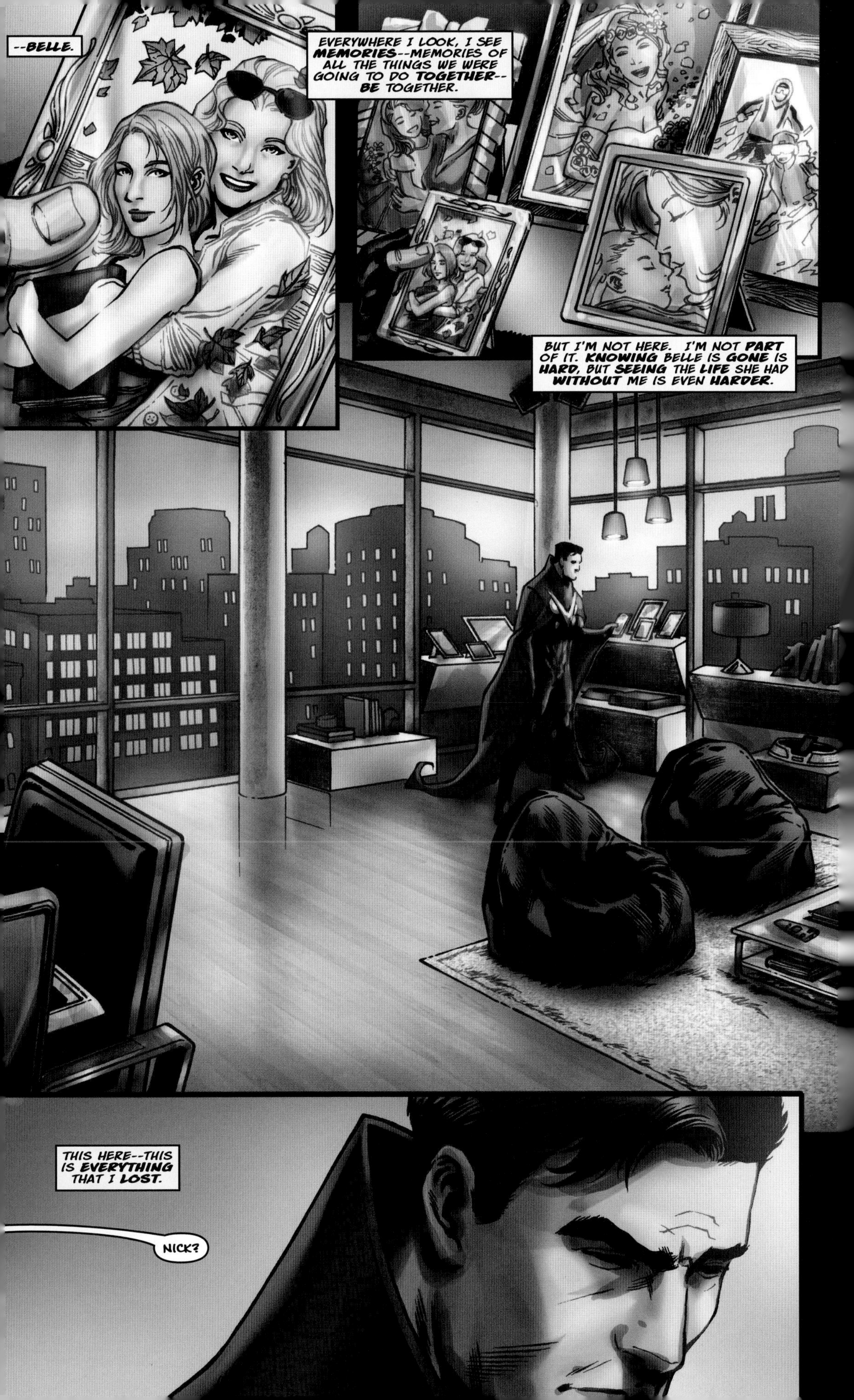
--BELLE.
EVERYWHERE I LOOK, I SEE MEMORIES--MEMORIES OF ALL THE THINGS WE WERE GOING TO DO TOGETHER--BE TOGETHER.
BUT I'M NOT HERE. I'M NOT PART OF IT. KNOWING BELLE IS GONE IS HARD, BUT SEEING THE LIFE SHE HAD WITHOUT ME IS EVEN HARDER.
THIS HERE--THIS IS EVERYTHING THAT I LOST.
NICK?

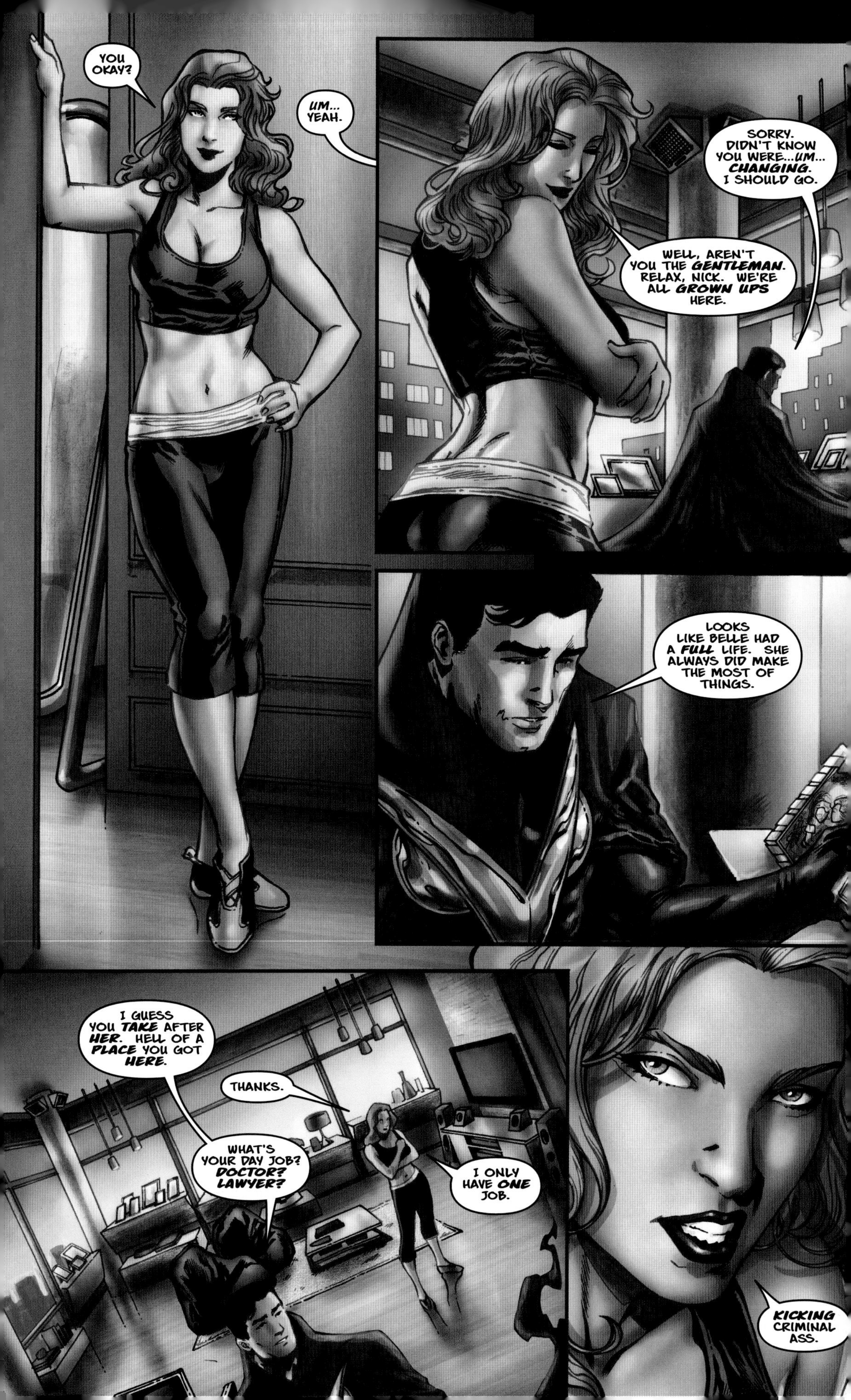
YOU OKAY?
UM... YEAH.
SORRY. DIDN'T KNOW YOU WERE...UM... CHANGING. I SHOULD GO.
WELL, AREN'T YOU THE GENTLEMAN. RELAX, NICK. WE'RE ALL GROWN UPS HERE.
LOOKS LIKE BELLE HAD A FULL LIFE. SHE ALWAYS DID MAKE THE MOST OF THINGS.
I GUESS YOU TAKE AFTER HER. HELL OF A PLACE YOU GOT HERE.
THANKS.
WHAT'S YOUR DAY JOB? DOCTOR? LAWYER?
I ONLY HAVE ONE JOB.
KICKING CRIMINAL ASS.

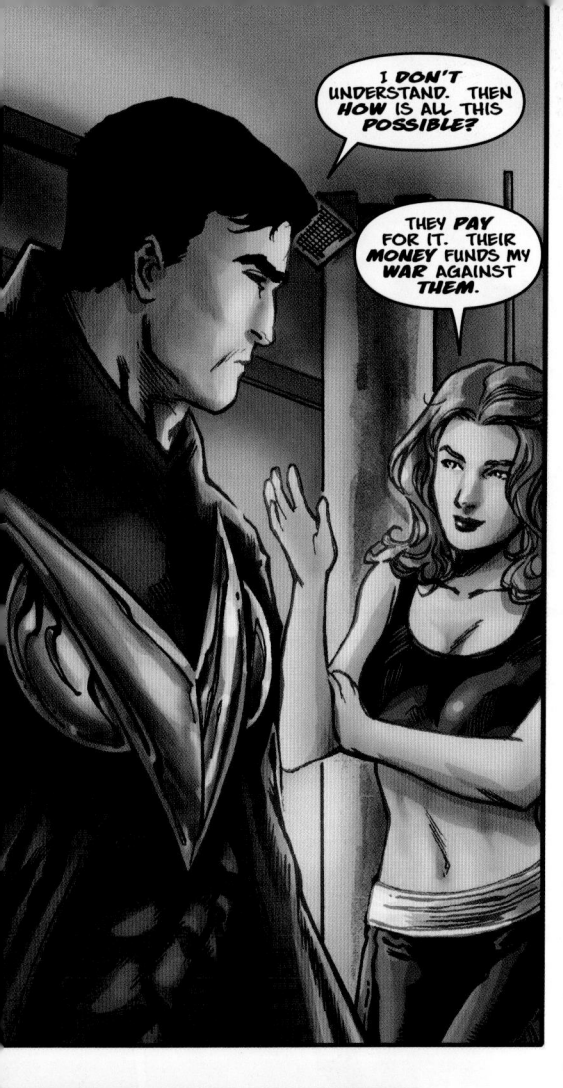

I DON'T UNDERSTAND. THEN HOW IS ALL THIS POSSIBLE?

THEY PAY FOR IT. THEIR MONEY FUNDS MY WAR AGAINST THEM.

LOVE THE IRONY, DON'T YOU?

YOU KEEP THEIR MONEY? BUT IT'S MADE ON THE MISERY OF OTHERS.

ROBBERY. LOAN-SHARKING. EXTORTION. DRUGS. PROSTITUTION.

I KNOW. I'M PUTTING IT TO GOOD USE.

NO. IT DOESN'T WORK THAT WAY. YOU CAN'T TAKE THEIR MONEY. IT'S TAINTED. DON'T YOU SEE THAT?

THIS ISN'T RIGHT. AND NEITHER IS THE WAY YOU HURT THEM.

EXCUSE ME?

IT'S AS IF YOU ENJOY INFLICTING PAIN ON THEM-- TORTURING THEM.

WHAT'S IT TO YOU?

THIS IS NOT THE WAY WE SET OUT TO DO THINGS--BELLE AND I.

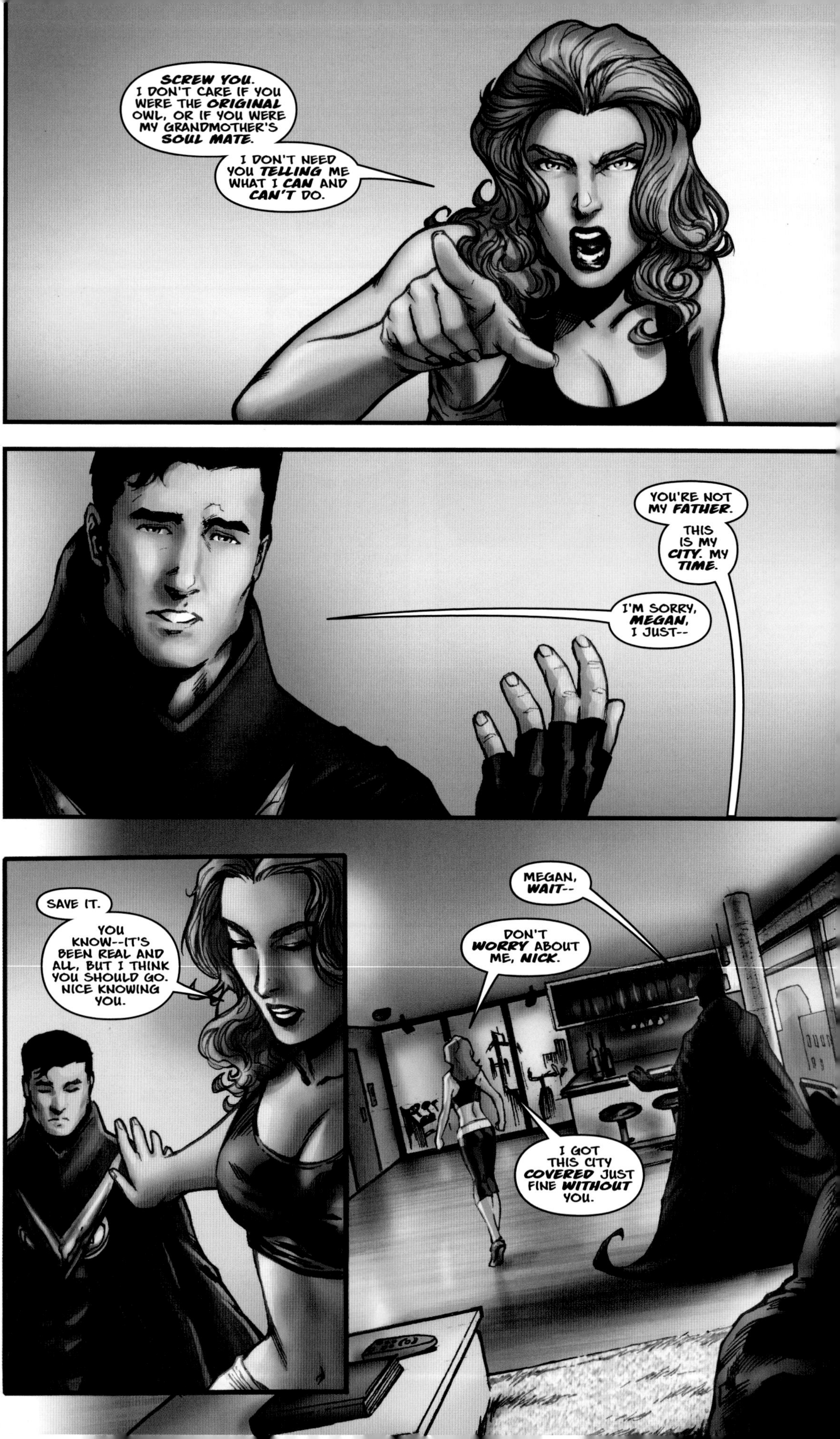
SCREW YOU. I DON'T CARE IF YOU WERE THE ORIGINAL OWL, OR IF YOU WERE MY GRANDMOTHER'S SOUL MATE.
I DON'T NEED YOU TELLING ME WHAT I CAN AND CAN'T DO.
I'M SORRY, MEGAN, I JUST--
YOU'RE NOT MY FATHER.
THIS IS MY CITY. MY TIME.
SAVE IT.
YOU KNOW--IT'S BEEN REAL AND ALL, BUT I THINK YOU SHOULD GO. NICE KNOWING YOU.
MEGAN, WAIT--
DON'T WORRY ABOUT ME, NICK.
I GOT THIS CITY COVERED JUST FINE WITHOUT YOU.

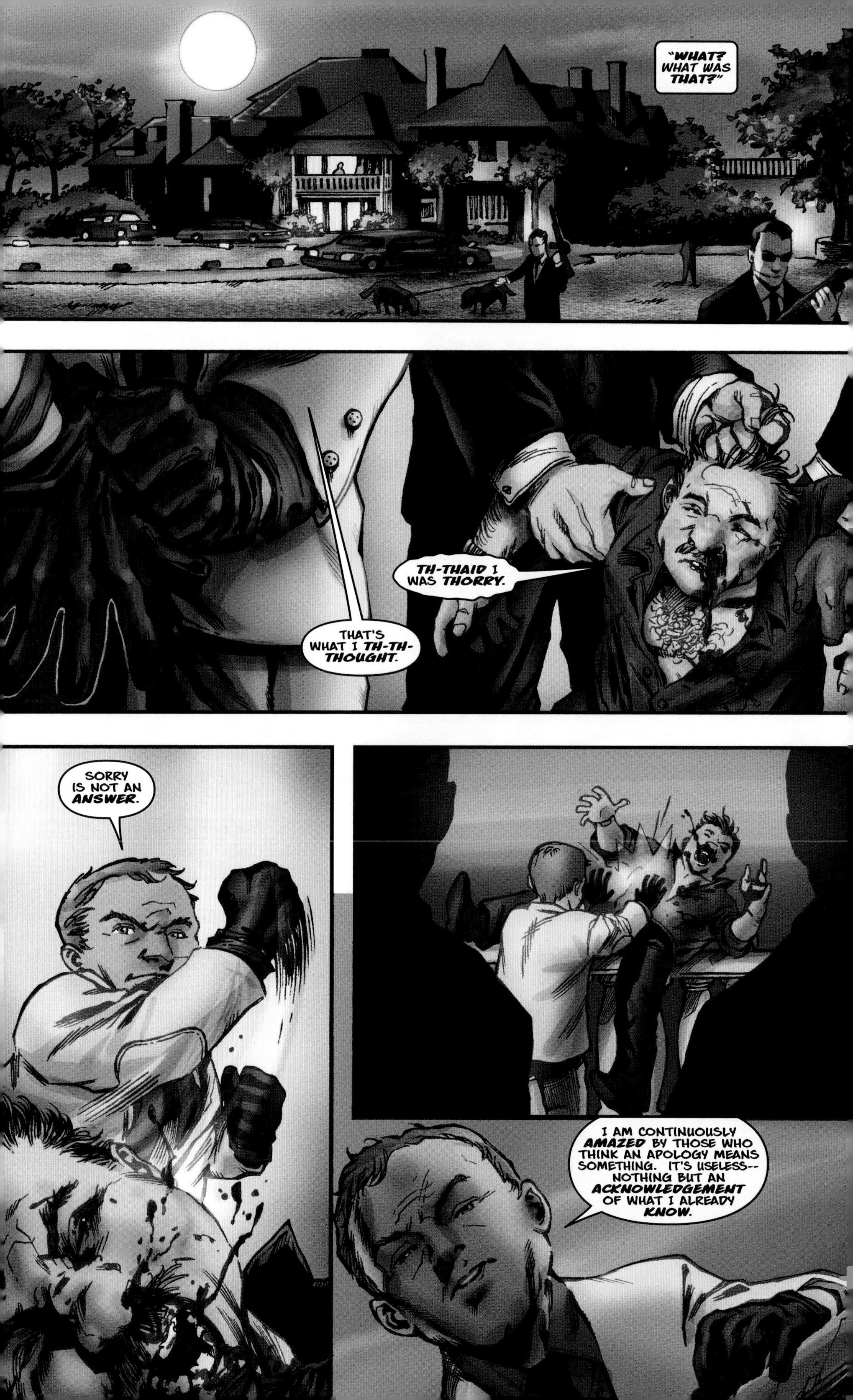
"WHAT? WHAT WAS THAT?"
TH-THAID I WAS THORRY.
THAT'S WHAT I TH-TH-THOUGHT.
SORRY IS NOT AN ANSWER.
I AM CONTINUOUSLY AMAZED BY THOSE WHO THINK AN APOLOGY MEANS SOMETHING. IT'S USELESS--NOTHING BUT AN ACKNOWLEDGEMENT OF WHAT I ALREADY KNOW.

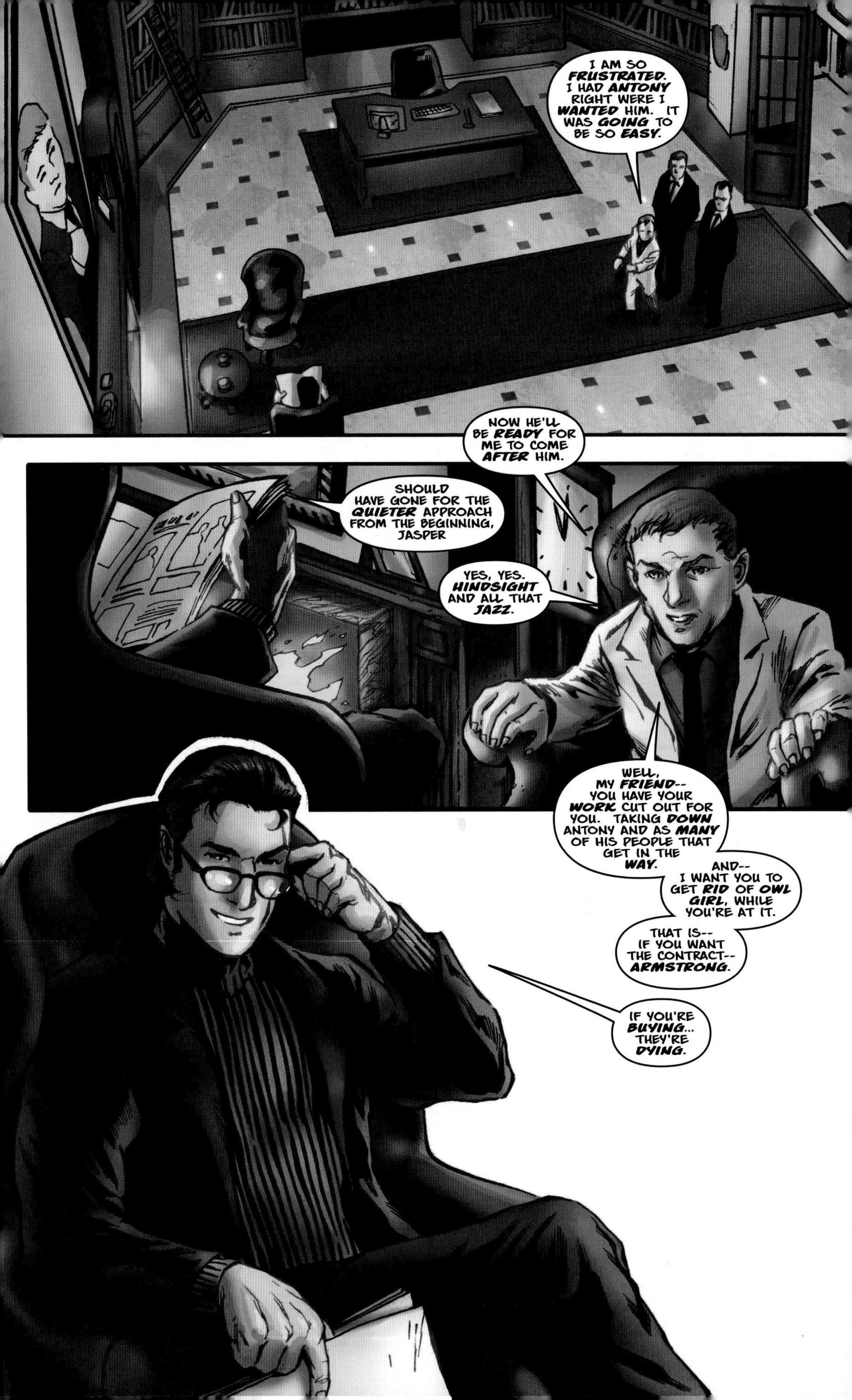
I AM SO FRUSTRATED. I HAD ANTONY RIGHT WERE I WANTED HIM. IT WAS GOING TO BE SO EASY.
NOW HE'LL BE READY FOR ME TO COME AFTER HIM.
SHOULD HAVE GONE FOR THE QUIETER APPROACH FROM THE BEGINNING, JASPER
YES, YES. HINDSIGHT AND ALL THAT JAZZ.
WELL, MY FRIEND-- YOU HAVE YOUR WORK CUT OUT FOR YOU. TAKING DOWN ANTONY AND AS MANY OF HIS PEOPLE THAT GET IN THE WAY.
AND-- I WANT YOU TO GET RID OF OWL GIRL, WHILE YOU'RE AT IT.
THAT IS-- IF YOU WANT THE CONTRACT-- ARMSTRONG.
IF YOU'RE BUYING... THEY'RE DYING.

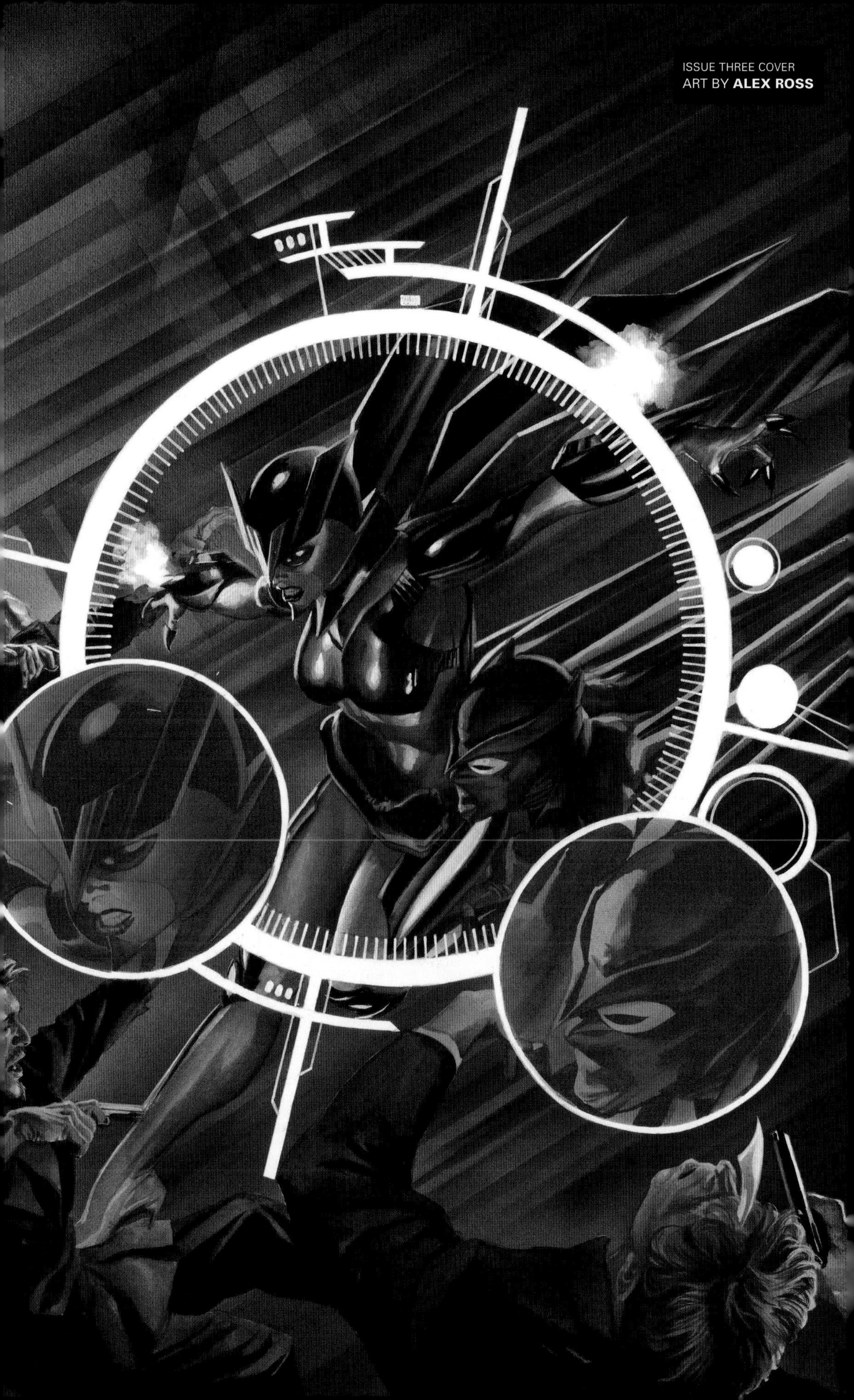

ISSUE THREE COVER
ART BY **ALEX ROSS**

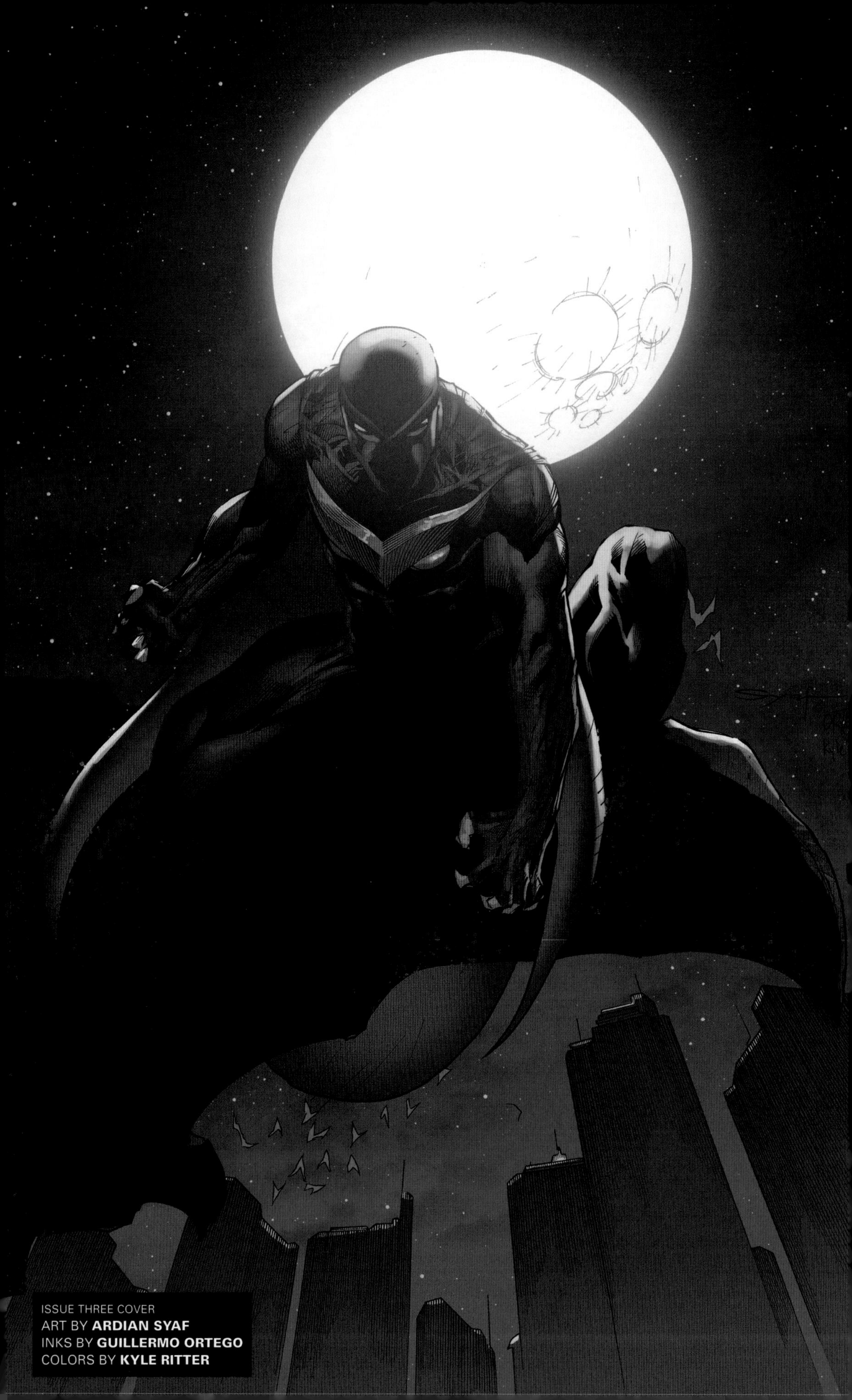

ISSUE THREE COVER
ART BY **ARDIAN SYAF**
INKS BY **GUILLERMO ORTEGO**
COLORS BY **KYLE RITTER**

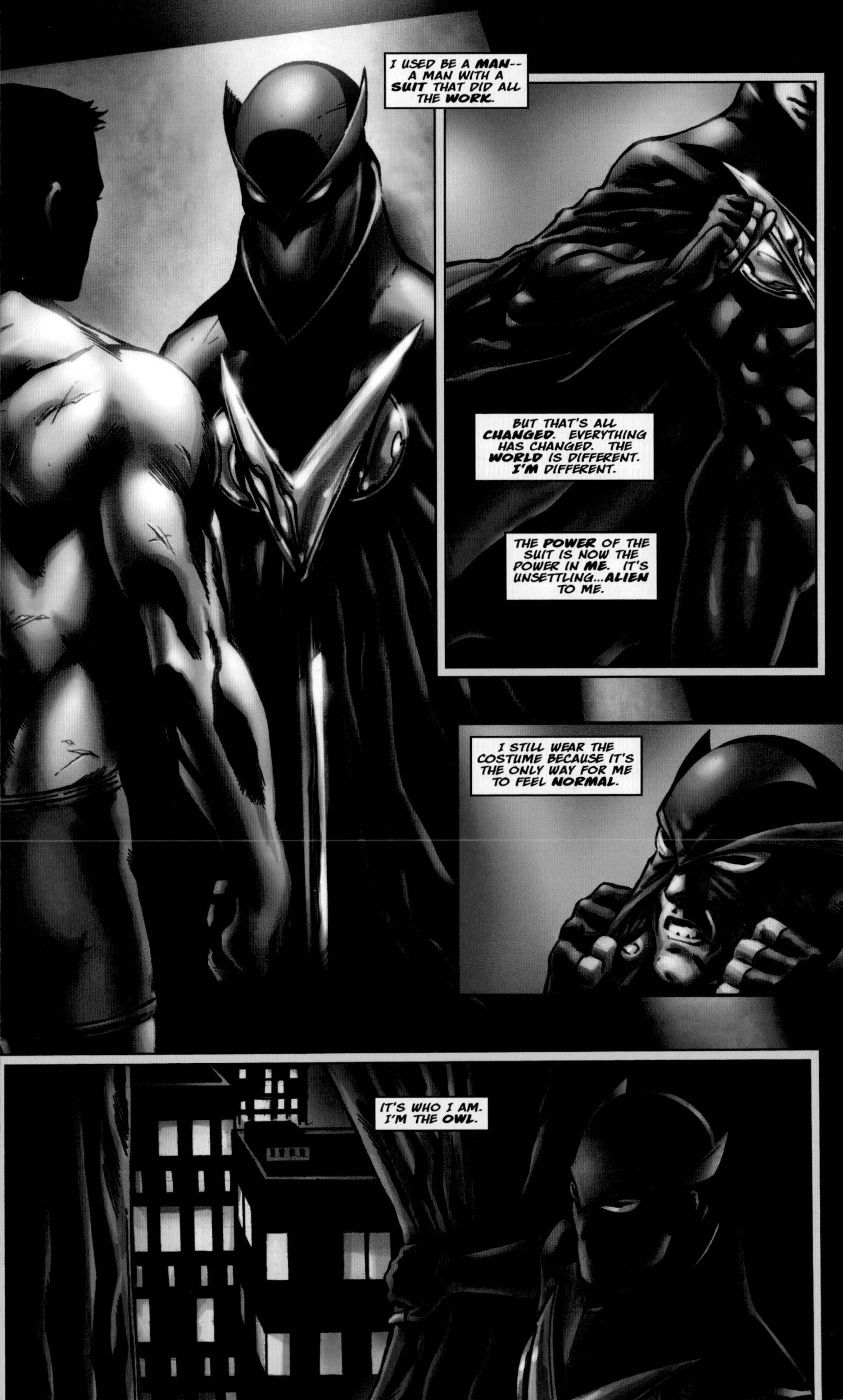
I USED BE A MAN--
A MAN WITH A
SUIT THAT DID ALL
THE WORK.
BUT THAT'S ALL
CHANGED. EVERYTHING
HAS CHANGED. THE
WORLD IS DIFFERENT.
I'M DIFFERENT.
THE POWER OF THE
SUIT IS NOW THE
POWER IN ME. IT'S
UNSETTLING...ALIEN
TO ME.
I STILL WEAR THE
COSTUME BECAUSE IT'S
THE ONLY WAY FOR ME
TO FEEL NORMAL.
IT'S WHO I AM.
I'M THE OWL.

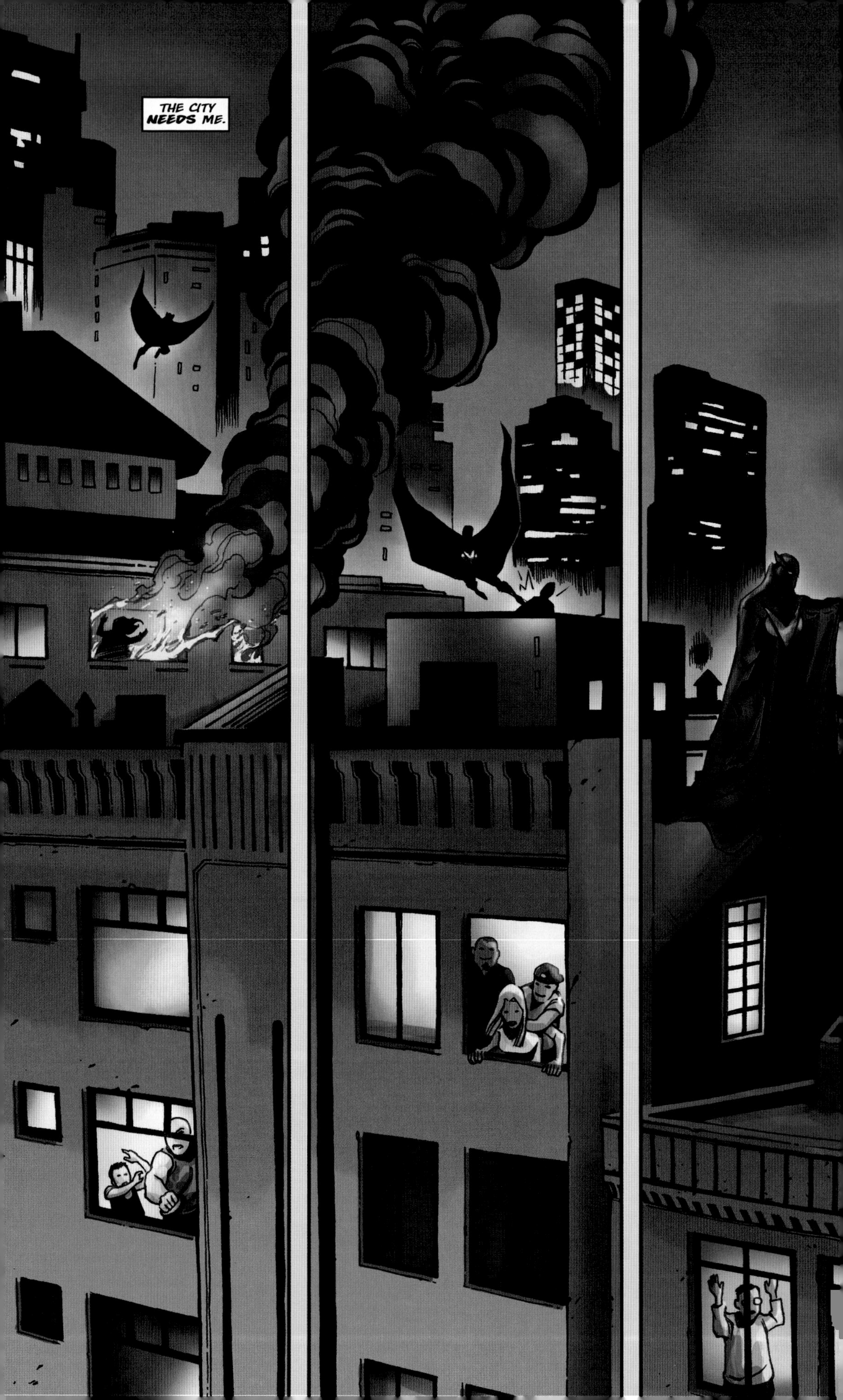
THE CITY NEEDS ME.

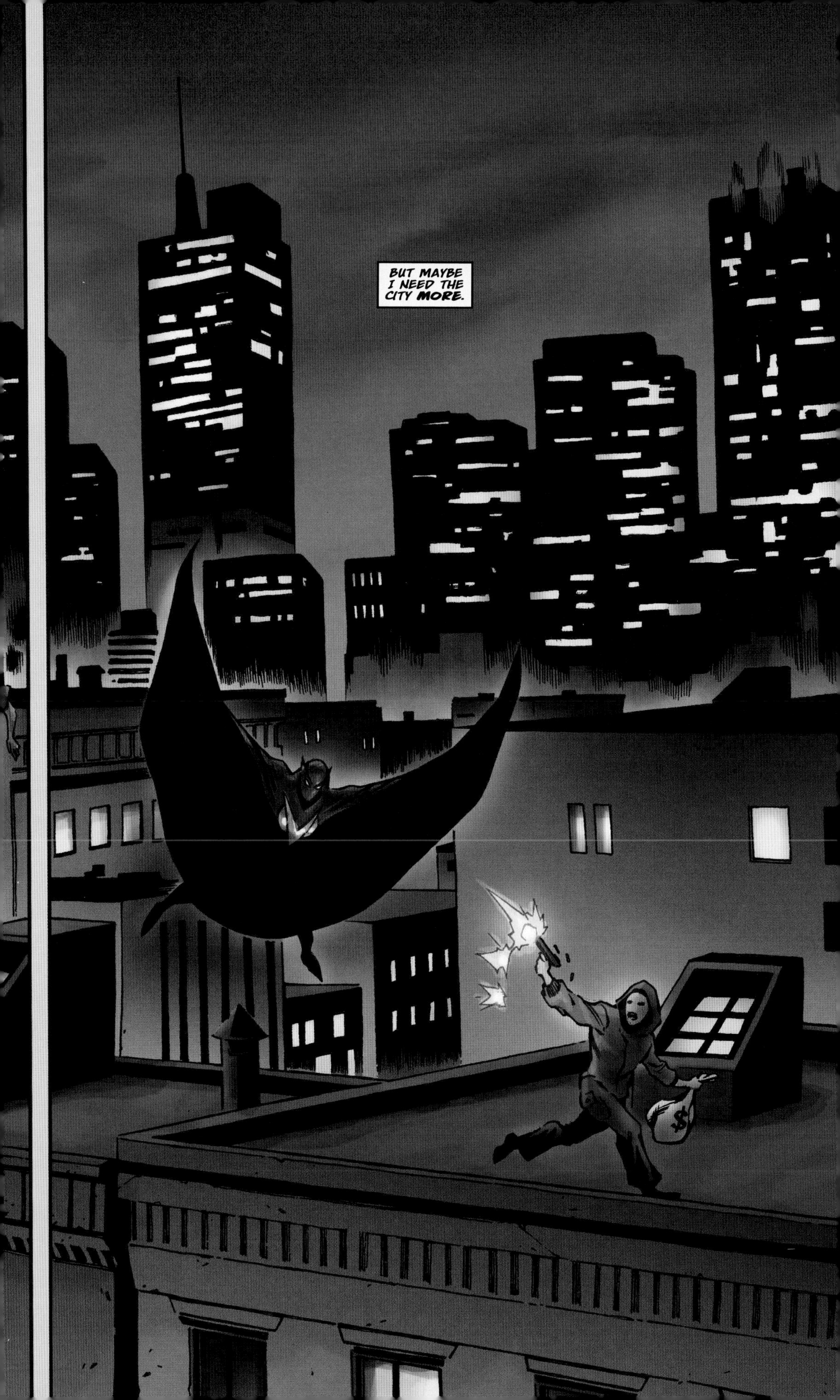
BUT MAYBE I NEED THE CITY MORE.

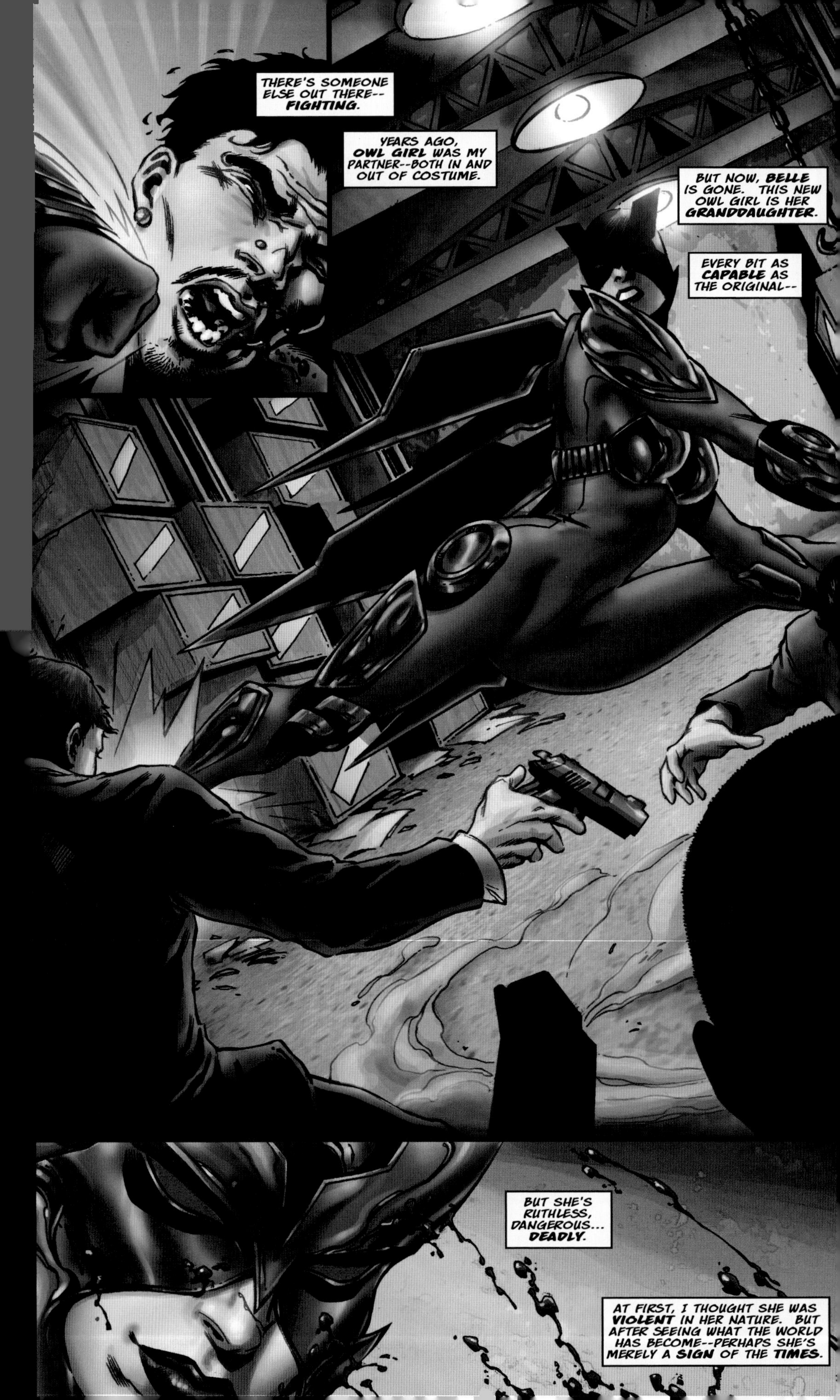
THERE'S SOMEONE ELSE OUT THERE-- FIGHTING.
YEARS AGO, OWL GIRL WAS MY PARTNER--BOTH IN AND OUT OF COSTUME.
BUT NOW, BELLE IS GONE. THIS NEW OWL GIRL IS HER GRANDDAUGHTER.
EVERY BIT AS CAPABLE AS THE ORIGINAL--
BUT SHE'S RUTHLESS, DANGEROUS... DEADLY.
AT FIRST, I THOUGHT SHE WAS VIOLENT IN HER NATURE. BUT AFTER SEEING WHAT THE WORLD HAS BECOME--PERHAPS SHE'S MERELY A SIGN OF THE TIMES.

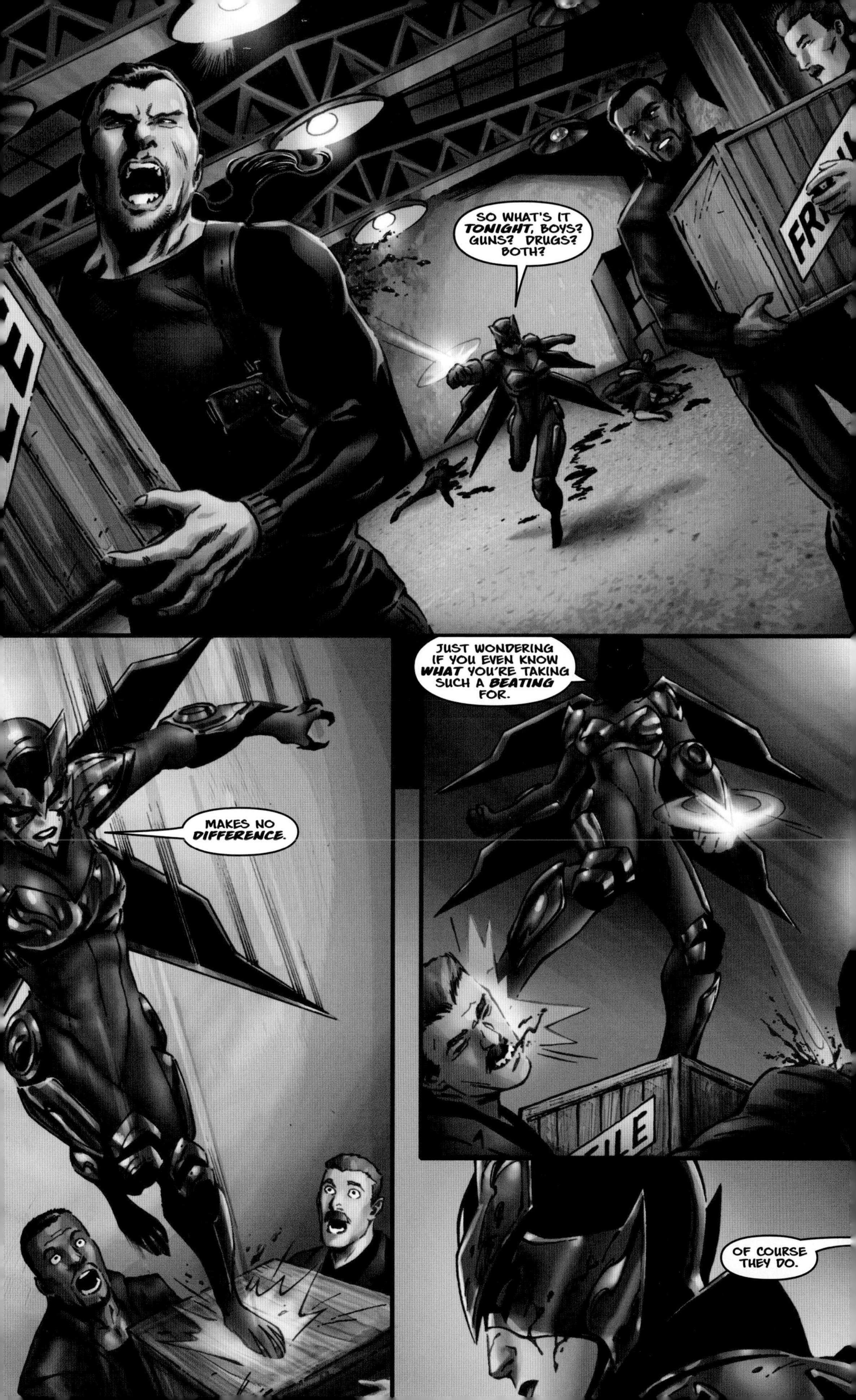

SO WHAT'S IT TONIGHT, BOYS? GUNS? DRUGS? BOTH?
MAKES NO DIFFERENCE.
JUST WONDERING IF YOU EVEN KNOW WHAT YOU'RE TAKING SUCH A BEATING FOR.
OF COURSE THEY DO.

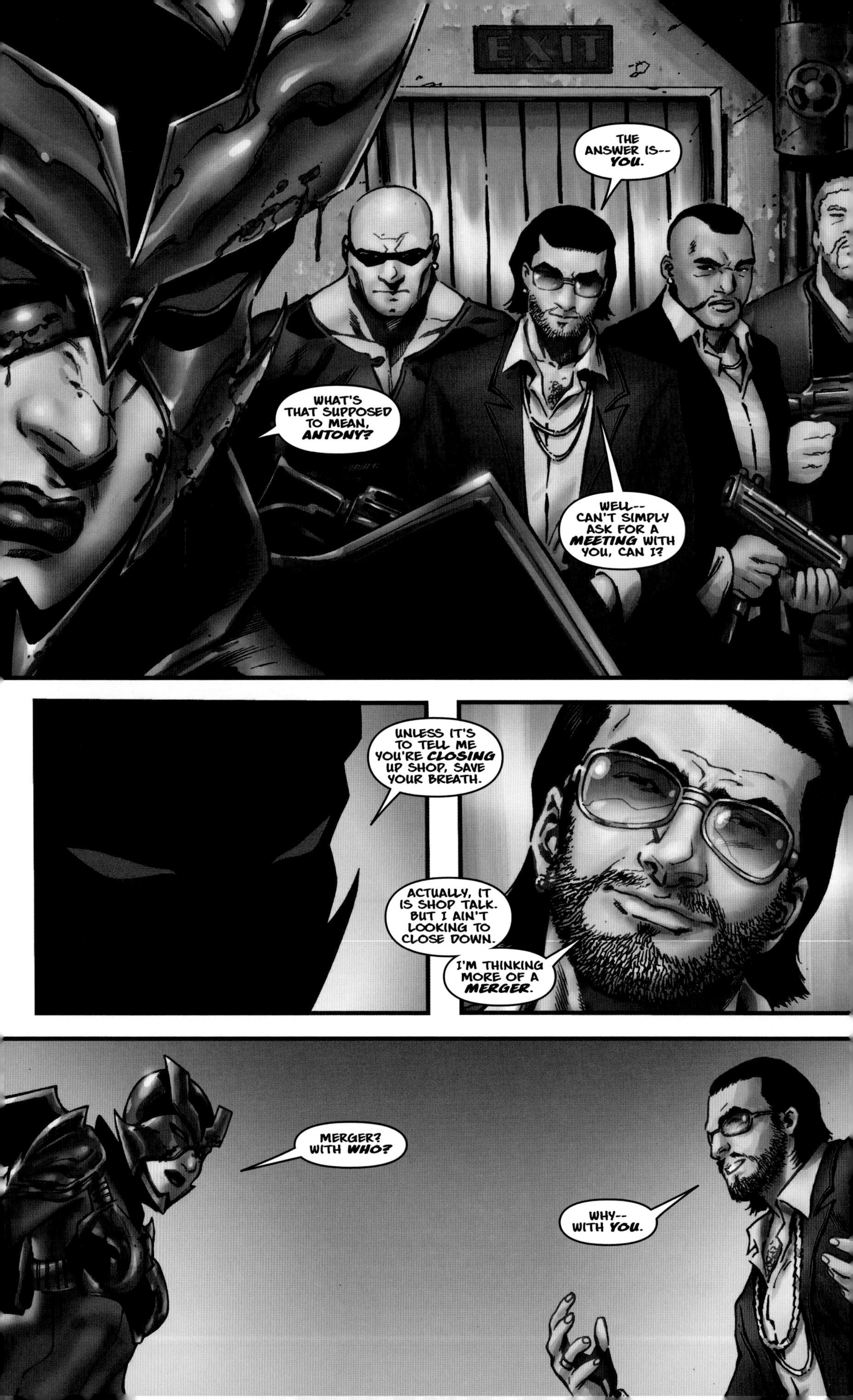
EXIT
THE ANSWER IS-- YOU.
WHAT'S THAT SUPPOSED TO MEAN, ANTONY?
WELL-- CAN'T SIMPLY ASK FOR A MEETING WITH YOU, CAN I?
UNLESS IT'S TO TELL ME YOU'RE CLOSING UP SHOP, SAVE YOUR BREATH.
ACTUALLY, IT IS SHOP TALK. BUT I AIN'T LOOKING TO CLOSE DOWN.
I'M THINKING MORE OF A MERGER.
MERGER? WITH WHO?
WHY-- WITH YOU.

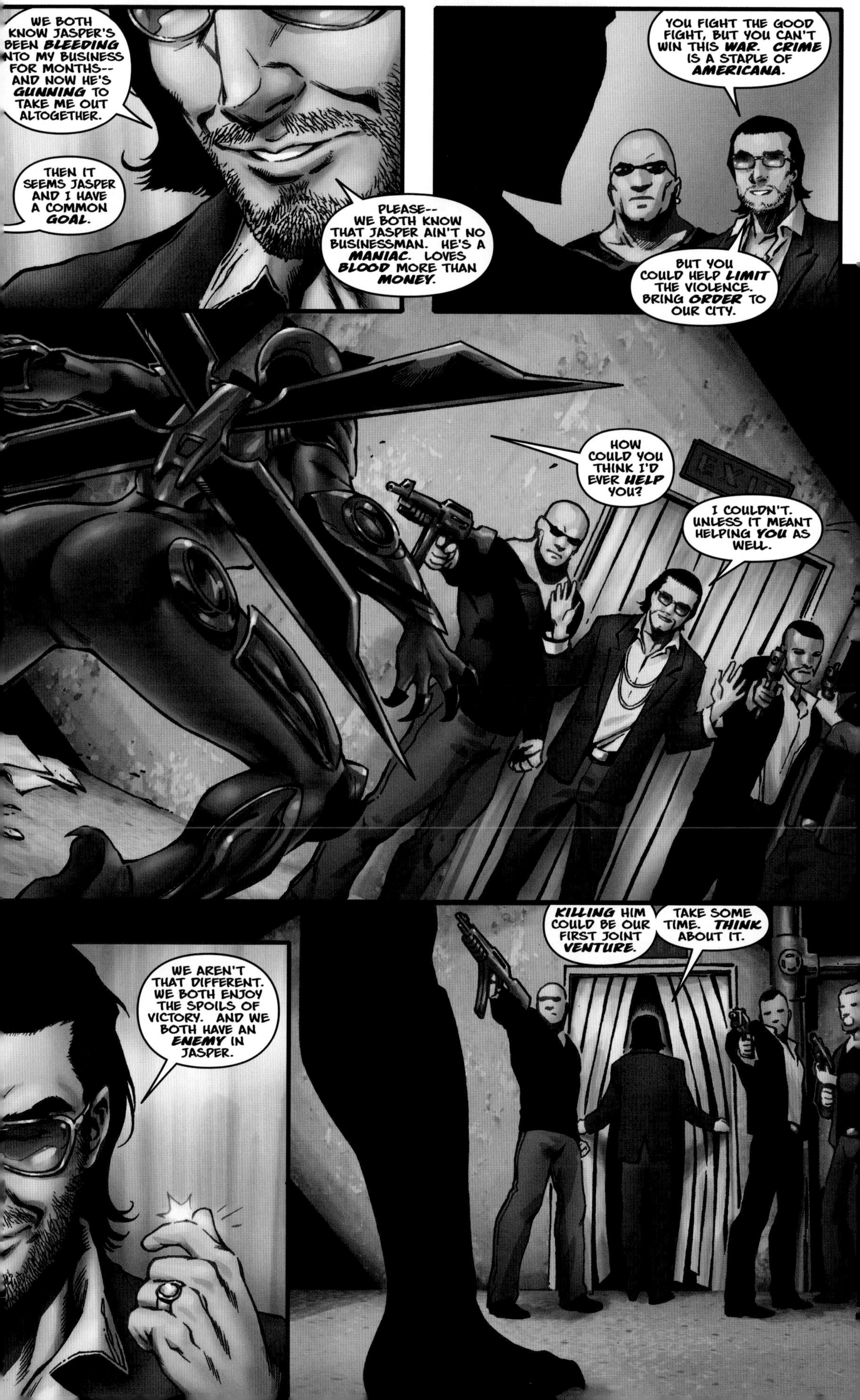

WE BOTH KNOW JASPER'S BEEN BLEEDING INTO MY BUSINESS FOR MONTHS-- AND NOW HE'S GUNNING TO TAKE ME OUT ALTOGETHER.
THEN IT SEEMS JASPER AND I HAVE A COMMON GOAL.
PLEASE-- WE BOTH KNOW THAT JASPER AIN'T NO BUSINESSMAN. HE'S A MANIAC. LOVES BLOOD MORE THAN MONEY.
YOU FIGHT THE GOOD FIGHT, BUT YOU CAN'T WIN THIS WAR. CRIME IS A STAPLE OF AMERICANA.
BUT YOU COULD HELP LIMIT THE VIOLENCE. BRING ORDER TO OUR CITY.
HOW COULD YOU THINK I'D EVER HELP YOU?
EXIT
I COULDN'T. UNLESS IT MEANT HELPING YOU AS WELL.
WE AREN'T THAT DIFFERENT. WE BOTH ENJOY THE SPOILS OF VICTORY. AND WE BOTH HAVE AN ENEMY IN JASPER.
KILLING HIM COULD BE OUR FIRST JOINT VENTURE.
TAKE SOME TIME. THINK ABOUT IT.

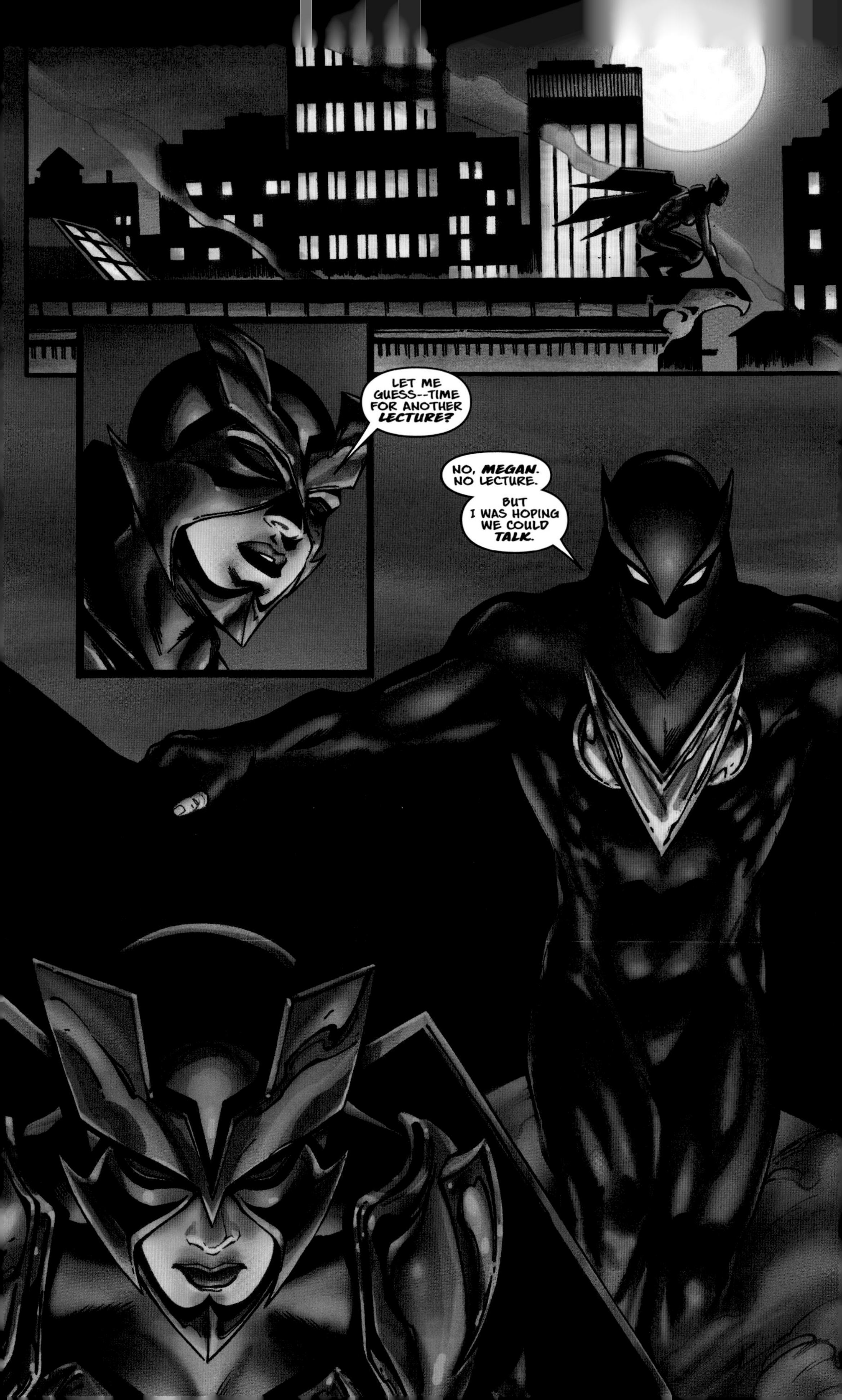
LET ME GUESS--TIME FOR ANOTHER LECTURE?
NO, MEGAN. NO LECTURE.
BUT I WAS HOPING WE COULD TALK.

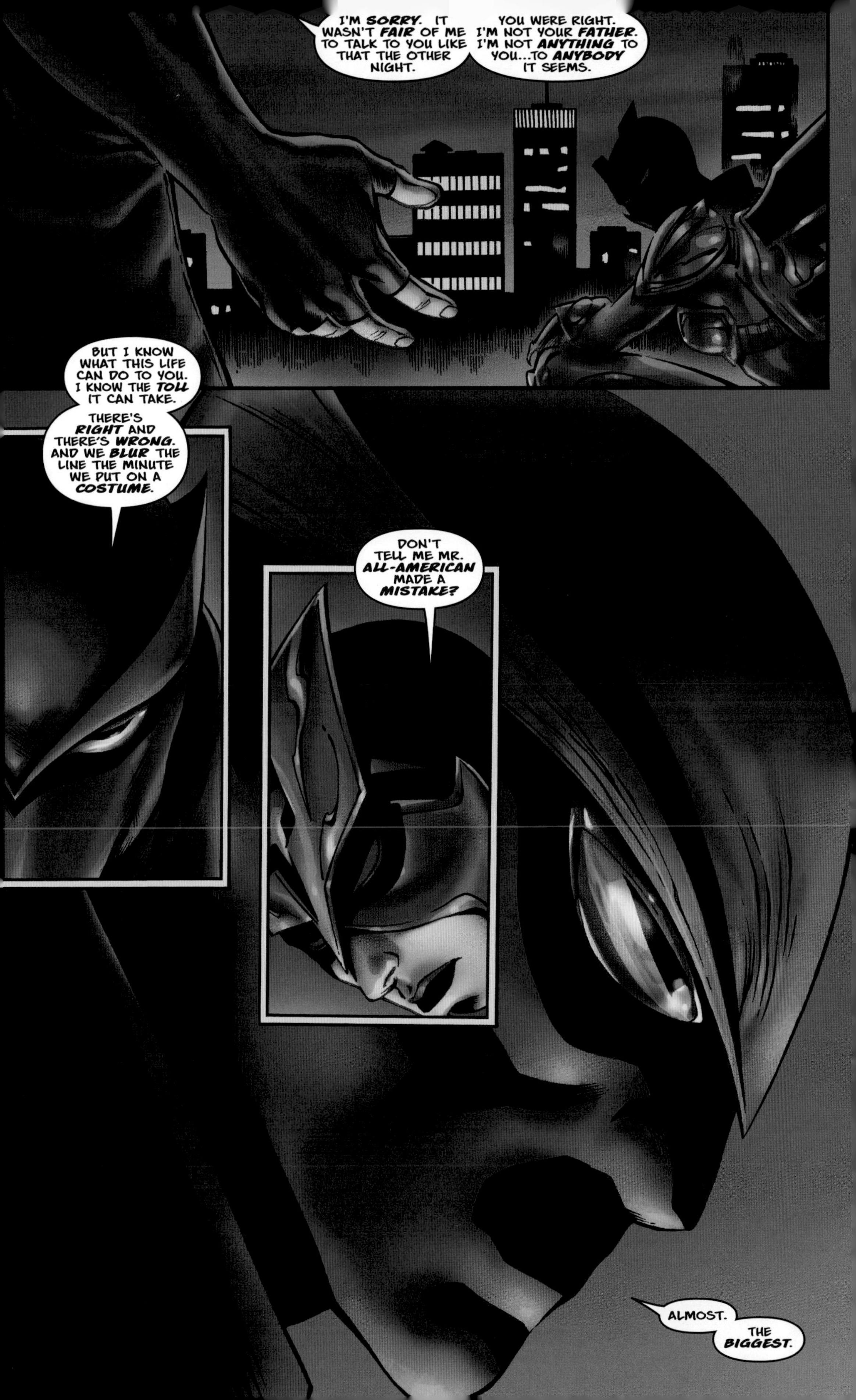
I'M SORRY. IT WASN'T FAIR OF ME TO TALK TO YOU LIKE THAT THE OTHER NIGHT.
YOU WERE RIGHT. I'M NOT YOUR FATHER. I'M NOT ANYTHING TO YOU...TO ANYBODY IT SEEMS.
BUT I KNOW WHAT THIS LIFE CAN DO TO YOU. I KNOW THE TOLL IT CAN TAKE.
THERE'S RIGHT AND THERE'S WRONG. AND WE BLUR THE LINE THE MINUTE WE PUT ON A COSTUME.
DON'T TELL ME MR. ALL-AMERICAN MADE A MISTAKE?
ALMOST. THE BIGGEST.

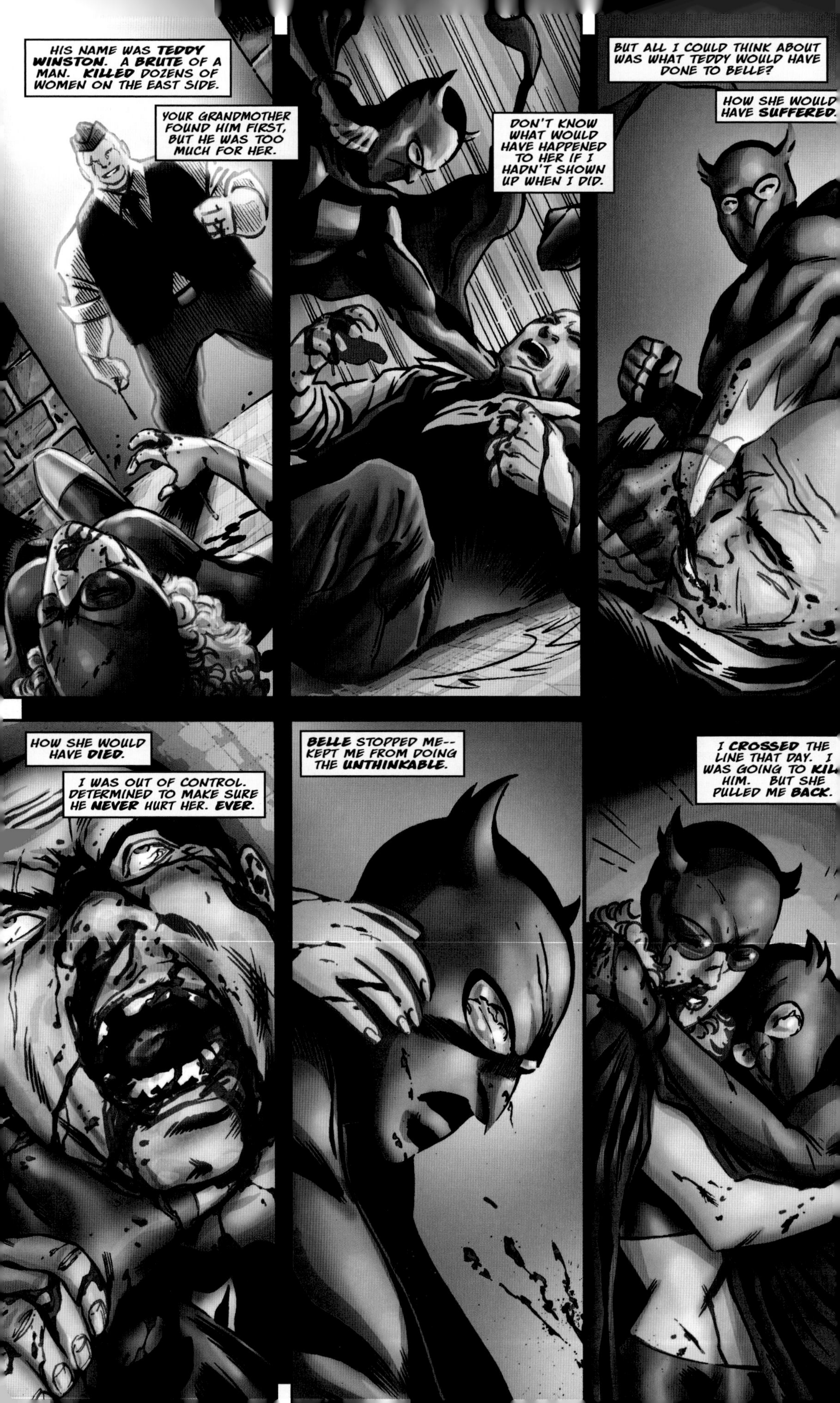

HIS NAME WAS TEDDY WINSTON. A BRUTE OF A MAN. KILLED DOZENS OF WOMEN ON THE EAST SIDE.
YOUR GRANDMOTHER FOUND HIM FIRST, BUT HE WAS TOO MUCH FOR HER.
DON'T KNOW WHAT WOULD HAVE HAPPENED TO HER IF I HADN'T SHOWN UP WHEN I DID.
BUT ALL I COULD THINK ABOUT WAS WHAT TEDDY WOULD HAVE DONE TO BELLE?
HOW SHE WOULD HAVE SUFFERED.
HOW SHE WOULD HAVE DIED.
I WAS OUT OF CONTROL. DETERMINED TO MAKE SURE HE NEVER HURT HER. EVER.
BELLE STOPPED ME-- KEPT ME FROM DOING THE UNTHINKABLE.
I CROSSED THE LINE THAT DAY. I WAS GOING TO KIL HIM. BUT SHE PULLED ME BACK.

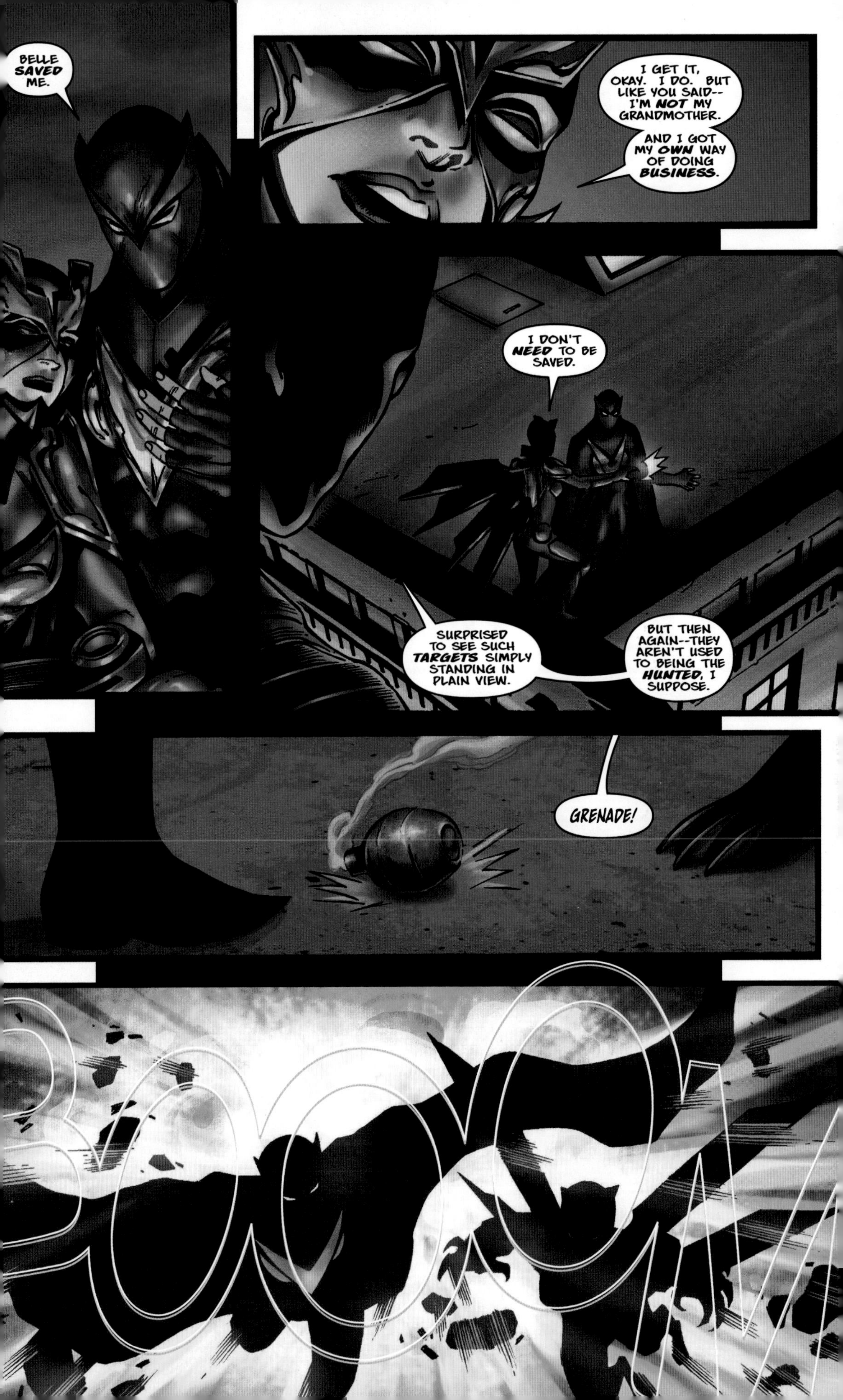
BELLE SAVED ME.
I GET IT, OKAY. I DO. BUT LIKE YOU SAID-- I'M NOT MY GRANDMOTHER.
AND I GOT MY OWN WAY OF DOING BUSINESS.
I DON'T NEED TO BE SAVED.
SURPRISED TO SEE SUCH TARGETS SIMPLY STANDING IN PLAIN VIEW.
BUT THEN AGAIN--THEY AREN'T USED TO BEING THE HUNTED, I SUPPOSE.
GRENADE!
BOOOOM

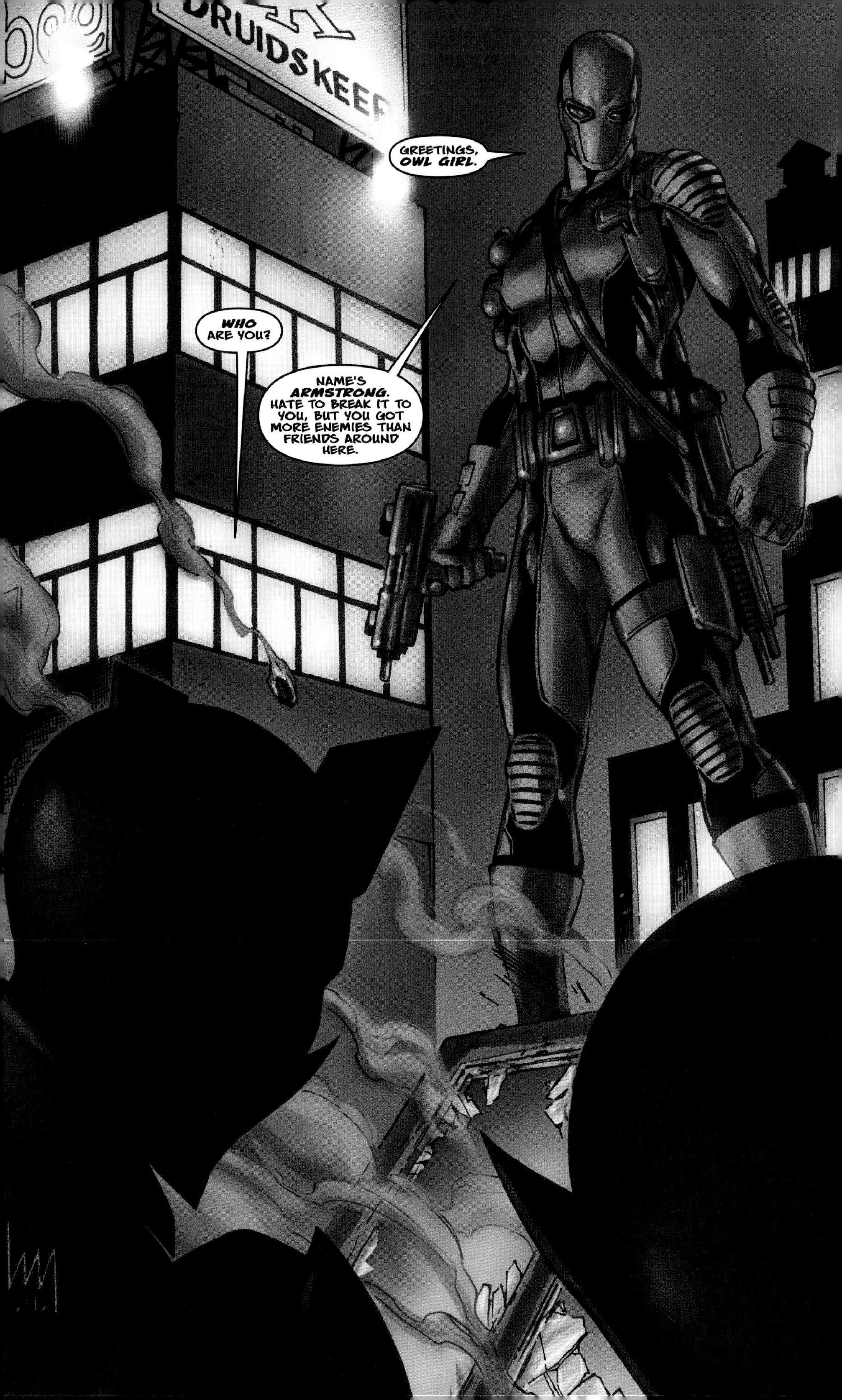
DRUIDSKEEP
GREETINGS, OWL GIRL.
WHO ARE YOU?
NAME'S ARMSTRONG. HATE TO BREAK IT TO YOU, BUT YOU GOT MORE ENEMIES THAN FRIENDS AROUND HERE.

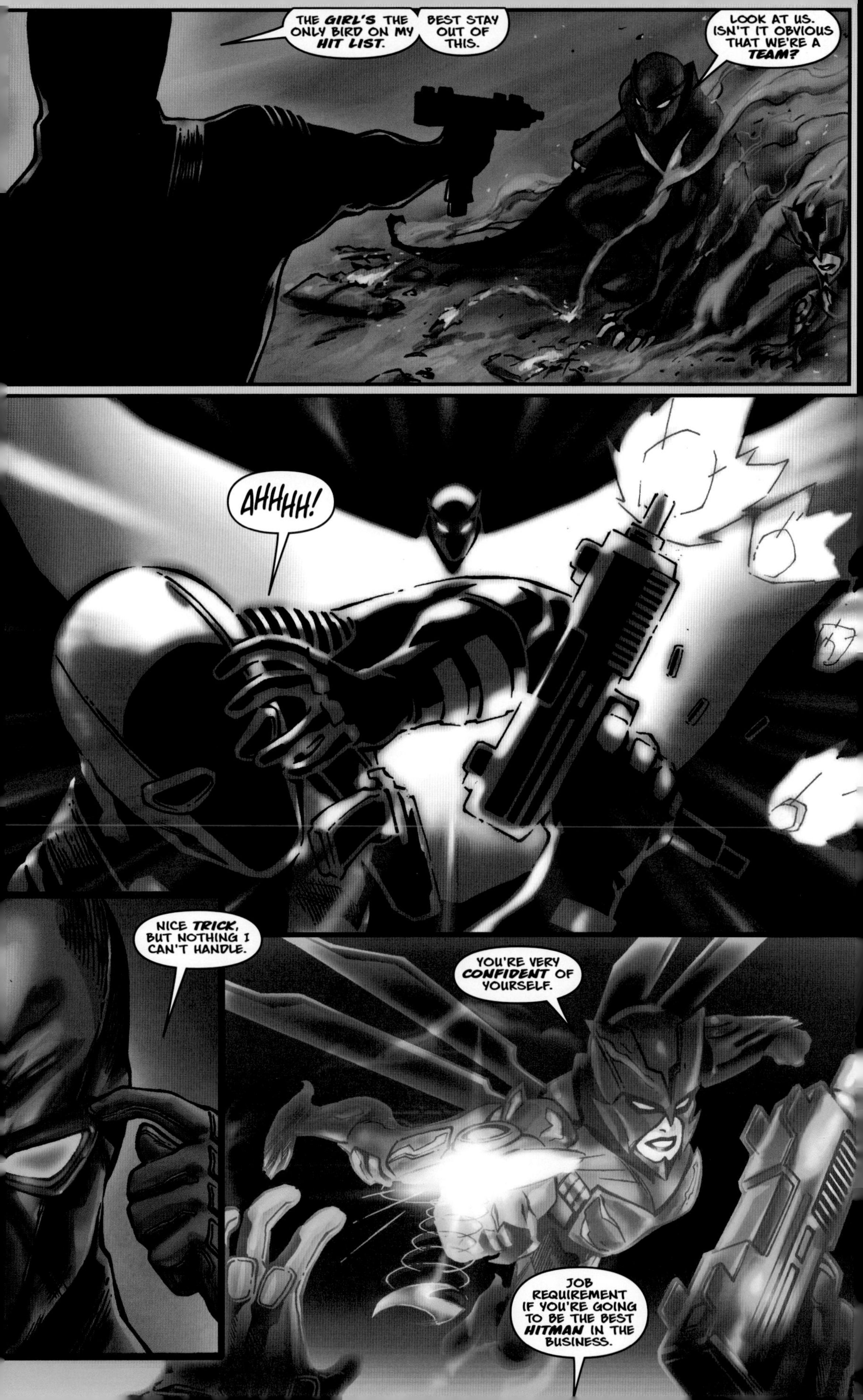
THE GIRL'S THE ONLY BIRD ON MY HIT LIST.
BEST STAY OUT OF THIS.
LOOK AT US. ISN'T IT OBVIOUS THAT WE'RE A TEAM?
AHHHH!
NICE TRICK, BUT NOTHING I CAN'T HANDLE.
YOU'RE VERY CONFIDENT OF YOURSELF.
JOB REQUIREMENT IF YOU'RE GOING TO BE THE BEST HITMAN IN THE BUSINESS.

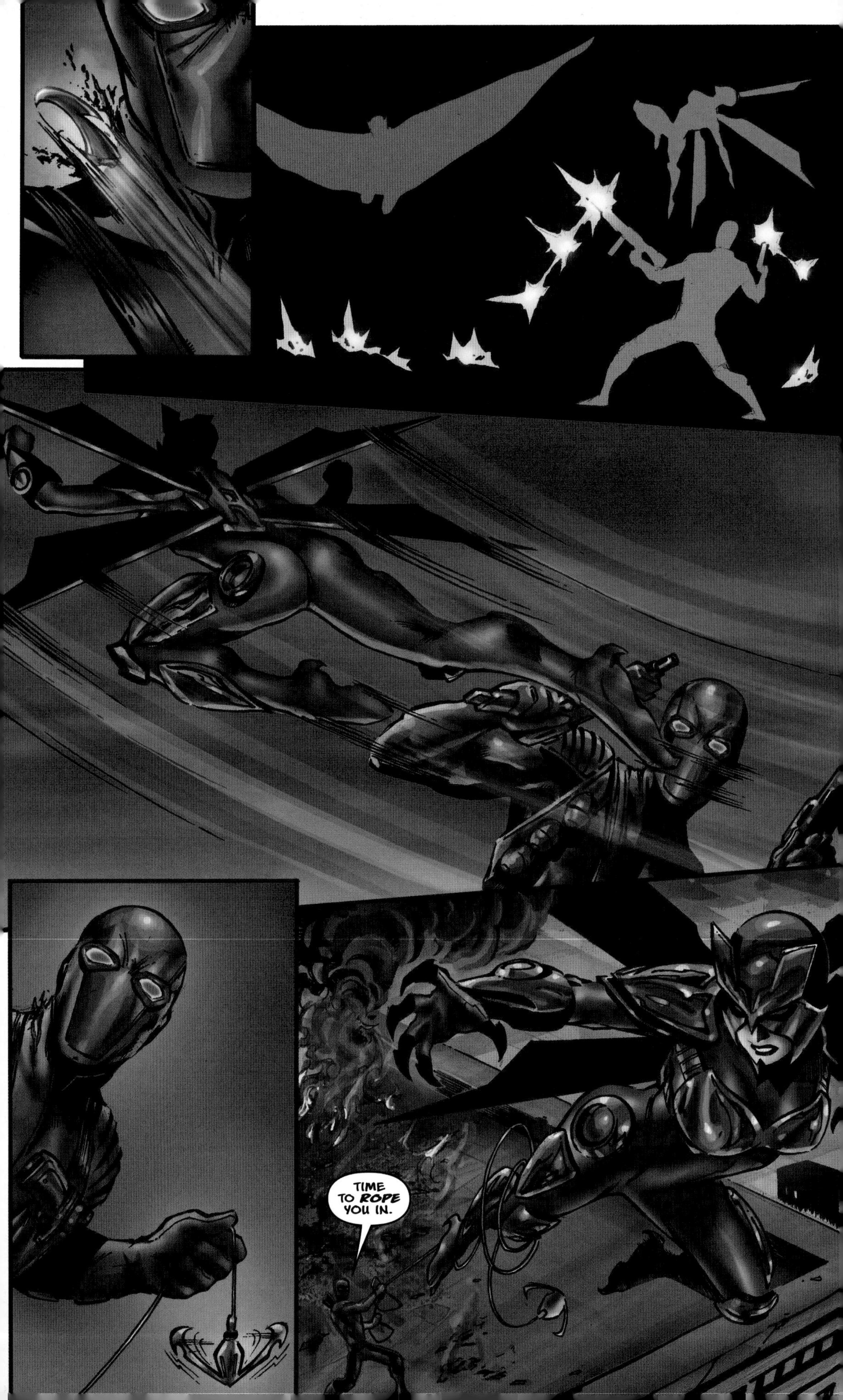
TIME TO ROPE YOU IN.

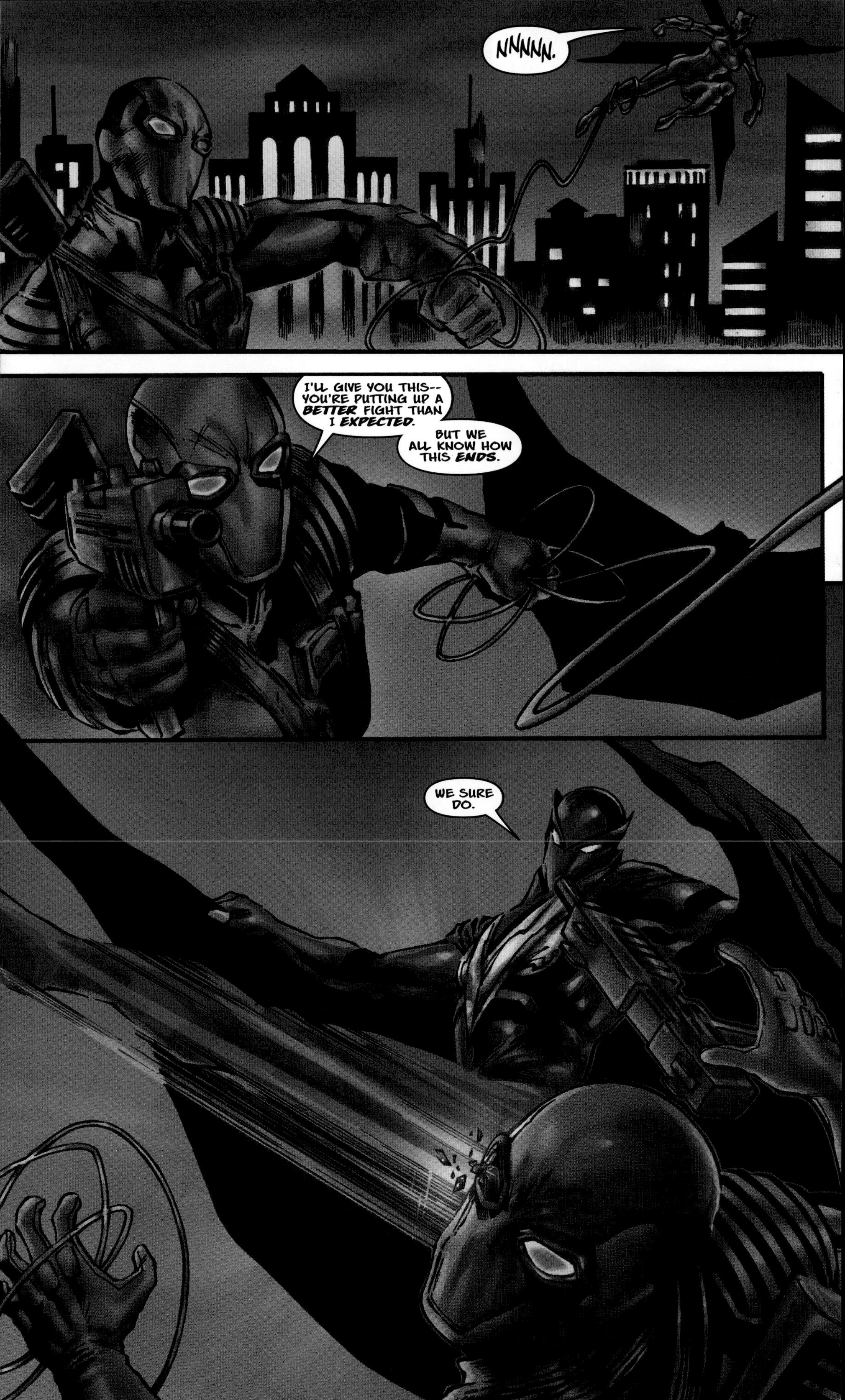
NNNNN.
I'LL GIVE YOU THIS-- YOU'RE PUTTING UP A BETTER FIGHT THAN I EXPECTED.
BUT WE ALL KNOW HOW THIS ENDS.
WE SURE DO.

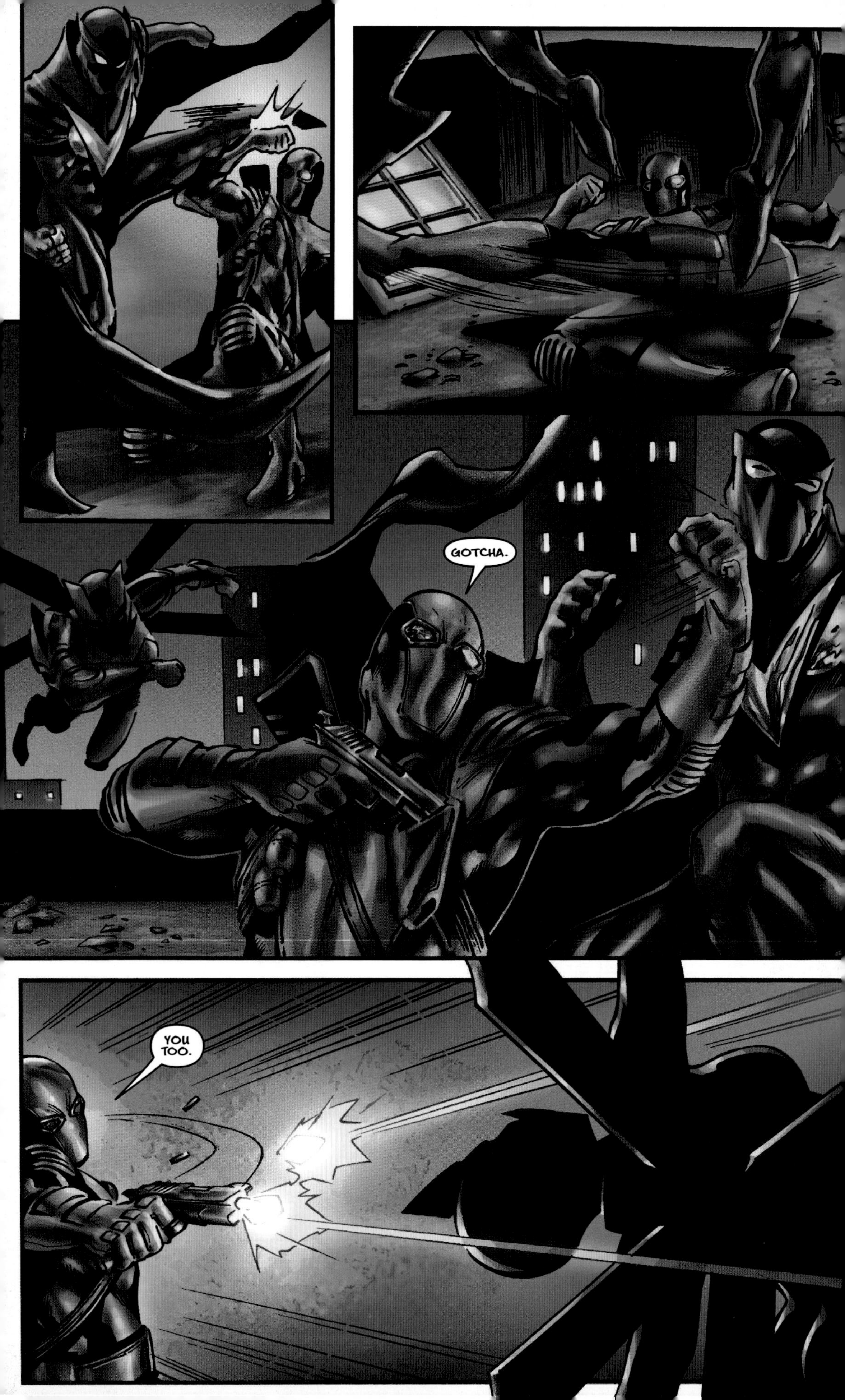
GOTCHA.
YOU TOO.

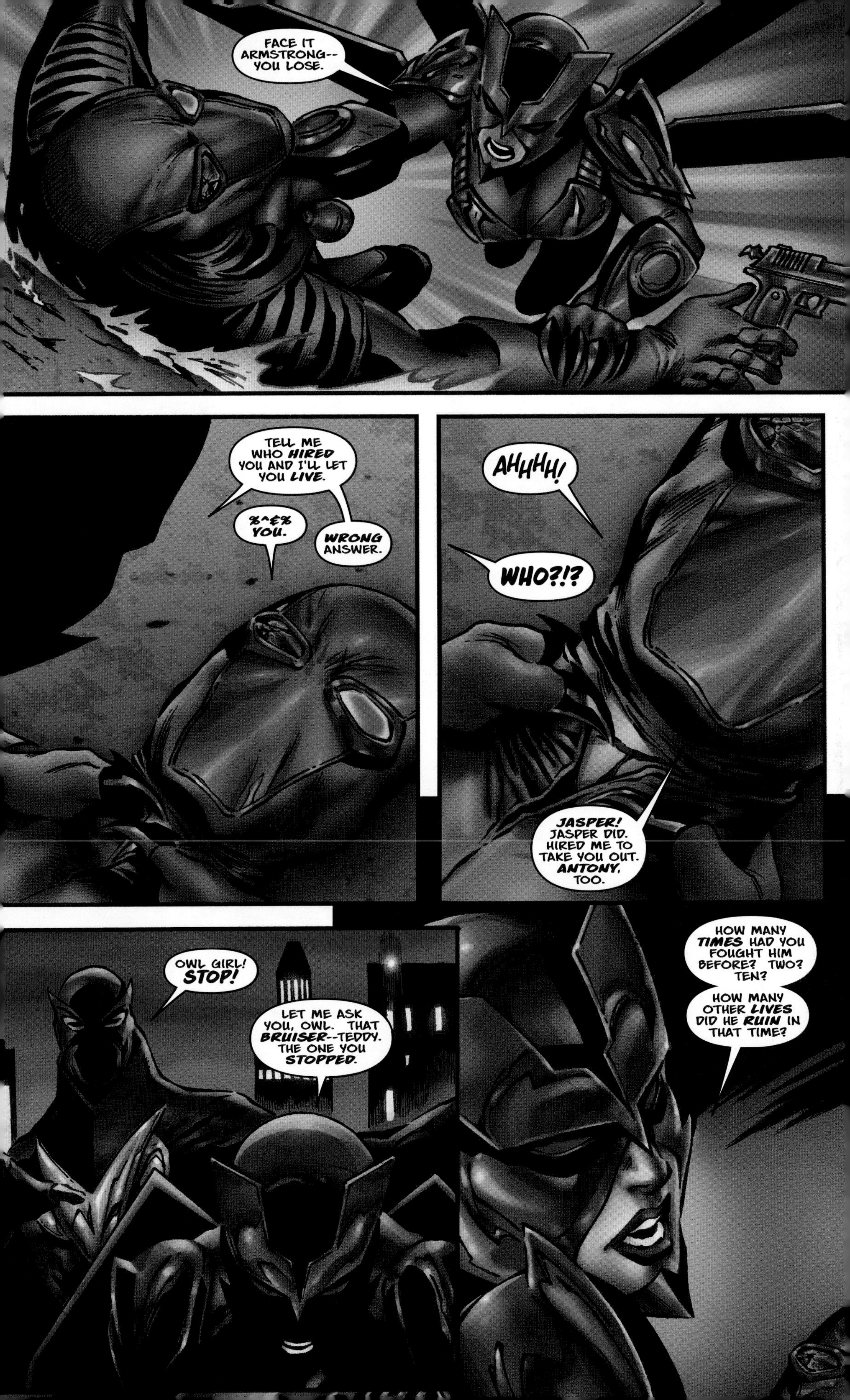

FACE IT ARMSTRONG-- YOU LOSE.
TELL ME WHO HIRED YOU AND I'LL LET YOU LIVE.
%^£% YOU.
WRONG ANSWER.
AHHHH!
WHO?!?
JASPER! JASPER DID. HIRED ME TO TAKE YOU OUT. ANTONY, TOO.
OWL GIRL! STOP!
LET ME ASK YOU, OWL. THAT BRUISER--TEDDY. THE ONE YOU STOPPED.
HOW MANY TIMES HAD YOU FOUGHT HIM BEFORE? TWO? TEN?
HOW MANY OTHER LIVES DID HE RUIN IN THAT TIME?

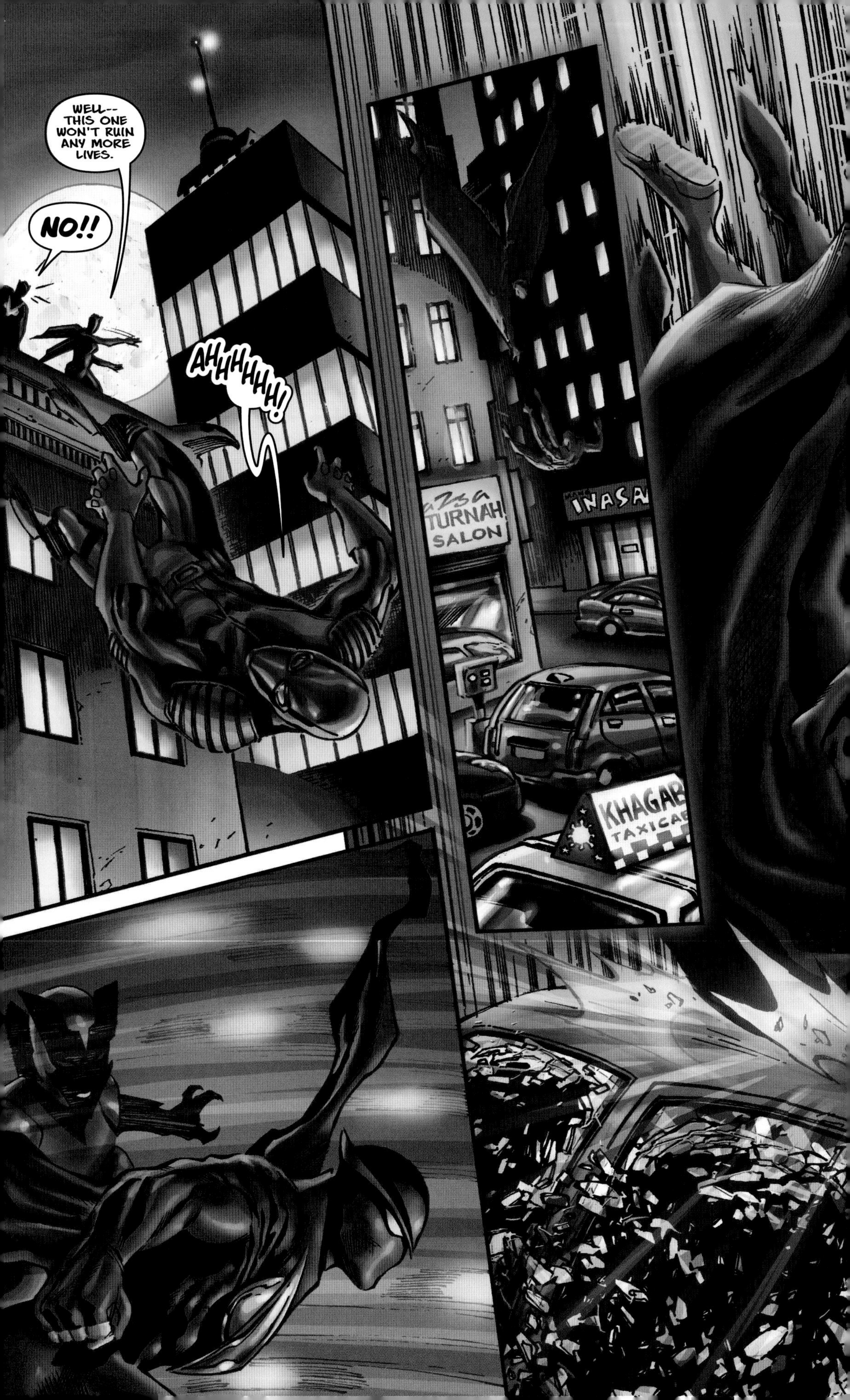
WELL-- THIS ONE WON'T RUIN ANY MORE LIVES.
NO!!
AHHHHHH!
TURNAH! SALON
INASA
KHAGAB TAXICAB

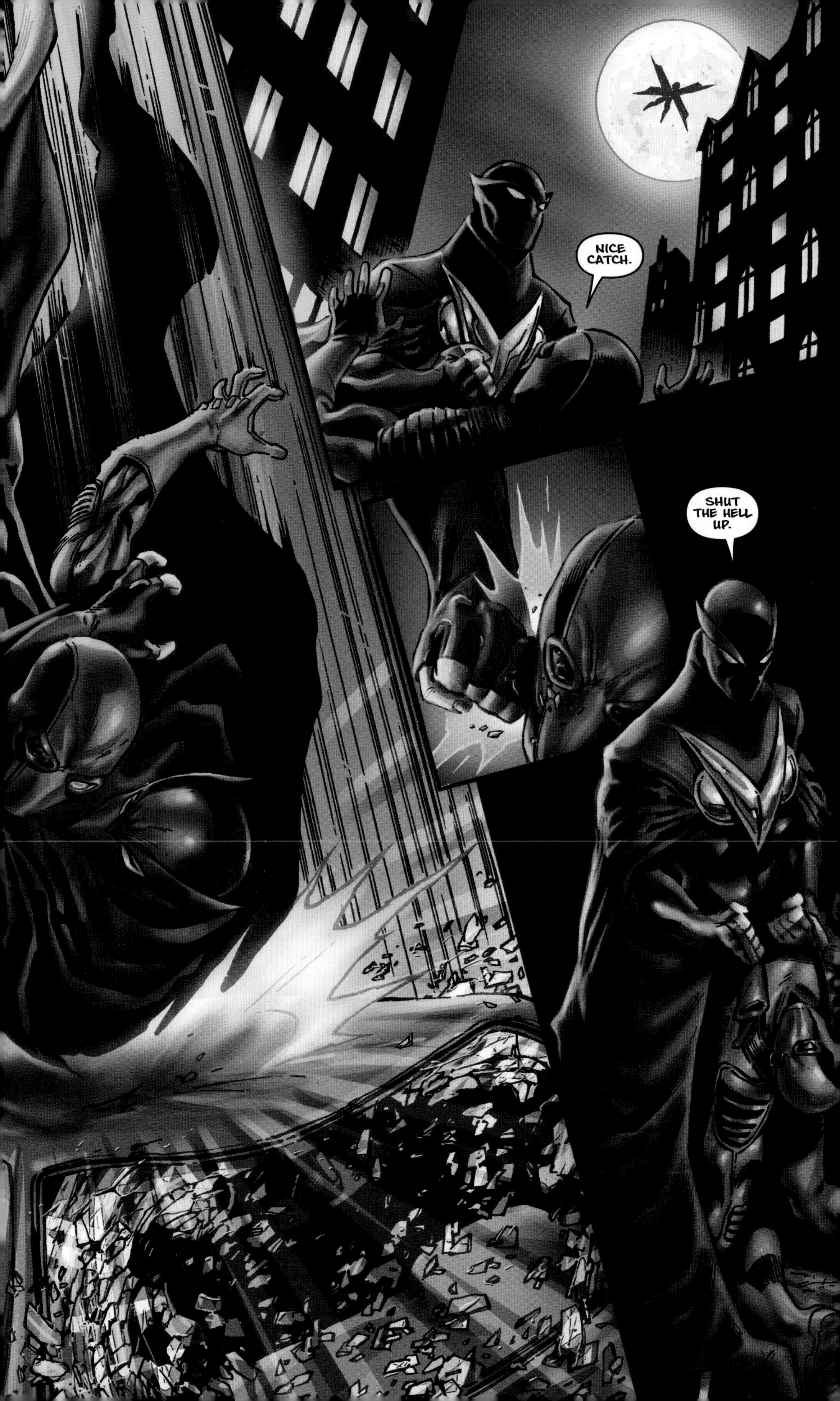
NICE CATCH.
SHUT THE HELL UP.

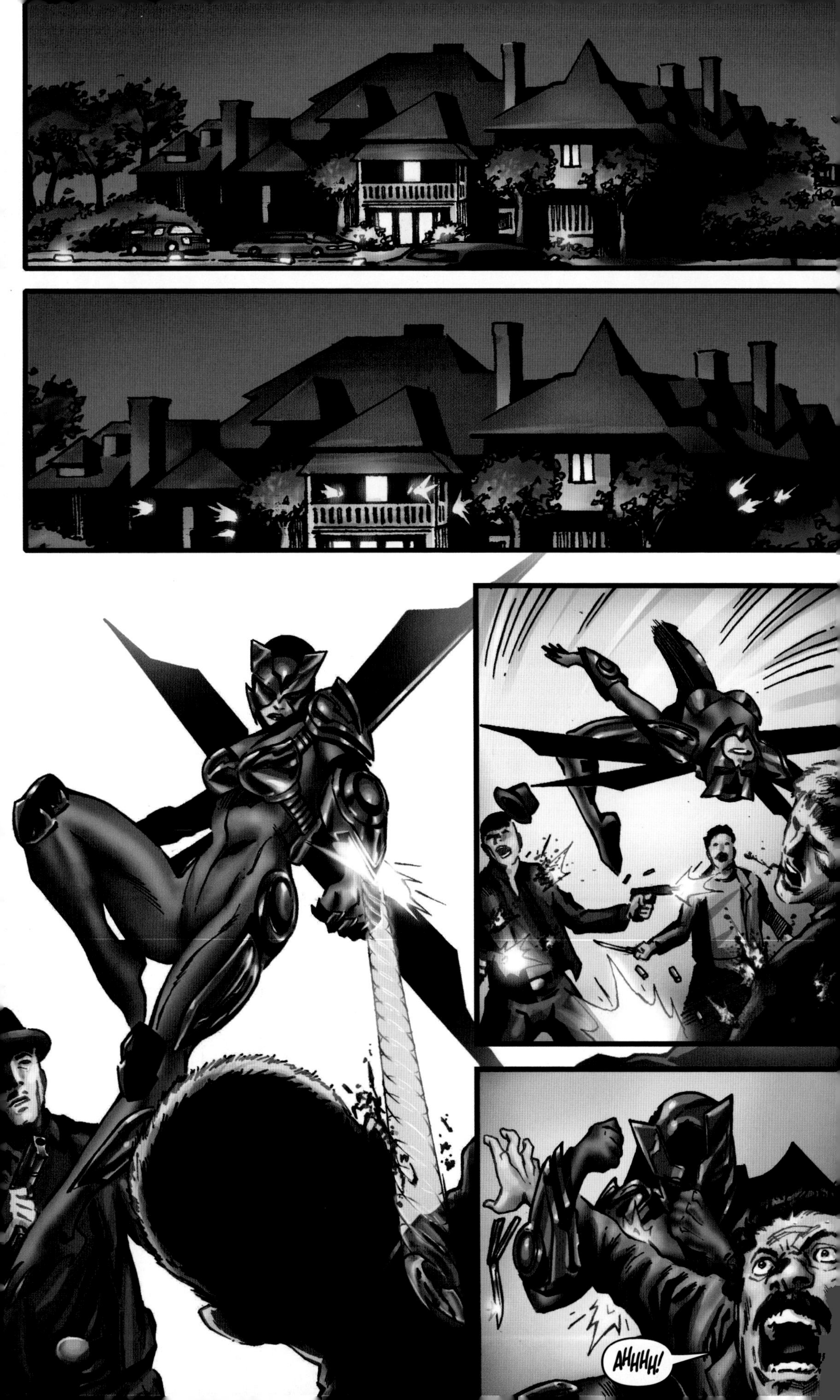
AHHHH!

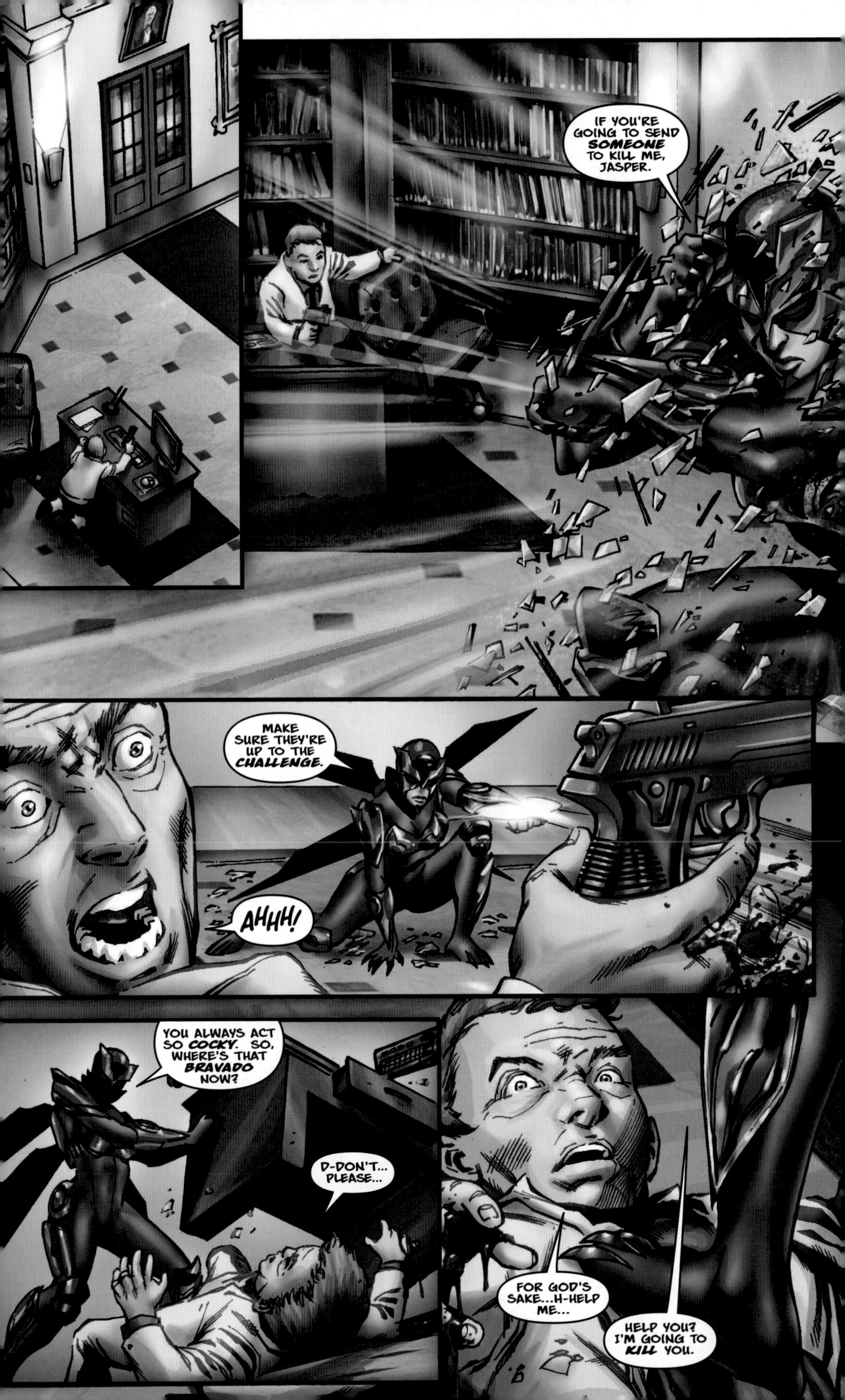
IF YOU'RE GOING TO SEND SOMEONE TO KILL ME, JASPER.
MAKE SURE THEY'RE UP TO THE CHALLENGE.
AHHH!
YOU ALWAYS ACT SO COCKY. SO, WHERE'S THAT BRAVADO NOW?
D-DON'T... PLEASE...
FOR GOD'S SAKE...H-HELP ME...
HELP YOU? I'M GOING TO KILL YOU.

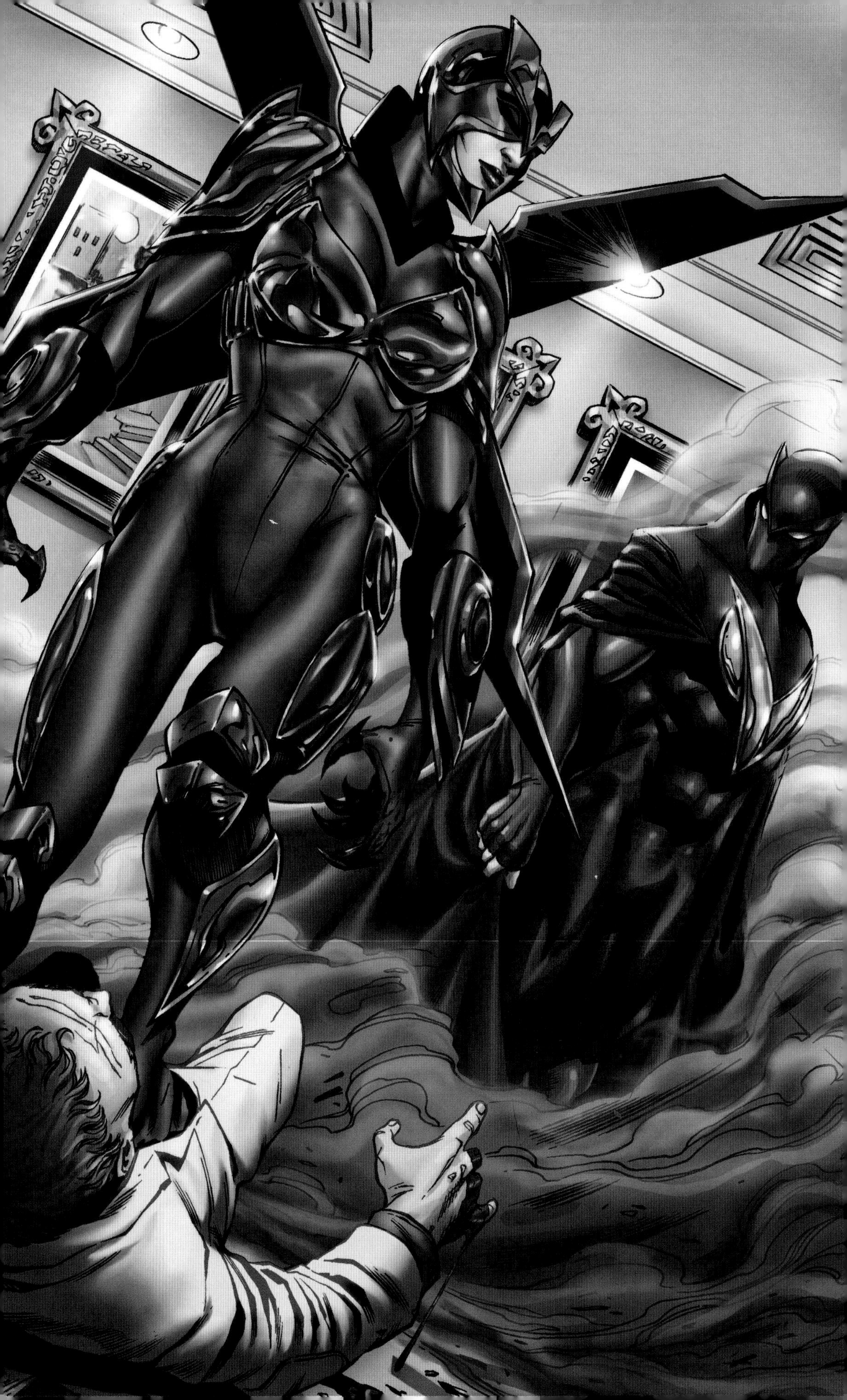

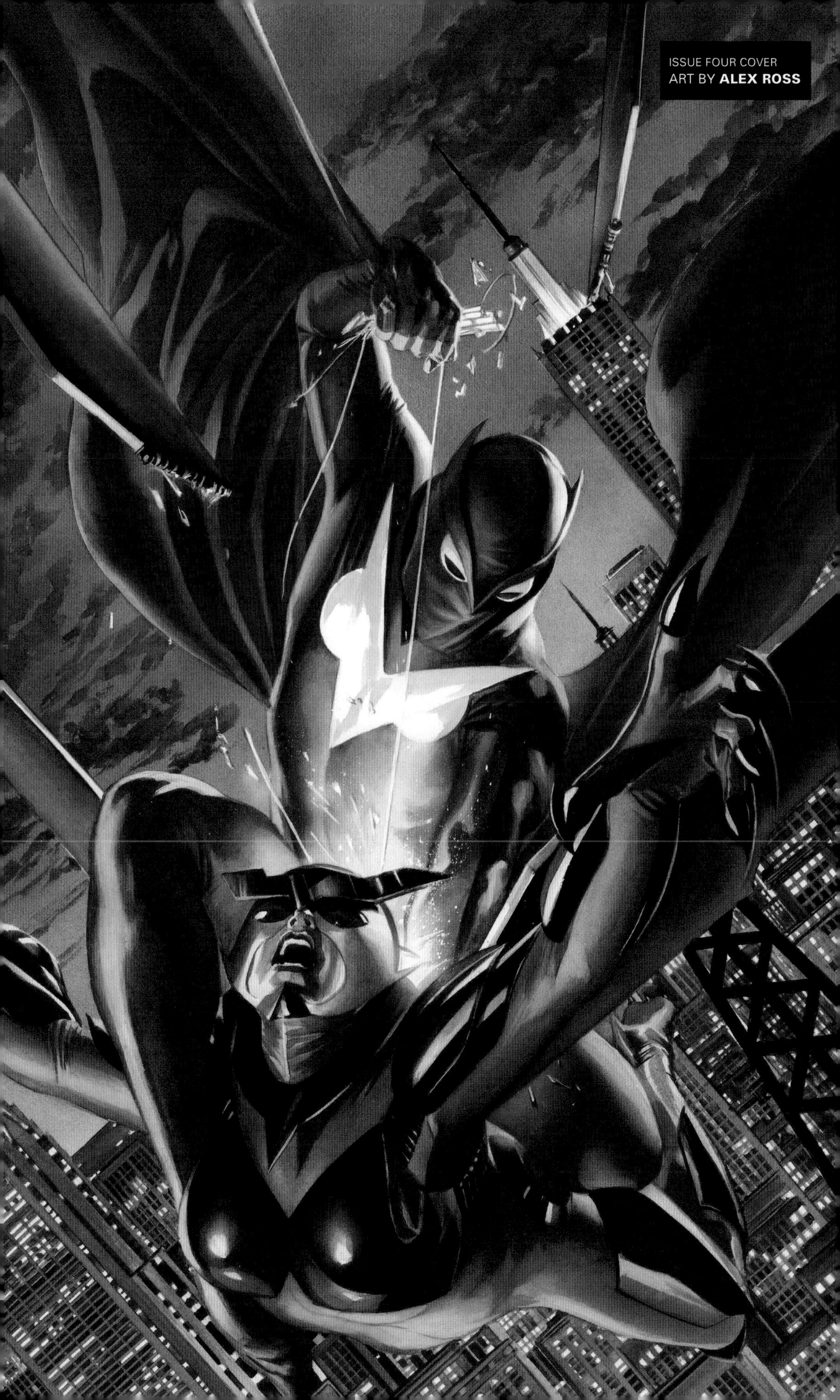

ISSUE FOUR COVER
ART BY **ALEX ROSS**

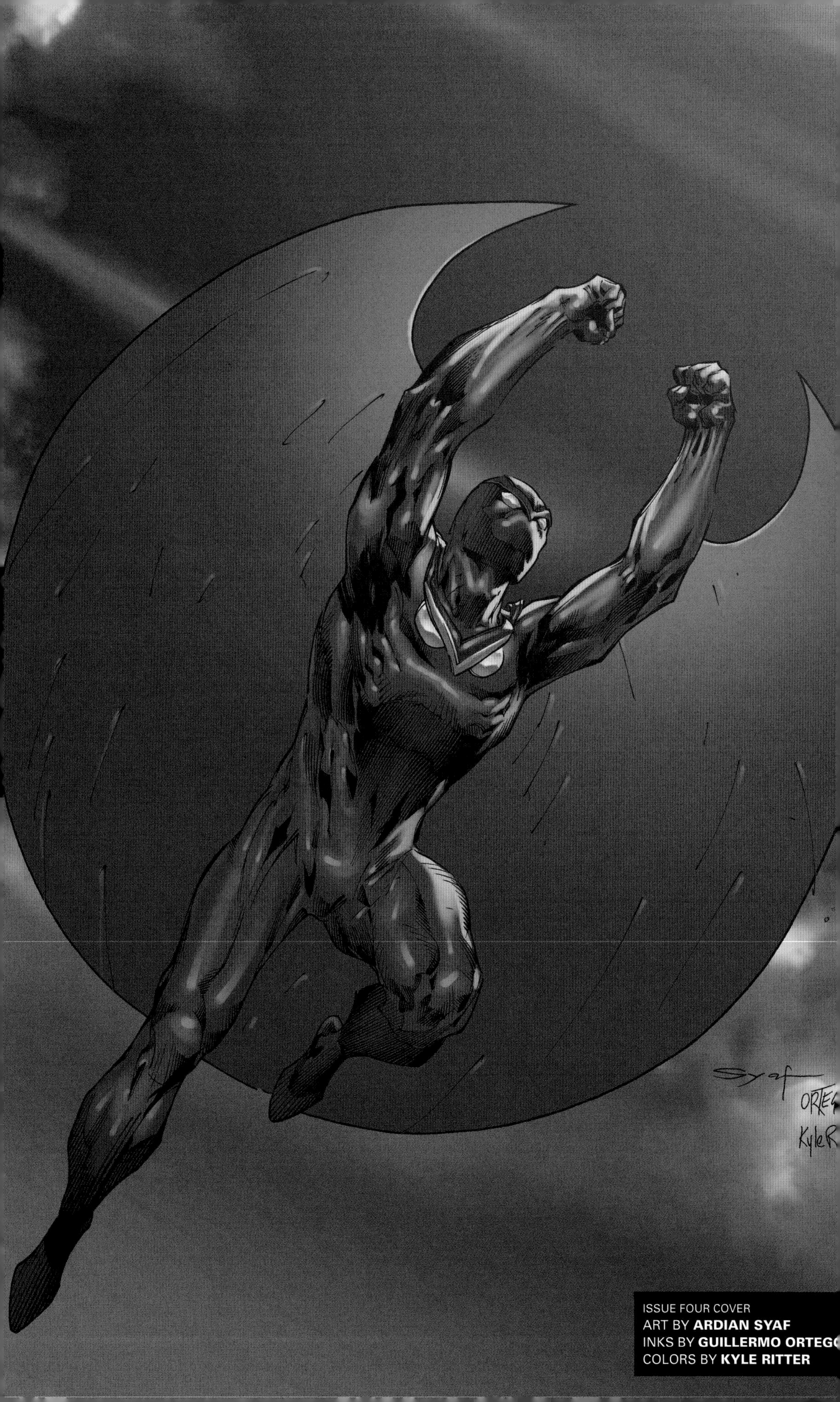

ISSUE FOUR COVER
ART BY **ARDIAN SYAF**
INKS BY **GUILLERMO ORTEGO**
COLORS BY **KYLE RITTER**

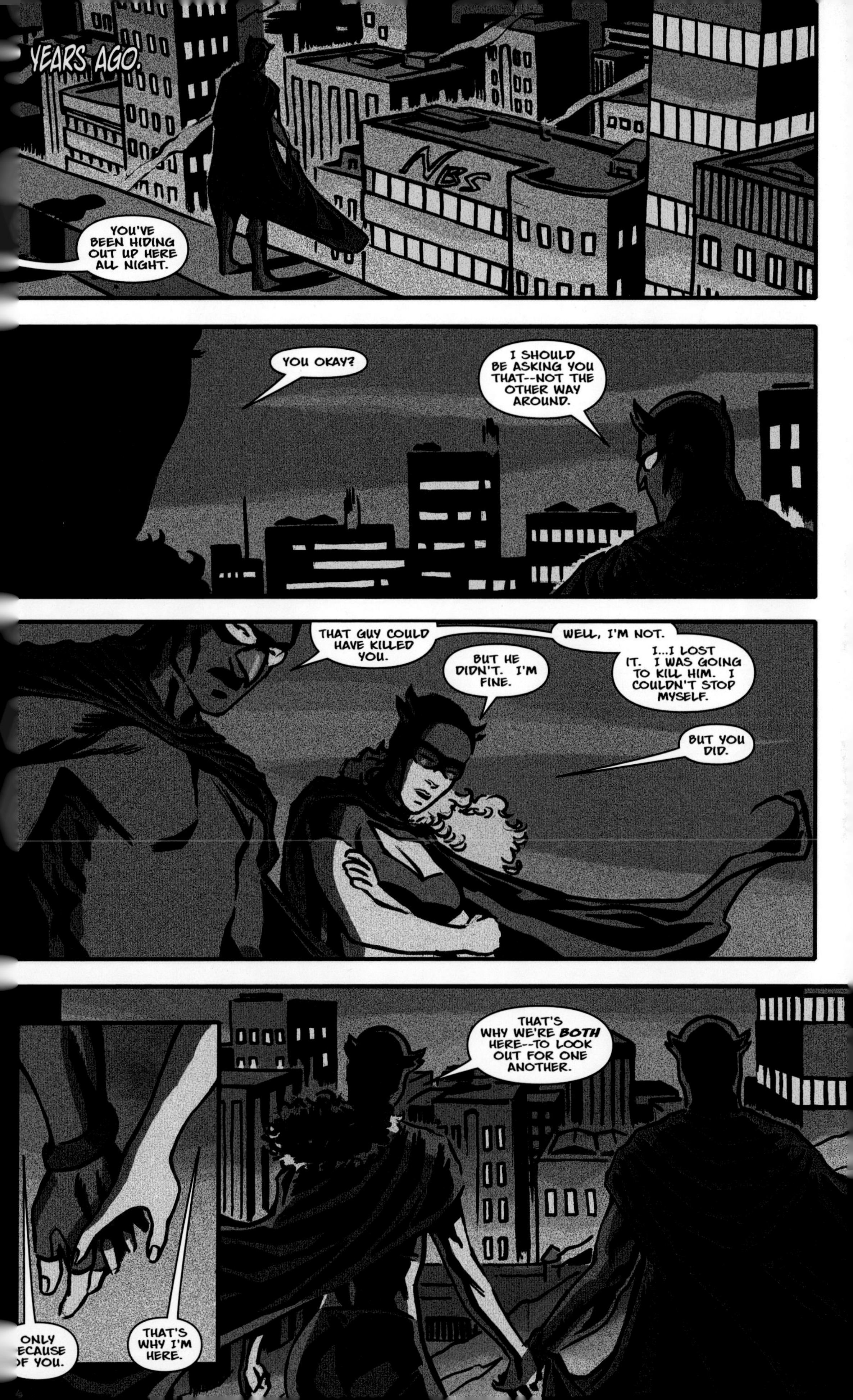
YEARS AGO.
YOU'VE BEEN HIDING OUT UP HERE ALL NIGHT.
YOU OKAY?
I SHOULD BE ASKING YOU THAT--NOT THE OTHER WAY AROUND.
THAT GUY COULD HAVE KILLED YOU.
BUT HE DIDN'T. I'M FINE.
WELL, I'M NOT.
I...I LOST IT. I WAS GOING TO KILL HIM. I COULDN'T STOP MYSELF.
BUT YOU DID.
THAT'S WHY WE'RE BOTH HERE--TO LOOK OUT FOR ONE ANOTHER.
ONLY ECAUSE OF YOU.
THAT'S WHY I'M HERE.

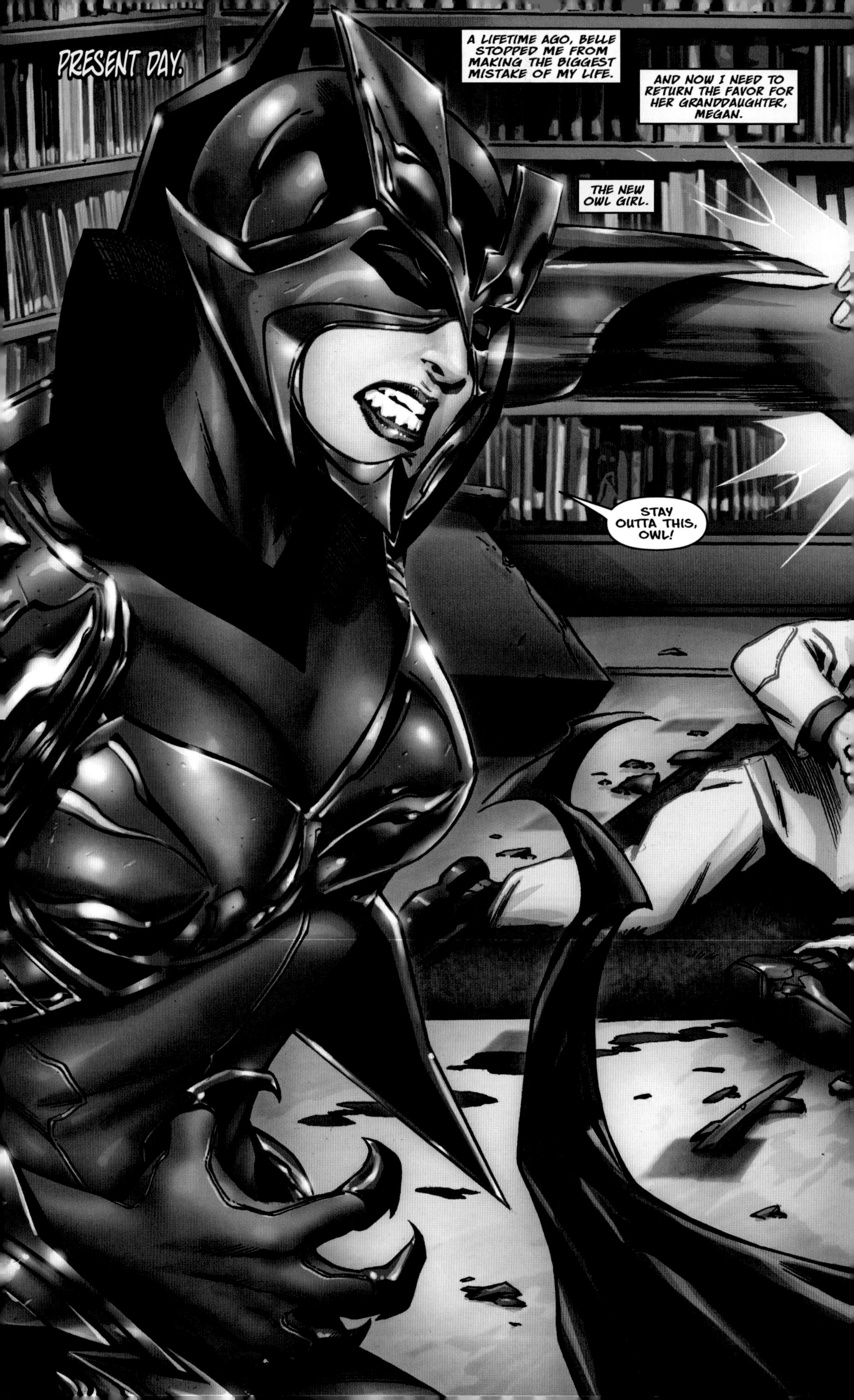
PRESENT DAY.
A LIFETIME AGO, BELLE STOPPED ME FROM MAKING THE BIGGEST MISTAKE OF MY LIFE.
AND NOW I NEED TO RETURN THE FAVOR FOR HER GRANDDAUGHTER, MEGAN.
THE NEW OWL GIRL.
STAY OUTTA THIS, OWL!

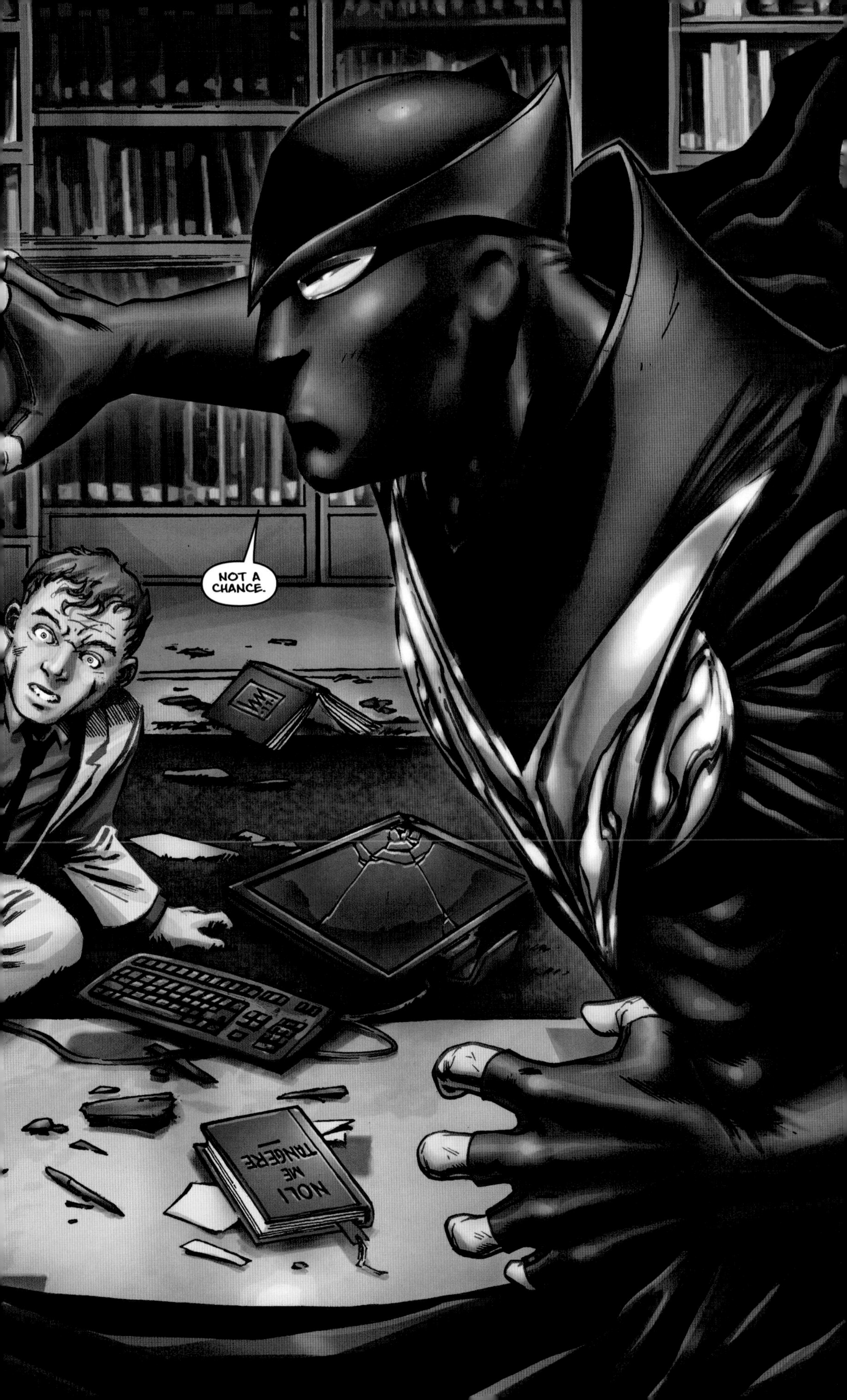

NOT A CHANCE.
NOLI ME TANGERE

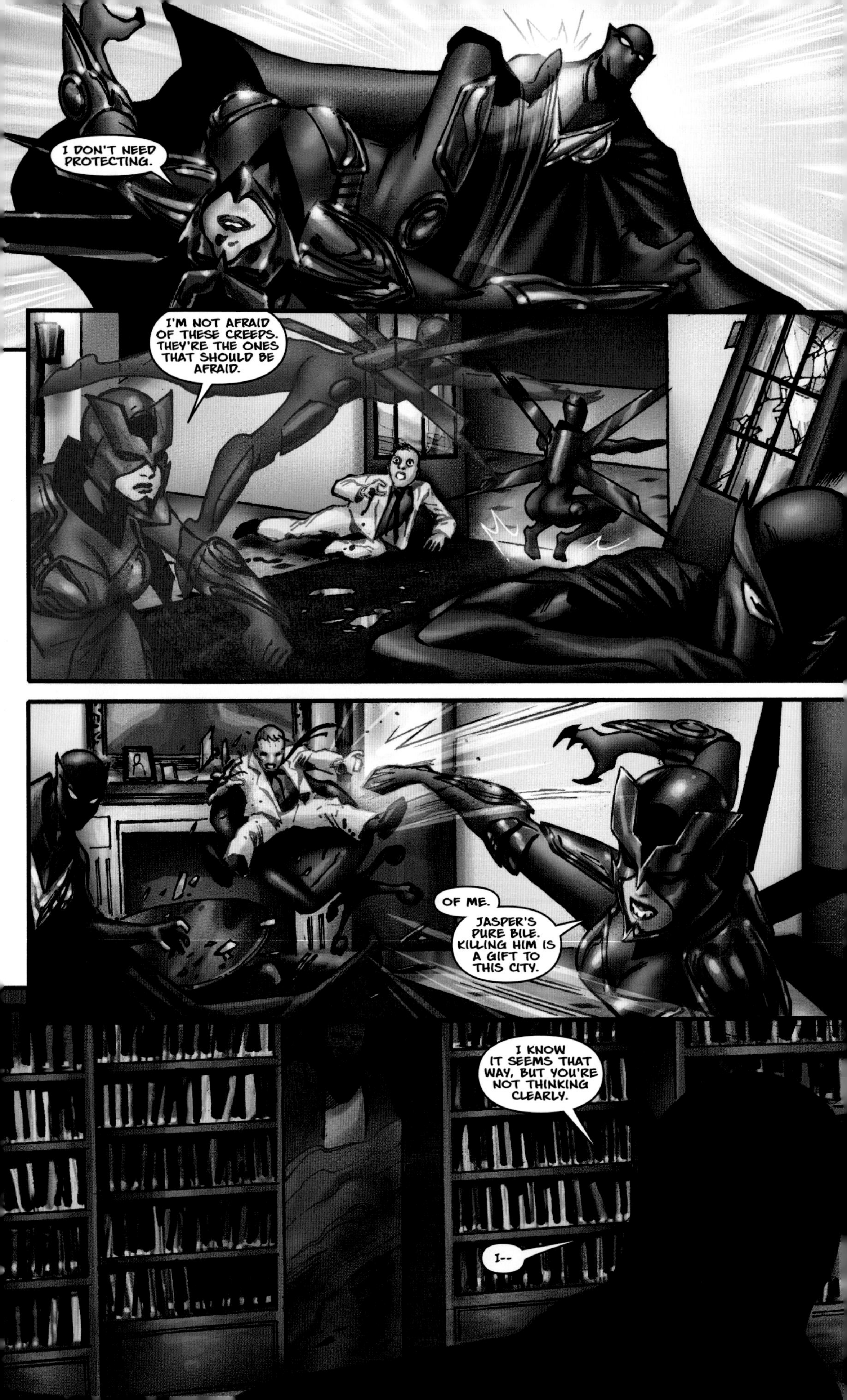
I DON'T NEED PROTECTING.
I'M NOT AFRAID OF THESE CREEPS. THEY'RE THE ONES THAT SHOULD BE AFRAID.
OF ME.
JASPER'S PURE BILE. KILLING HIM IS A GIFT TO THIS CITY.
I KNOW IT SEEMS THAT WAY, BUT YOU'RE NOT THINKING CLEARLY.
I--

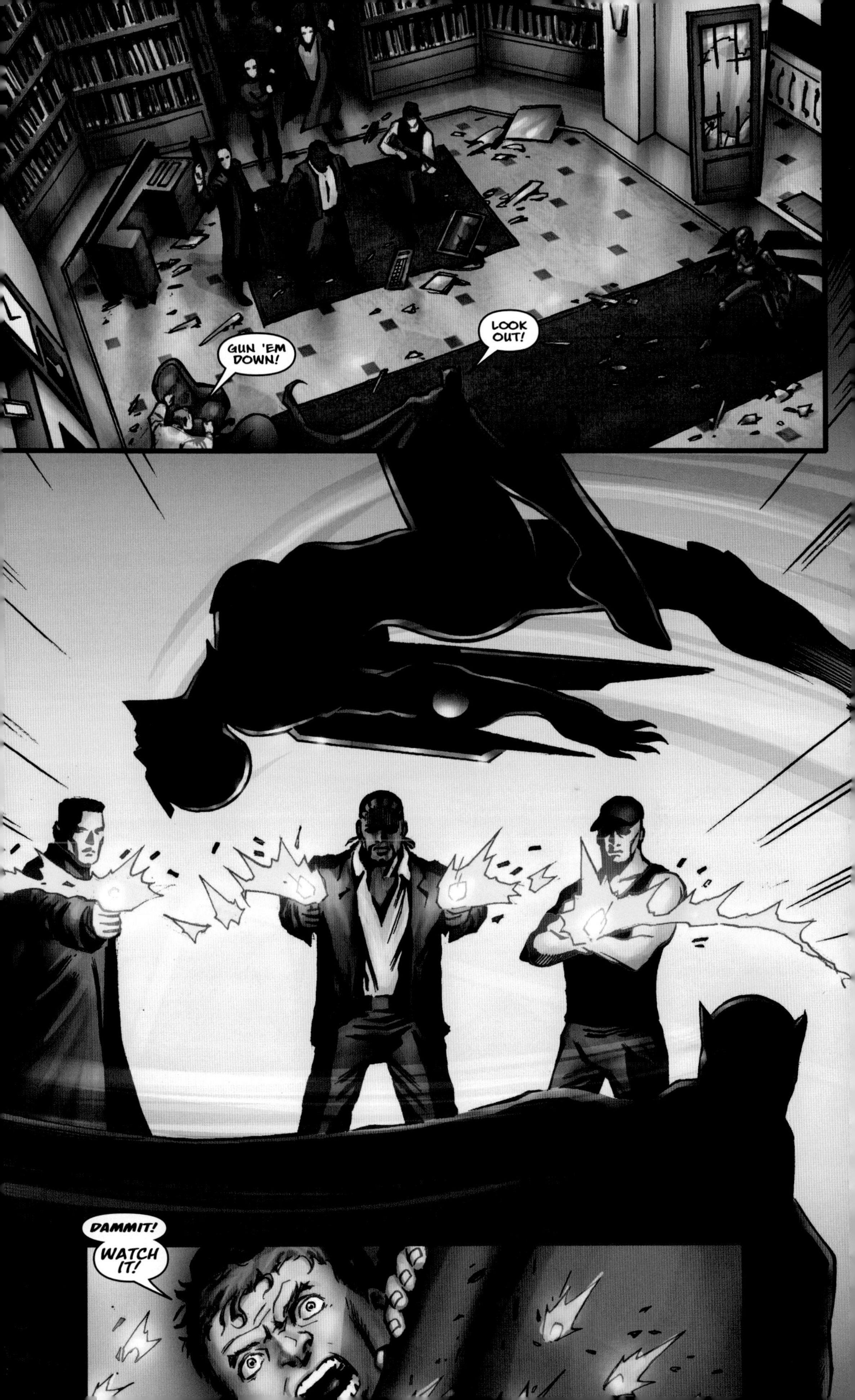
GUN 'EM DOWN!
LOOK OUT!
DAMMIT!
WATCH IT!

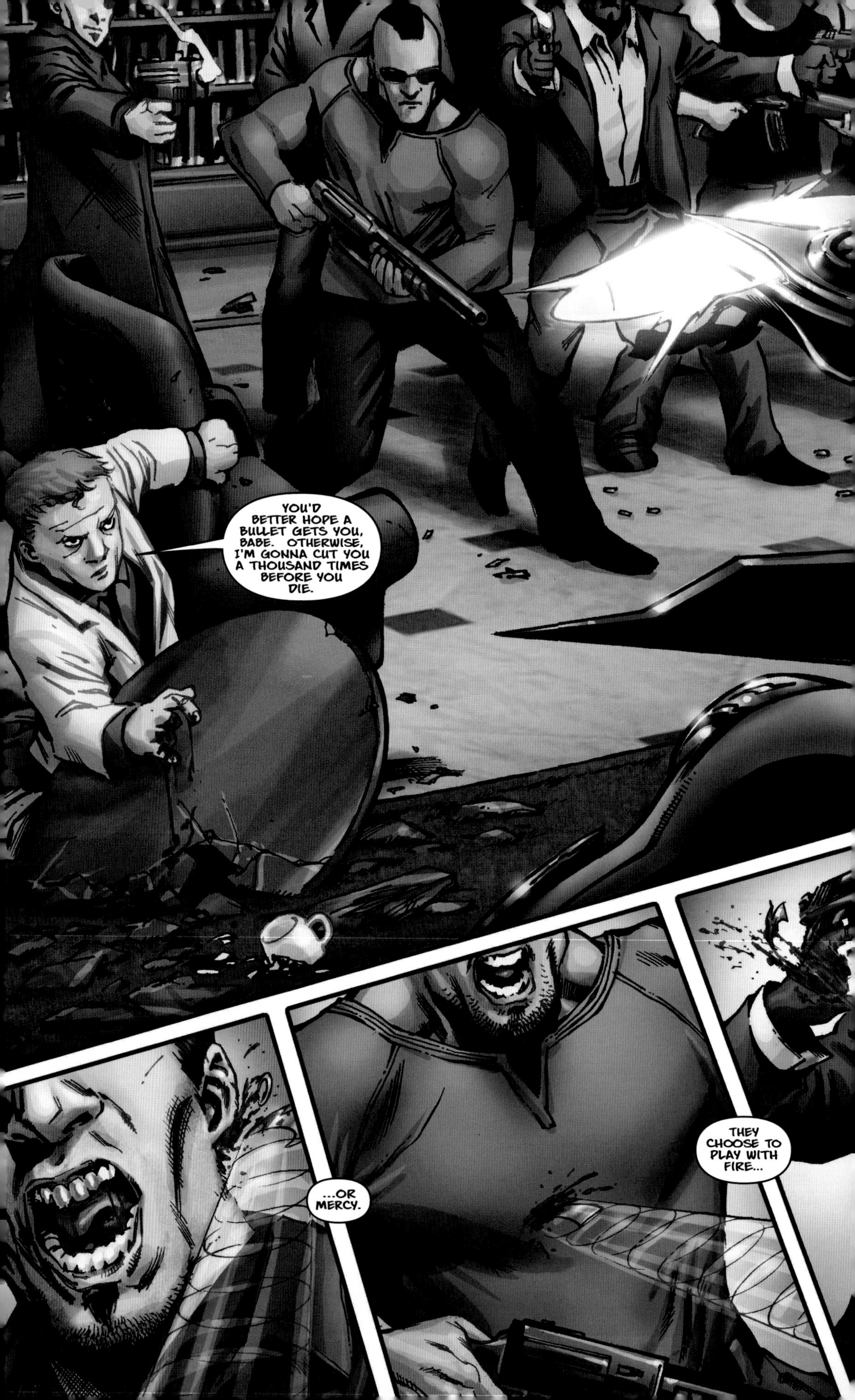
YOU'D BETTER HOPE A BULLET GETS YOU, BABE. OTHERWISE, I'M GONNA CUT YOU A THOUSAND TIMES BEFORE YOU DIE.
THEY CHOOSE TO PLAY WITH FIRE...
...OR MERCY.

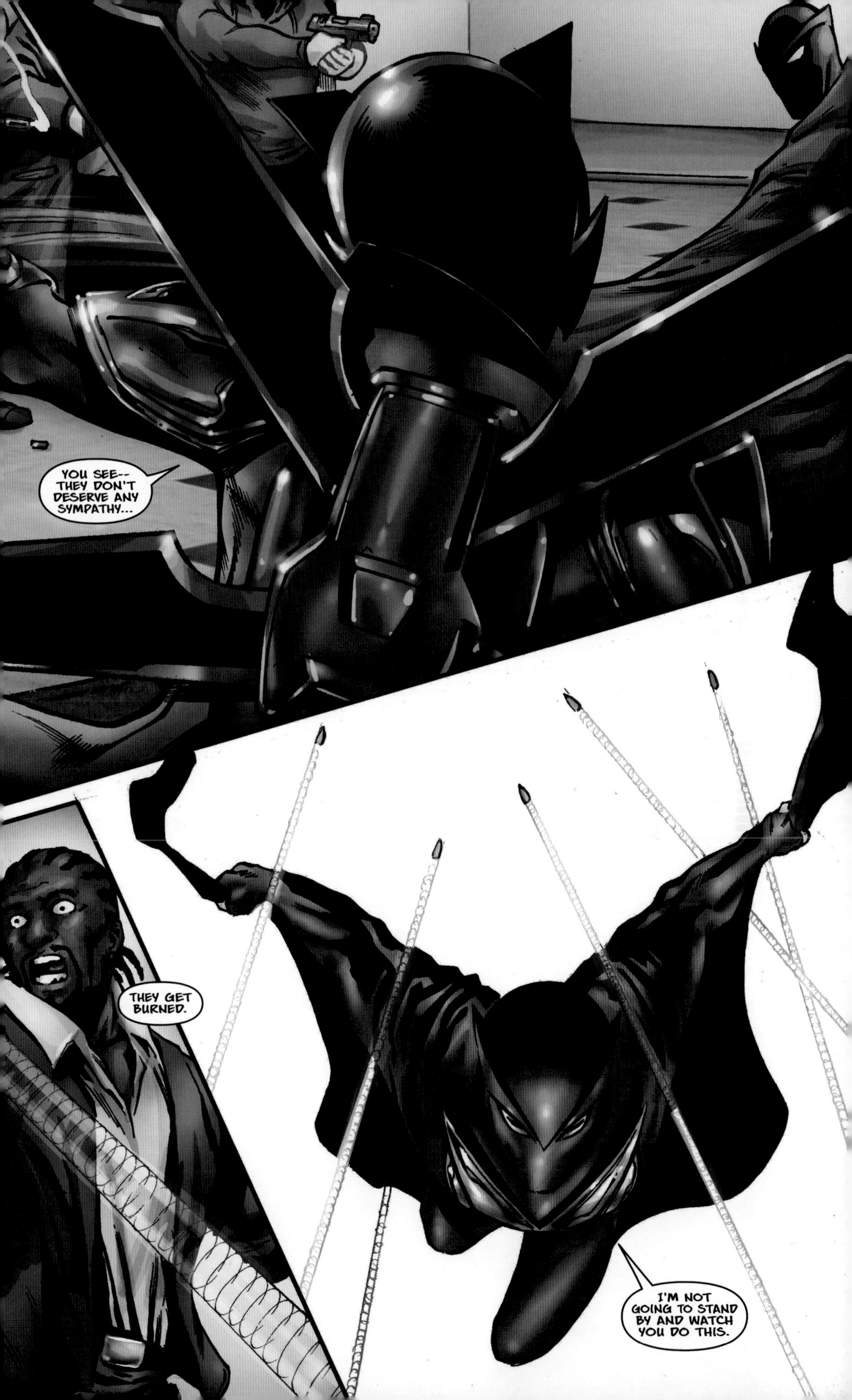
YOU SEE--
THEY DON'T DESERVE ANY SYMPATHY...
THEY GET BURNED.
I'M NOT GOING TO STAND BY AND WATCH YOU DO THIS.

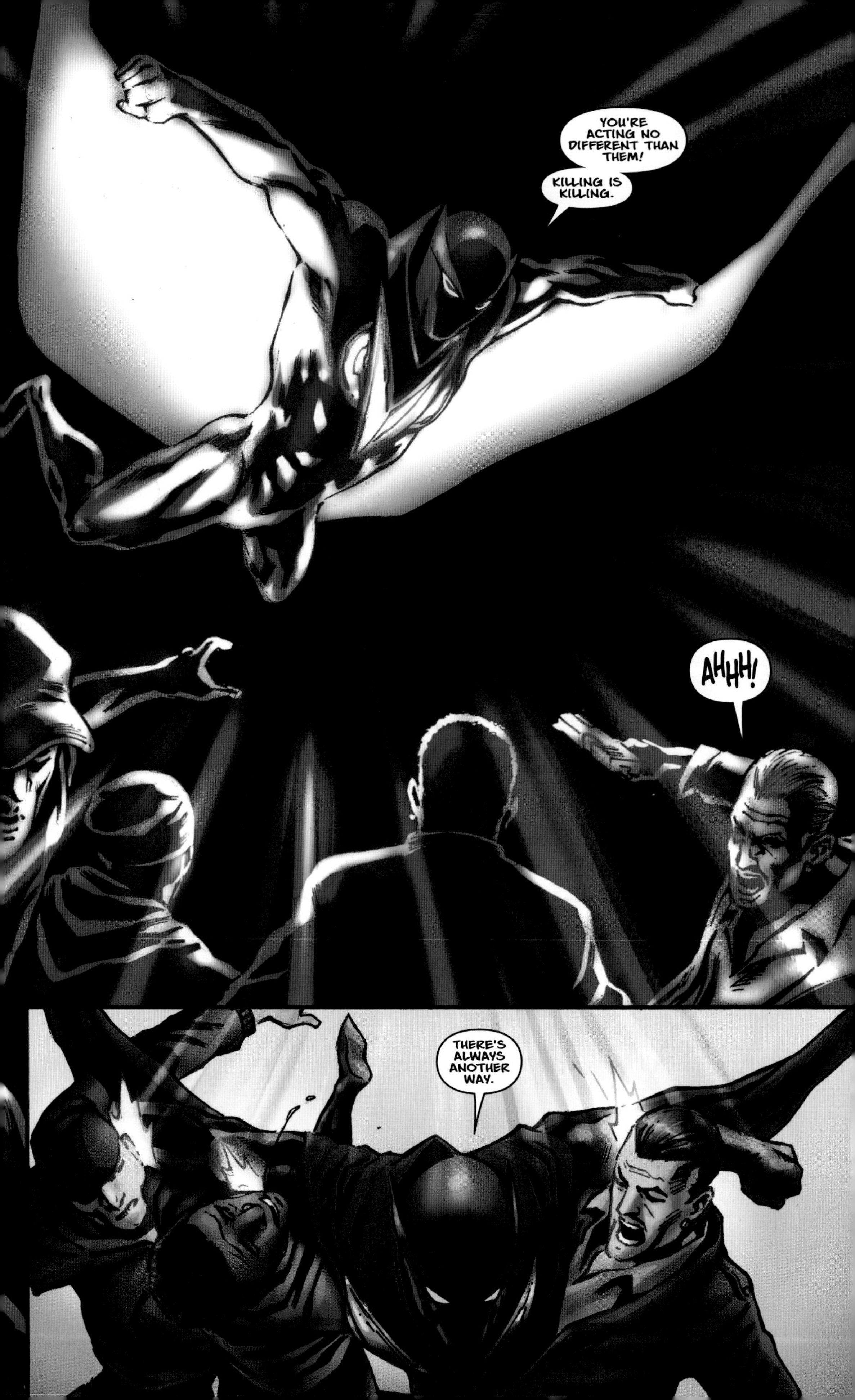
YOU'RE ACTING NO DIFFERENT THAN THEM!
KILLING IS KILLING.
AHHH!
THERE'S ALWAYS ANOTHER WAY.

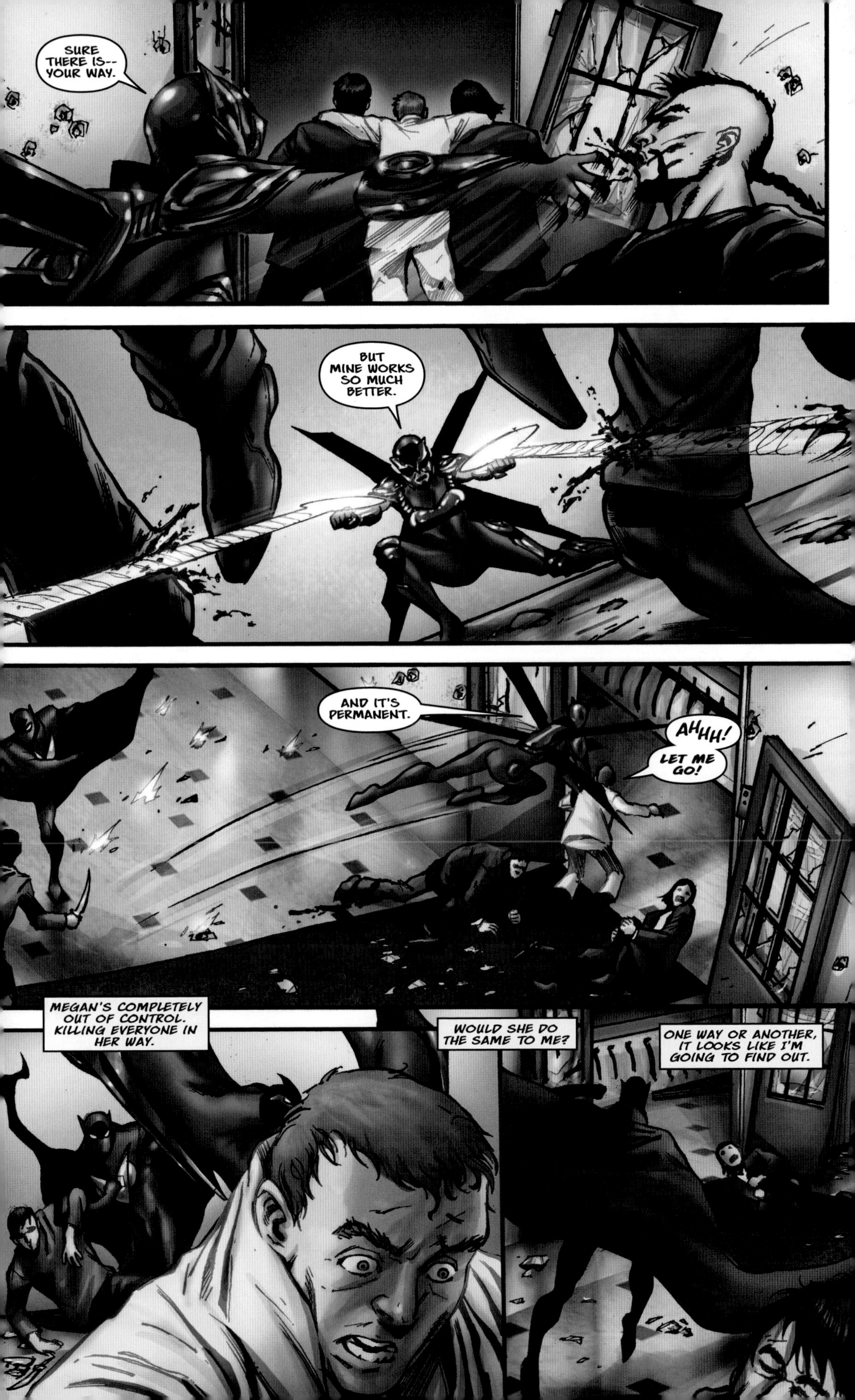
SURE THERE IS-- YOUR WAY.
BUT MINE WORKS SO MUCH BETTER.
AND IT'S PERMANENT.
AHHH!
LET ME GO!
MEGAN'S COMPLETELY OUT OF CONTROL. KILLING EVERYONE IN HER WAY.
WOULD SHE DO THE SAME TO ME?
ONE WAY OR ANOTHER, IT LOOKS LIKE I'M GOING TO FIND OUT.

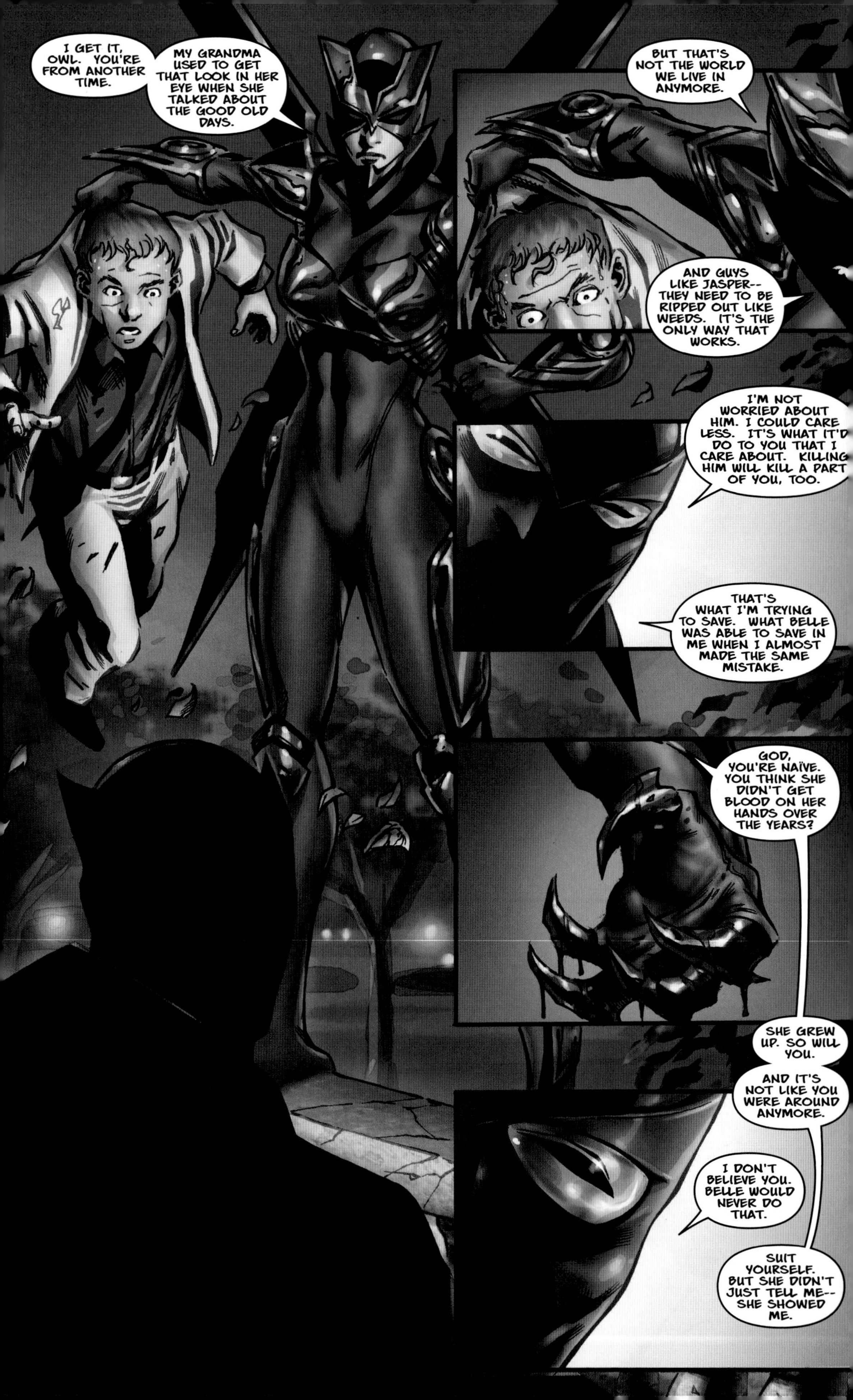

I GET IT, OWL. YOU'RE FROM ANOTHER TIME.
MY GRANDMA USED TO GET THAT LOOK IN HER EYE WHEN SHE TALKED ABOUT THE GOOD OLD DAYS.
BUT THAT'S NOT THE WORLD WE LIVE IN ANYMORE.
AND GUYS LIKE JASPER-- THEY NEED TO BE RIPPED OUT LIKE WEEDS. IT'S THE ONLY WAY THAT WORKS.
I'M NOT WORRIED ABOUT HIM. I COULD CARE LESS. IT'S WHAT IT'D DO TO YOU THAT I CARE ABOUT. KILLING HIM WILL KILL A PART OF YOU, TOO.
THAT'S WHAT I'M TRYING TO SAVE. WHAT BELLE WAS ABLE TO SAVE IN ME WHEN I ALMOST MADE THE SAME MISTAKE.
GOD, YOU'RE NAÏVE. YOU THINK SHE DIDN'T GET BLOOD ON HER HANDS OVER THE YEARS?
SHE GREW UP. SO WILL YOU.
AND IT'S NOT LIKE YOU WERE AROUND ANYMORE.
I DON'T BELIEVE YOU. BELLE WOULD NEVER DO THAT.
SUIT YOURSELF. BUT SHE DIDN'T JUST TELL ME-- SHE SHOWED ME.

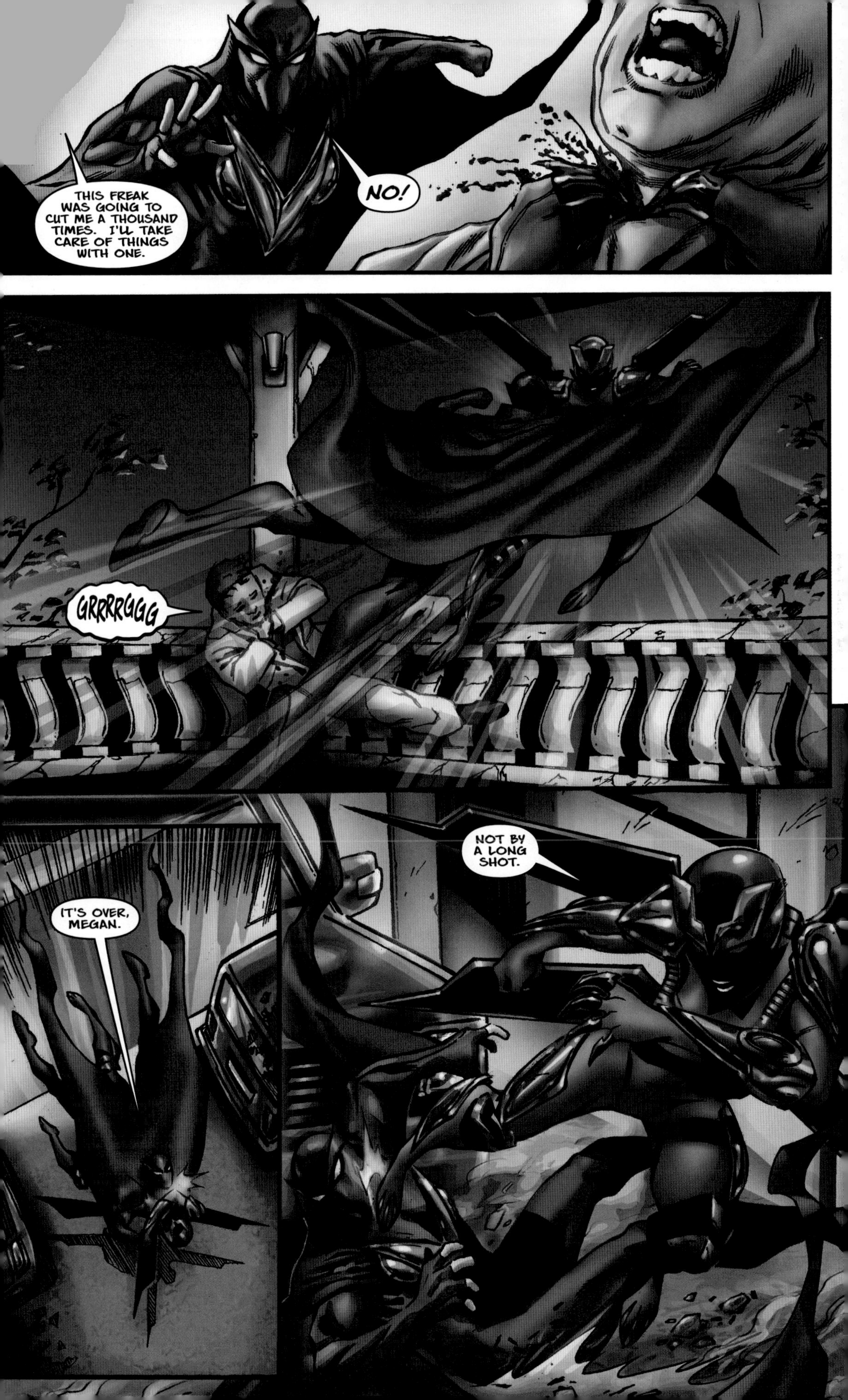
THIS FREAK WAS GOING TO CUT ME A THOUSAND TIMES. I'LL TAKE CARE OF THINGS WITH ONE.
NO!
GRRRRGGG
IT'S OVER, MEGAN.
NOT BY A LONG SHOT.

CAN'T REASON WITH HER ANYMORE. SHE'S TOO FAR GONE.
TIME TO TREAT HER LIKE ANY OTHER VILLAIN.
SORRY, BELLE.
NNNNN!
ABOUT TIME YOU TOOK THE KID'S GLOVES OFF.
BUT YOU LOST BEFORE WE EVEN STARTED, NICK.
BECAUSE I'LL GO THAT EXTRA MILE. AND YOU WON'T.
LET ME ASK YOU, DID YOU AND MY GRANDMA EVER WRESTLE AROUND?
DO YOU GO FOR THE ROUGH STUFF?

YOU MAY LOOK YOUNG, BUT YOU'RE JUST AN OLD MAN. OLD FASHIONED. AND OUT DATED.

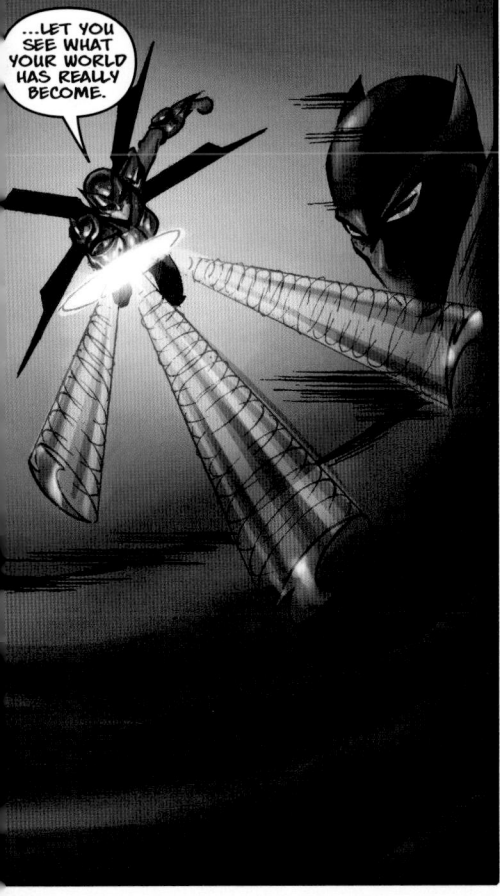

...LET YOU SEE WHAT YOUR WORLD HAS REALLY BECOME.

THIS AIN'T A FIGHT YOU CAN WIN WITHOUT GETTING YOUR HANDS DIRTY.

I DON'T CARE WHAT YOU SAY. BELLE WOULDN'T HAVE WANTED THIS FOR YOU.

SHE WAS BETTER THAN THAT. BUT CLEARLY, YOU'RE NOT. I SEE THAT NOW.

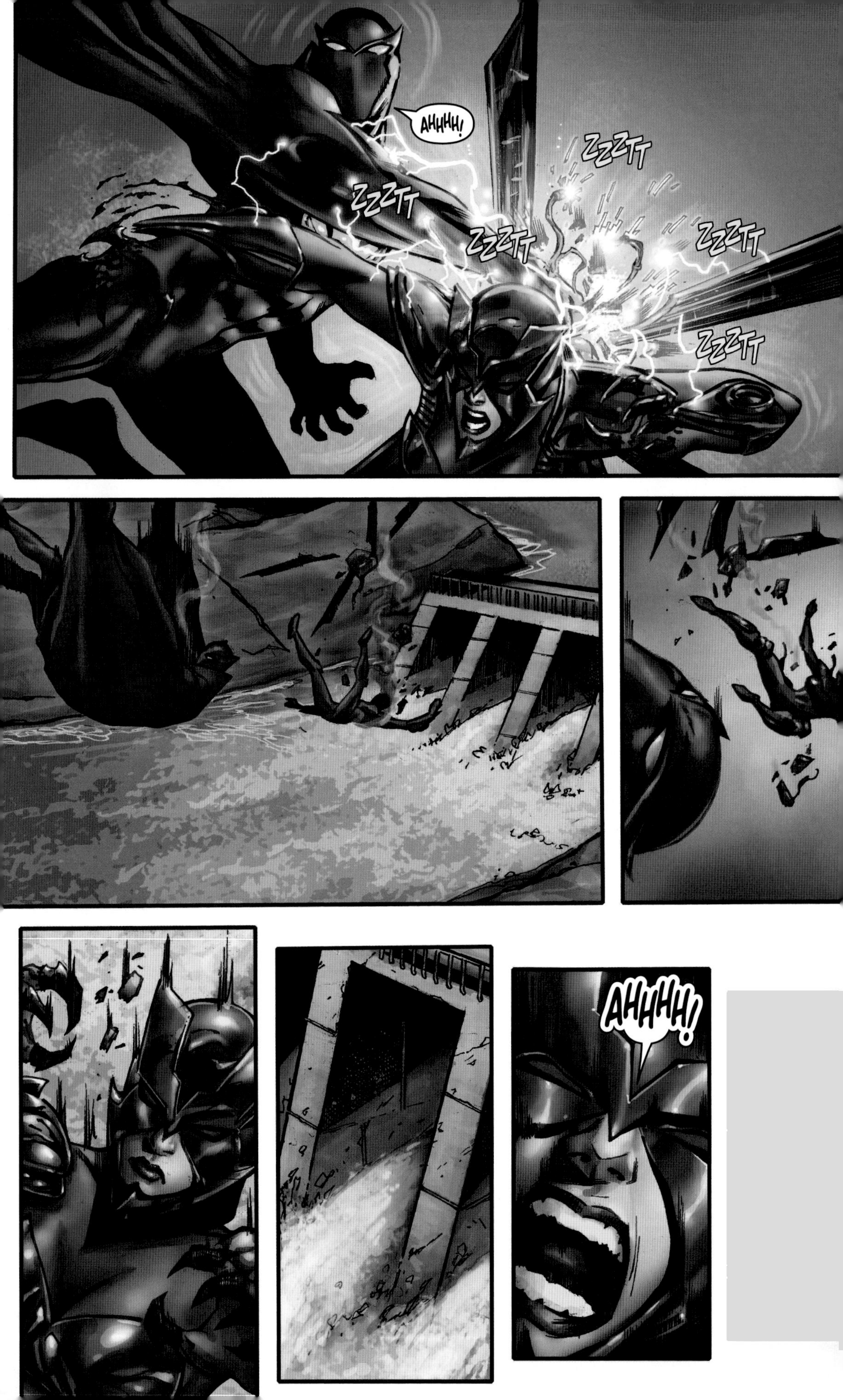
AHHHH!
ZZZTT
ZZZTT
ZZZTT
ZZZTT
ZZZTT
AHHHH!

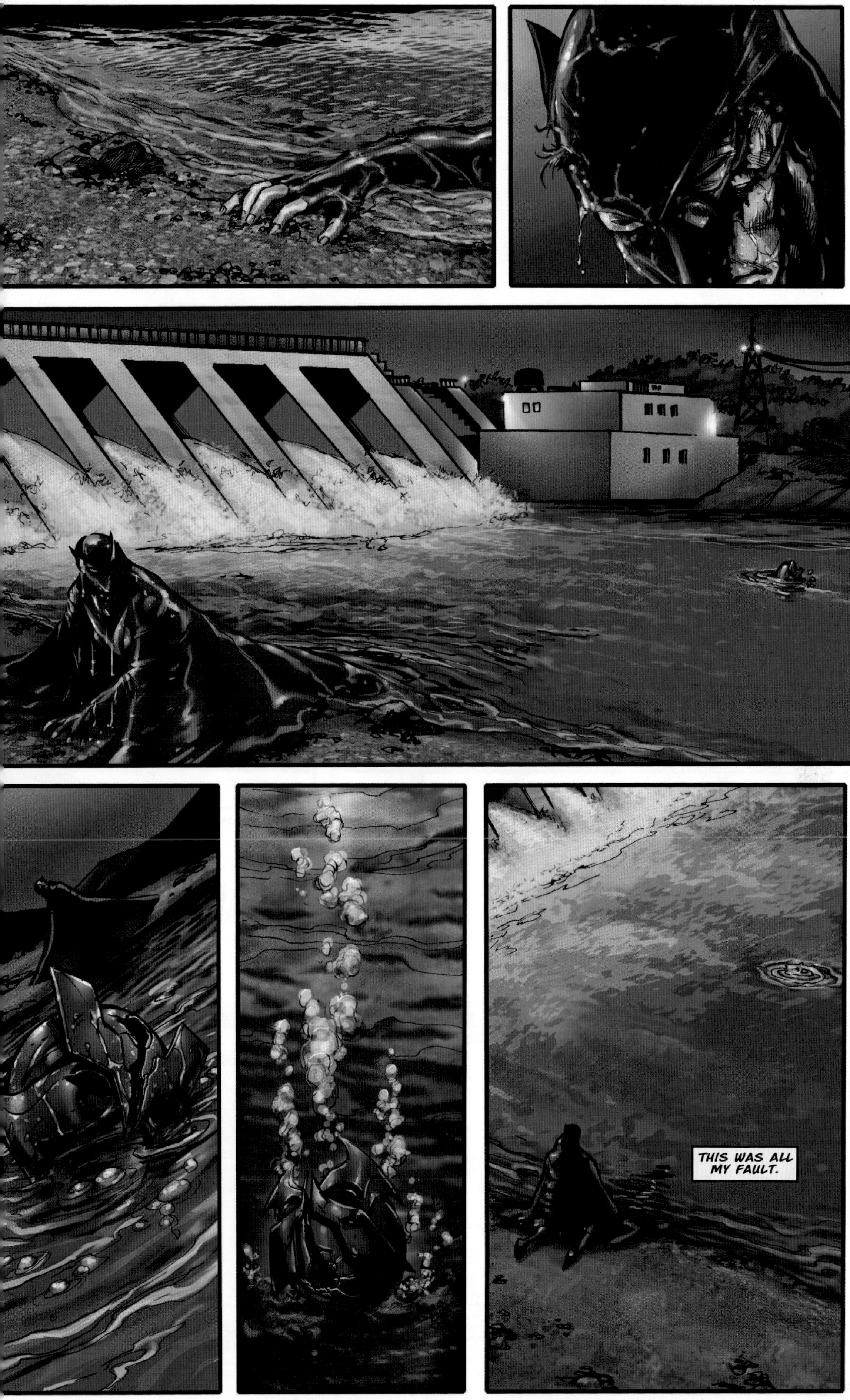
THIS WAS ALL MY FAULT.

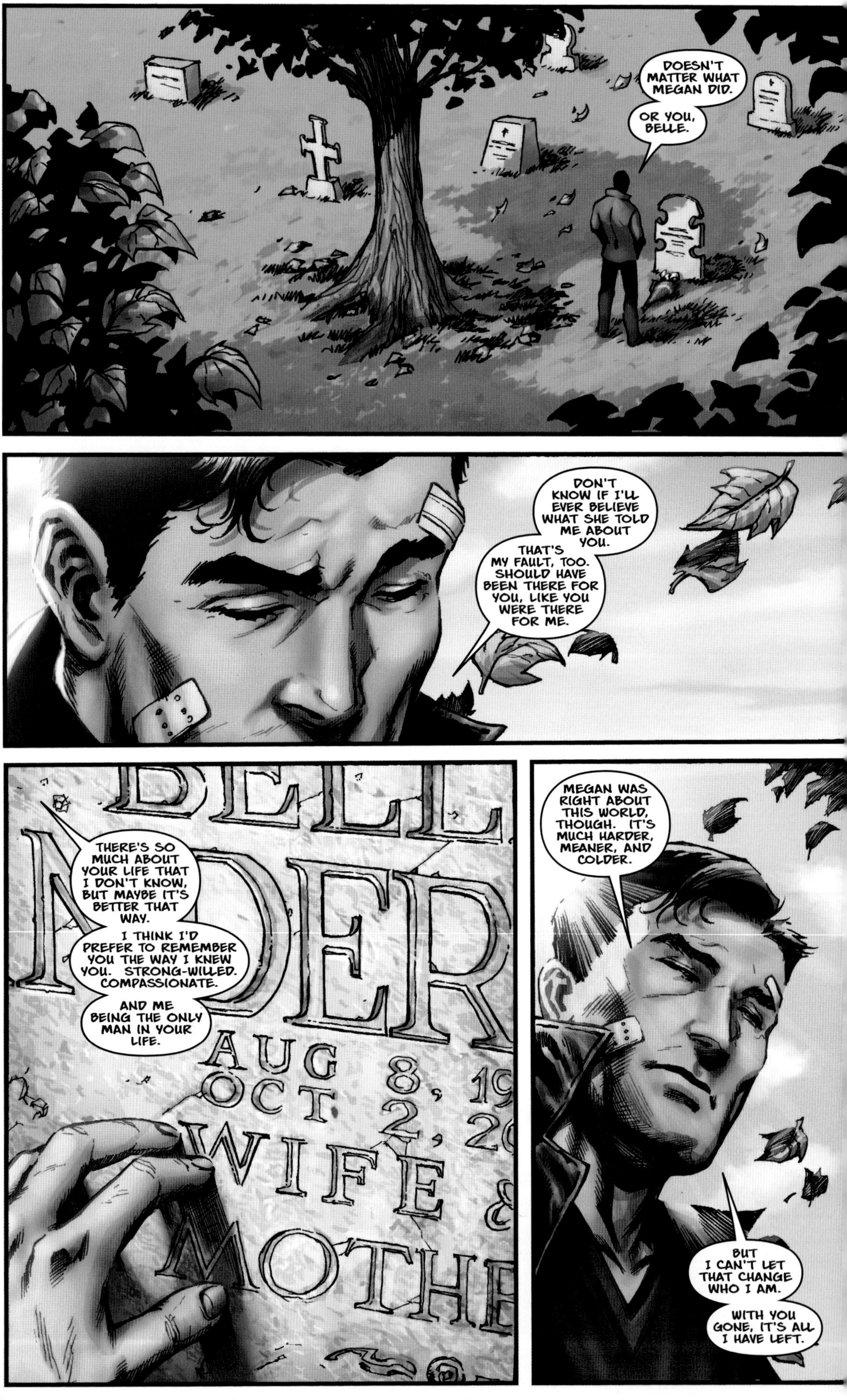

DOESN'T MATTER WHAT MEGAN DID.
OR YOU, BELLE.
DON'T KNOW IF I'LL EVER BELIEVE WHAT SHE TOLD ME ABOUT YOU.
THAT'S MY FAULT, TOO. SHOULD HAVE BEEN THERE FOR YOU, LIKE YOU WERE THERE FOR ME.
THERE'S SO MUCH ABOUT YOUR LIFE THAT I DON'T KNOW, BUT MAYBE IT'S BETTER THAT WAY.
I THINK I'D PREFER TO REMEMBER YOU THE WAY I KNEW YOU. STRONG-WILLED. COMPASSIONATE.
AND ME BEING THE ONLY MAN IN YOUR LIFE.
MEGAN WAS RIGHT ABOUT THIS WORLD, THOUGH. IT'S MUCH HARDER, MEANER, AND COLDER.
BUT I CAN'T LET THAT CHANGE WHO I AM.
WITH YOU GONE, IT'S ALL I HAVE LEFT.

LATER.

ENJOY THE PARTY, FELLAS. WITH JASPER AND OWL GIRL BOTH GONE, WE GOT SMOOTH SAILING.

GET READY FOR ANOTHER GOLDEN AGE HERE IN YORKTOWN.

HMMM. YOU LIKE THE BIG TOYS, EH?

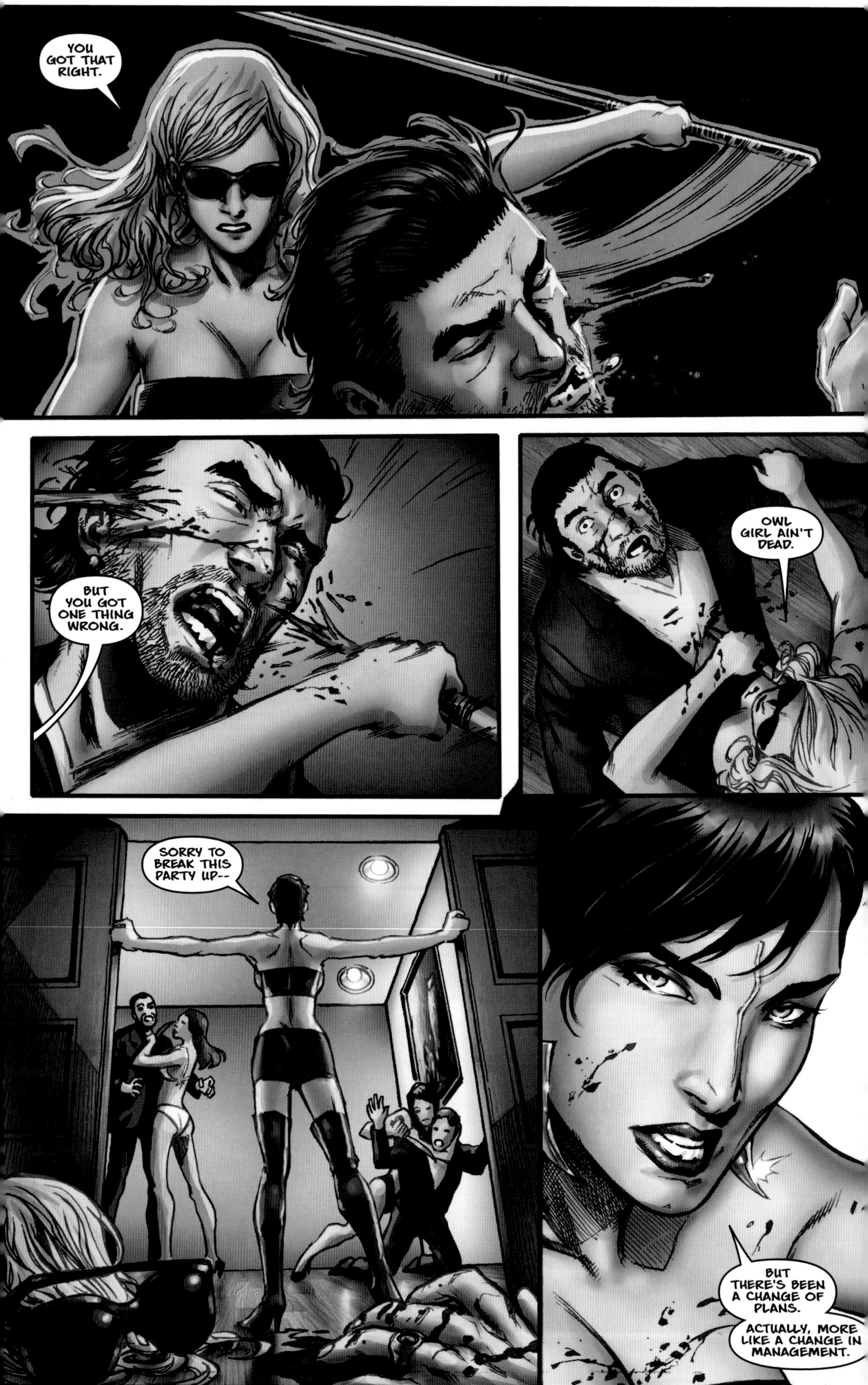
YOU GOT THAT RIGHT.
BUT YOU GOT ONE THING WRONG.
OWL GIRL AIN'T DEAD.
SORRY TO BREAK THIS PARTY UP--
BUT THERE'S BEEN A CHANGE OF PLANS.
ACTUALLY, MORE LIKE A CHANGE IN MANAGEMENT.

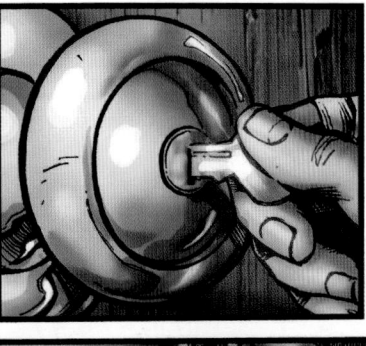

KKRRRTHHH

KKRRRTHHH

KKRRRTHHH

KKRRRTHHH

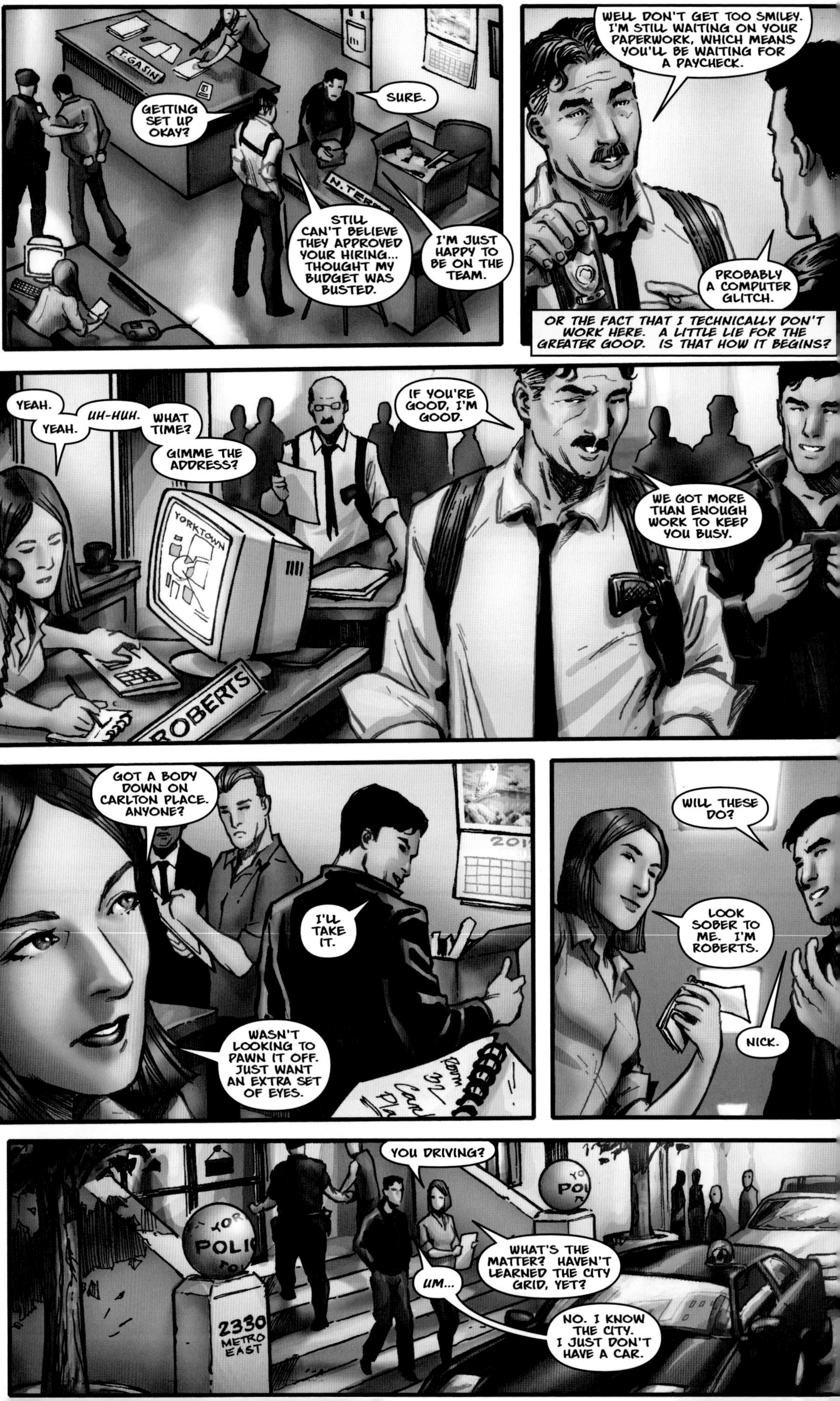
T.GASIN
GETTING SET UP OKAY?
SURE.
STILL CAN'T BELIEVE THEY APPROVED YOUR HIRING... THOUGHT MY BUDGET WAS BUSTED.
I'M JUST HAPPY TO BE ON THE TEAM.
WELL DON'T GET TOO SMILEY. I'M STILL WAITING ON YOUR PAPERWORK, WHICH MEANS YOU'LL BE WAITING FOR A PAYCHECK.
PROBABLY A COMPUTER GLITCH.
OR THE FACT THAT I TECHNICALLY DON'T WORK HERE. A LITTLE LIE FOR THE GREATER GOOD. IS THAT HOW IT BEGINS?
YEAH.
YEAH.
UH-HUH.
WHAT TIME?
GIMME THE ADDRESS?
IF YOU'RE GOOD, I'M GOOD.
WE GOT MORE THAN ENOUGH WORK TO KEEP YOU BUSY.
YORKTOWN
ROBERTS
GOT A BODY DOWN ON CARLTON PLACE. ANYONE?
I'LL TAKE IT.
WASN'T LOOKING TO PAWN IT OFF. JUST WANT AN EXTRA SET OF EYES.
WILL THESE DO?
LOOK SOBER TO ME. I'M ROBERTS.
NICK.
YOU DRIVING?
UM...
WHAT'S THE MATTER? HAVEN'T LEARNED THE CITY GRID, YET?
NO. I KNOW THE CITY. I JUST DON'T HAVE A CAR.
2330 METRO EAST

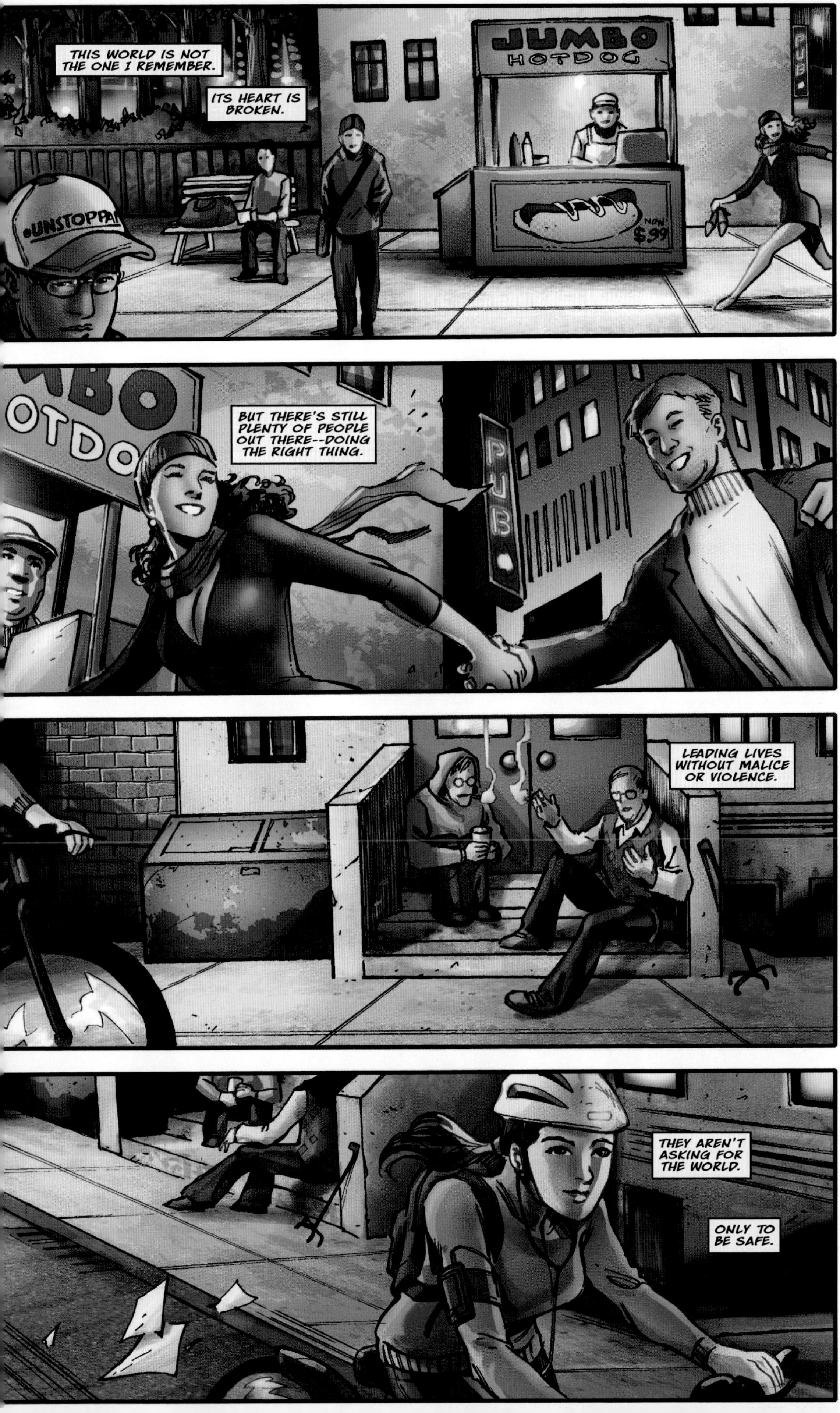
THIS WORLD IS NOT THE ONE I REMEMBER.
ITS HEART IS BROKEN.
JUMBO HOTDOG
PUB
#UNSTOPPA
NOW! $.99
BUT THERE'S STILL PLENTY OF PEOPLE OUT THERE--DOING THE RIGHT THING.
LEADING LIVES WITHOUT MALICE OR VIOLENCE.
THEY AREN'T ASKING FOR THE WORLD.
ONLY TO BE SAFE.

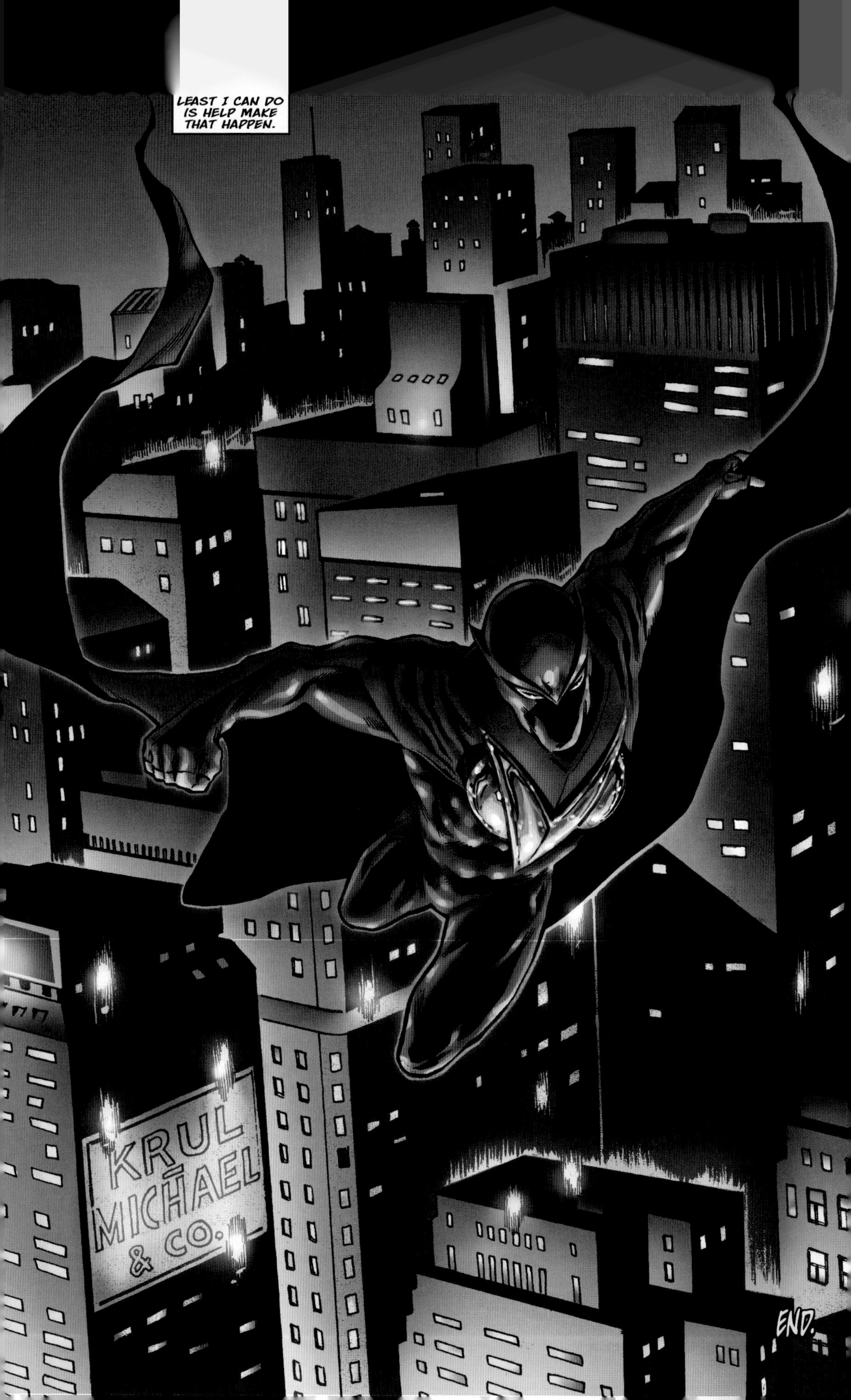
LEAST I CAN DO IS HELP MAKE THAT HAPPEN.
KRUL MICHAEL & CO.
END.

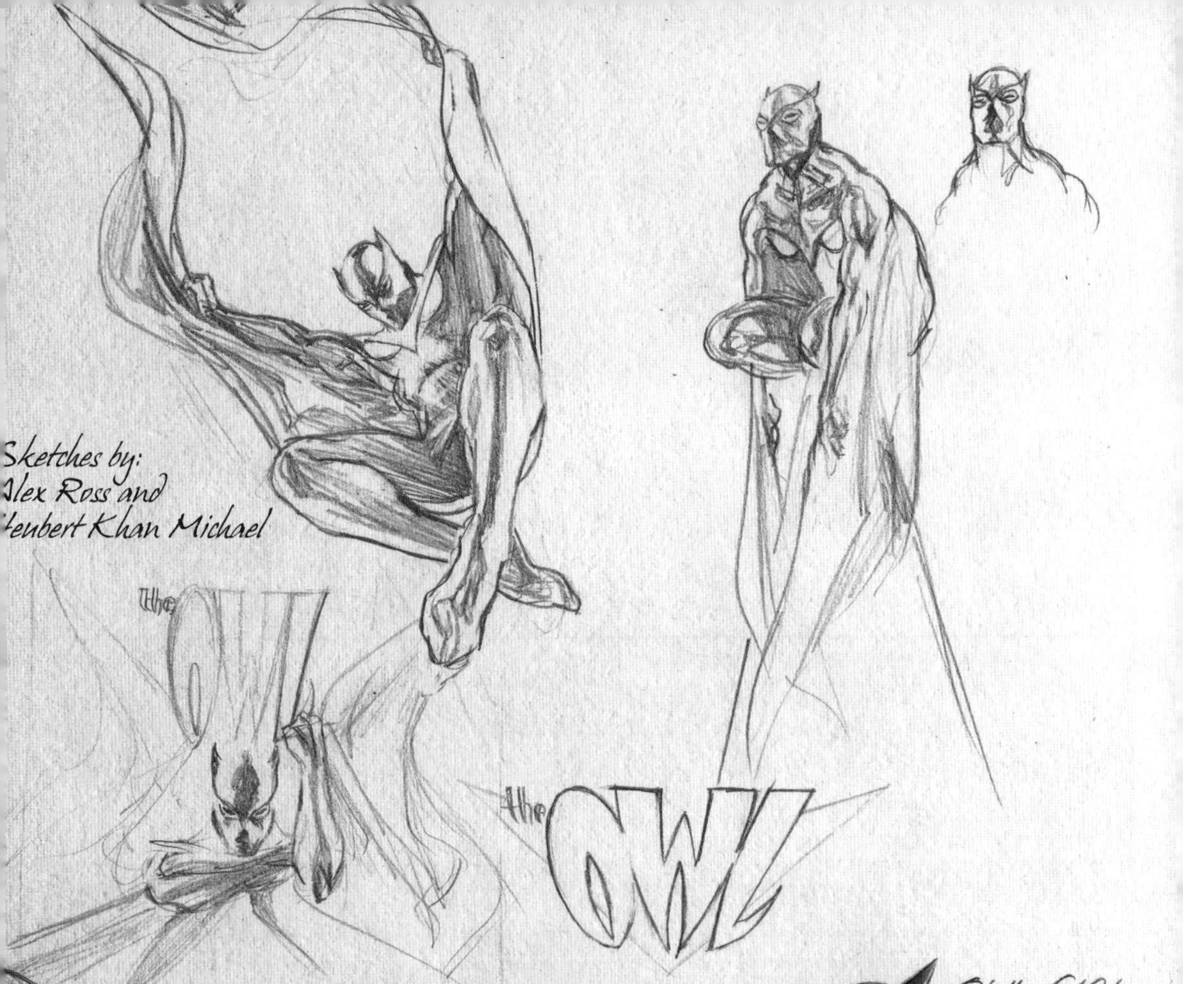
the OWL
the OWL

Sketches by:
Alex Ross and
Heubert Khan Michael

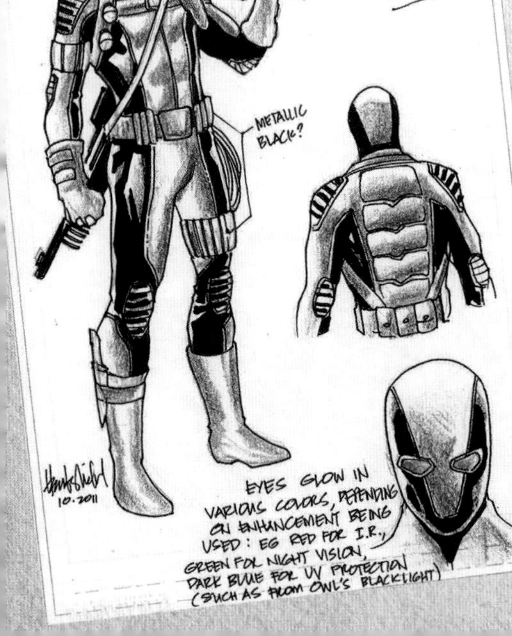
-ARMSTRONG-
ANY SUGGESTIONS ON COLORS?
—NO BRIGHT COLORS (FOR STEALTH)
—SUIT'S SIMILAR TO A MOTORCYCLE RACER'S: PROTECTS W/O AFFECTING MOBILITY
METALLIC BLACK?
10.2011
EYES GLOW IN VARIOUS COLORS, DEPENDING ON ENHANCEMENT BEING USED: EG RED FOR I.R., GREEN FOR NIGHT VISION, DARK BLUE FOR UV PROTECTION (SUCH AS FROM OWL'S BLACKLIGHT)

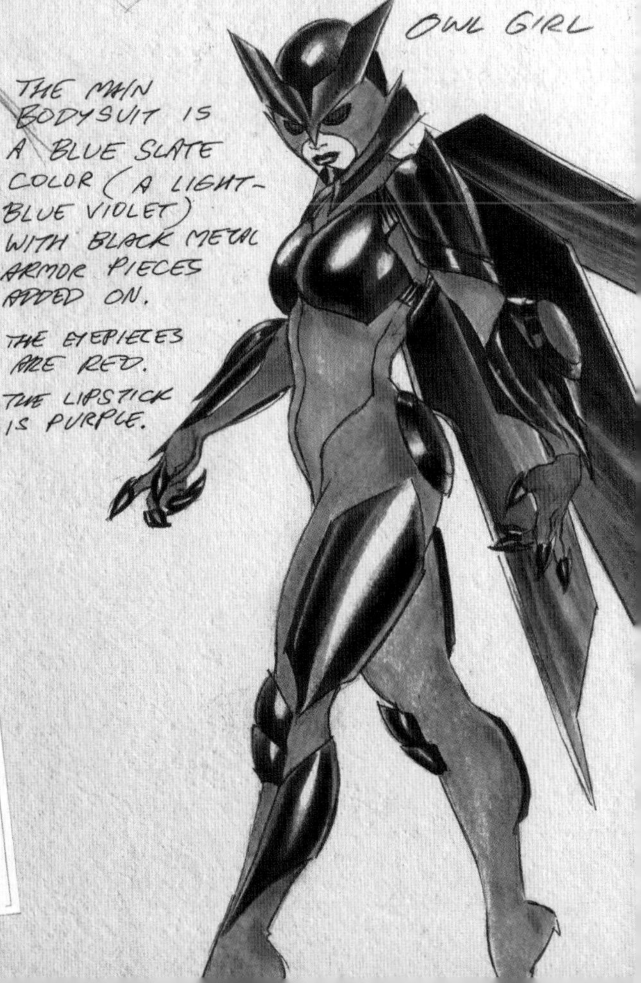
OWL GIRL
THE MAIN BODYSUIT IS A BLUE SLATE COLOR (A LIGHT-BLUE VIOLET) WITH BLACK METAL ARMOR PIECES ADDED ON.
THE EYEPIECES ARE RED.
THE LIPSTICK IS PURPLE.

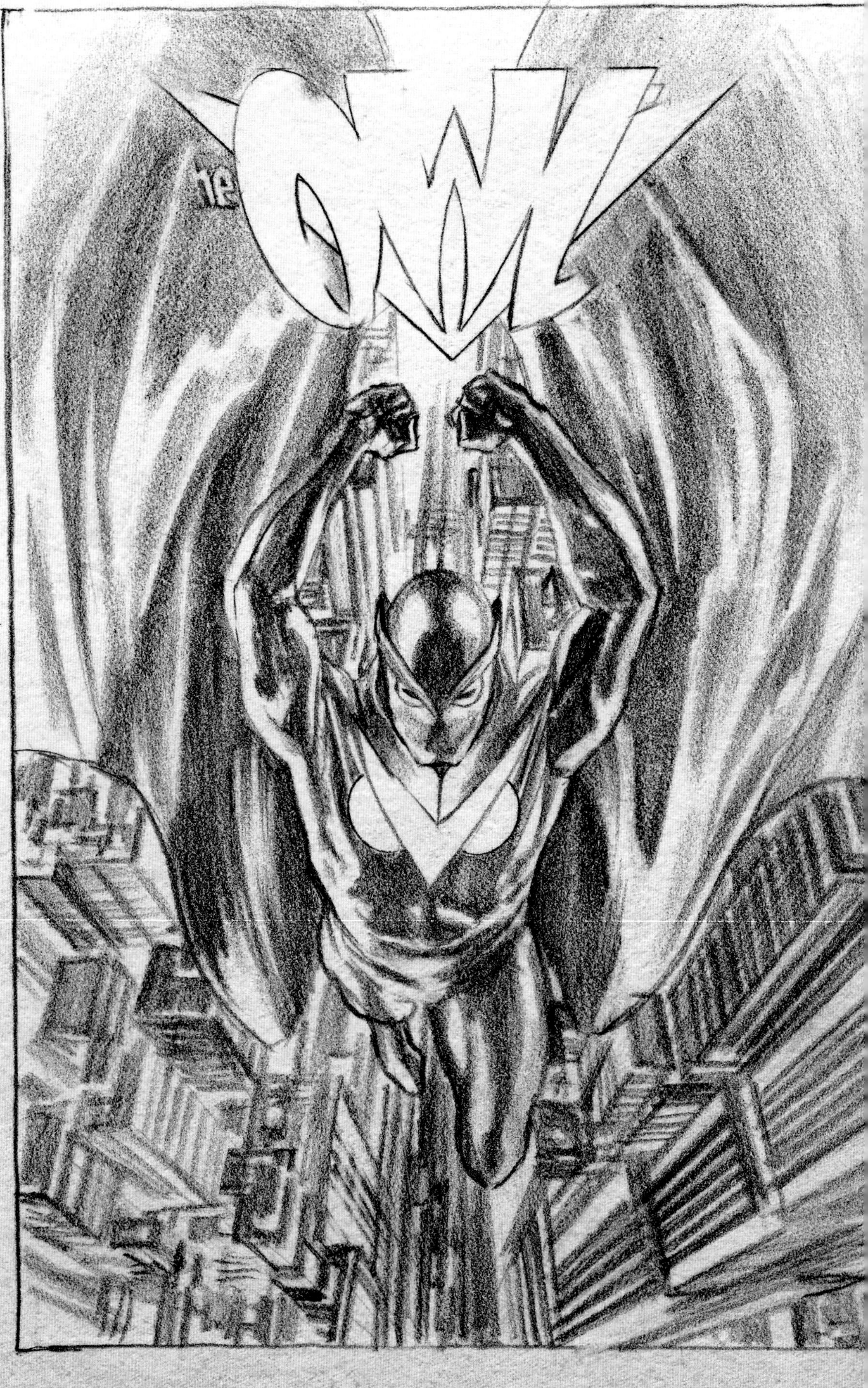
OWL

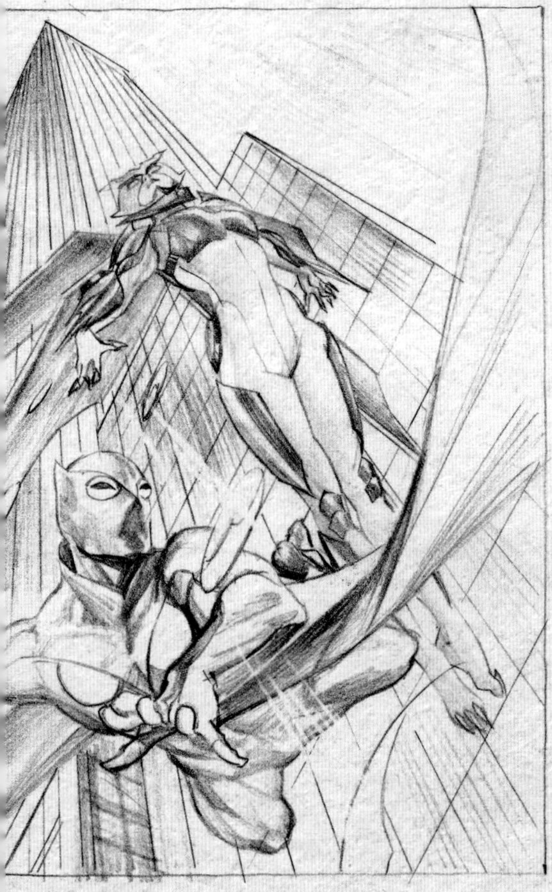

Alex Ross' original cover thumbnails

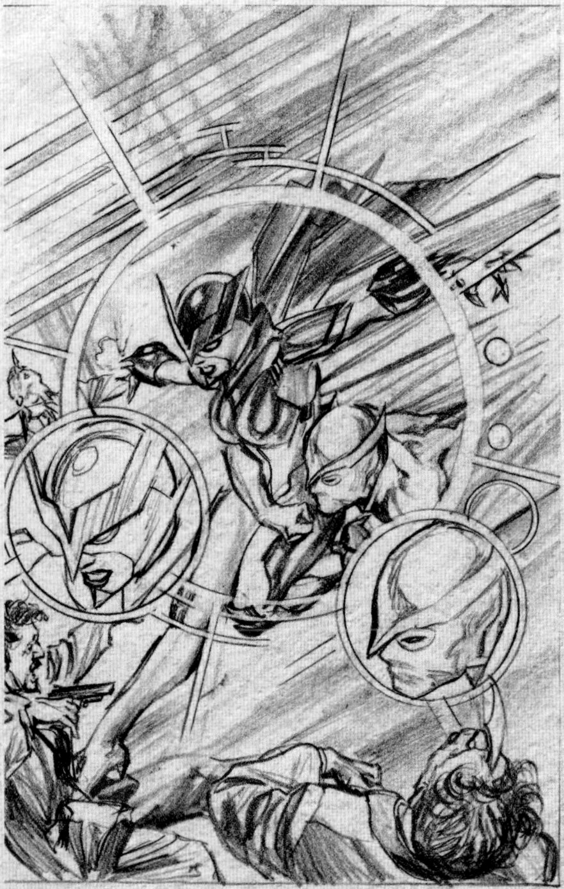

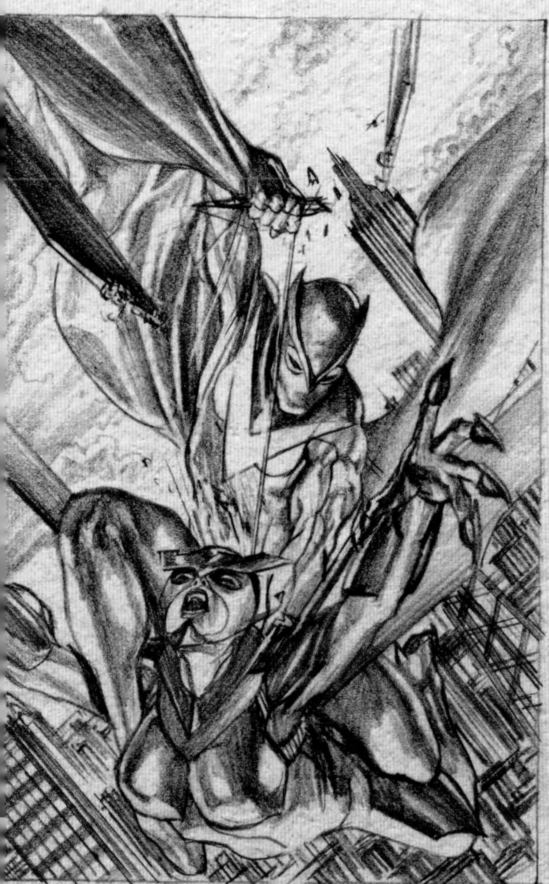

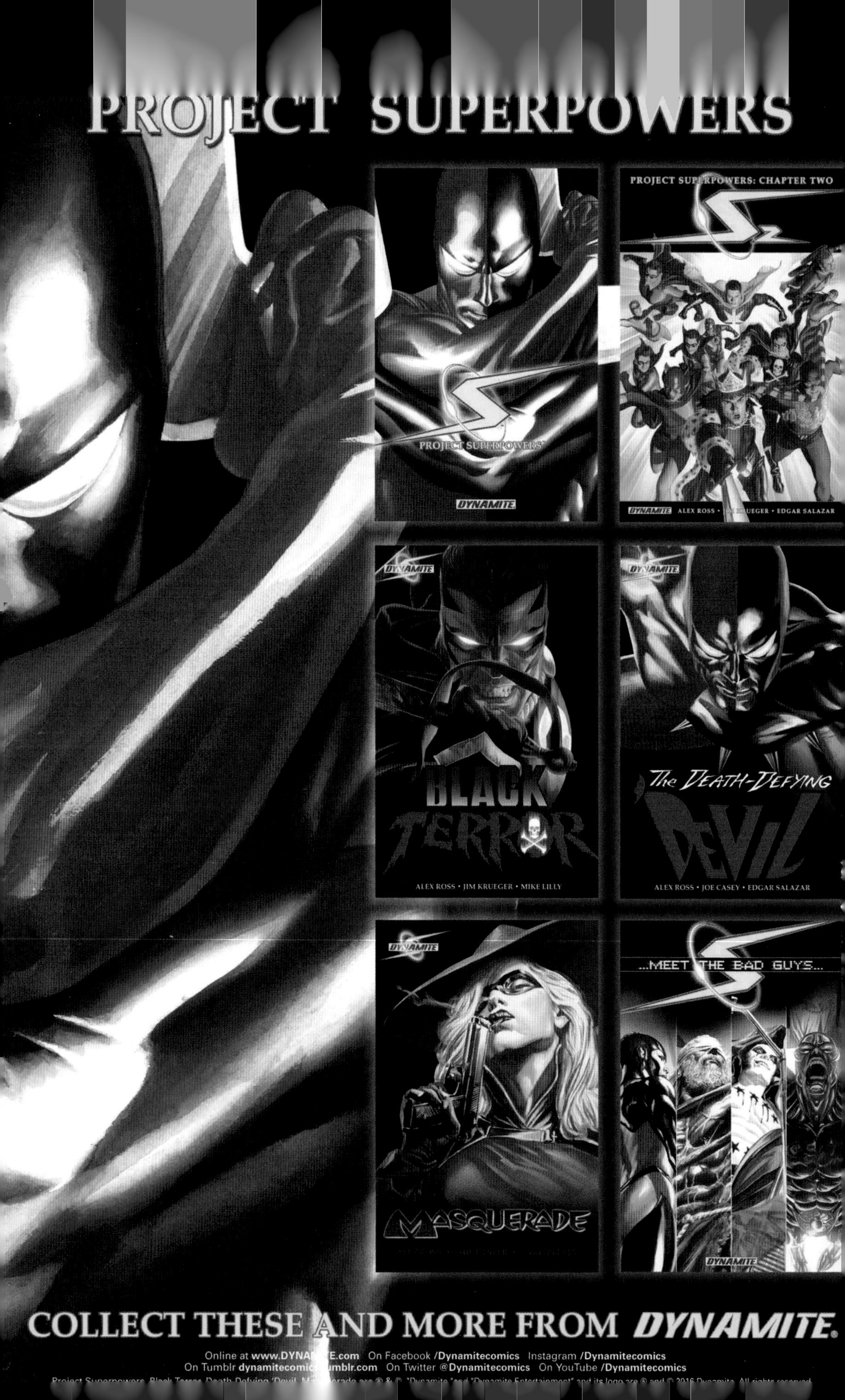

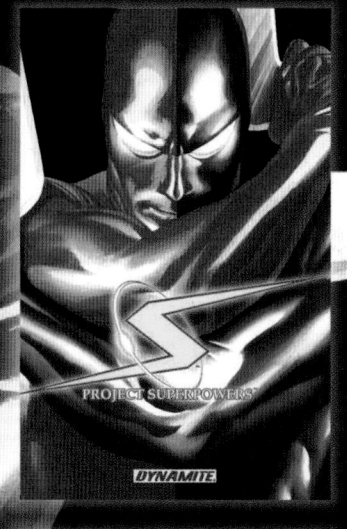

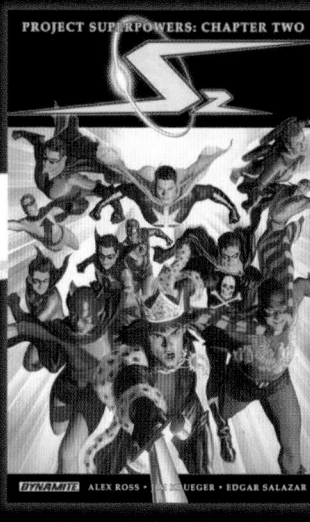

PROJECT SUPERPOWERS
PROJECT SUPERPOWERS
DYNAMITE
PROJECT SUPERPOWERS: CHAPTER TWO
DYNAMITE ALEX ROSS • EDGAR SALAZAR
DYNAMITE
BLACK TERROR
ALEX ROSS • JIM KRUEGER • MIKE LILLY
DYNAMITE
The DEATH-DEFYING DEVIL
ALEX ROSS • JOE CASEY • EDGAR SALAZAR
DYNAMITE
MASQUERADE
...MEET THE BAD GUYS...
DYNAMITE
COLLECT THESE AND MORE FROM DYNAMITE
Online at www.DYNAMITE.com On Facebook /Dynamitecomics Instagram /Dynamitecomics
On Tumblr dynamitecomics.tumblr.com On Twitter @Dynamitecomics On YouTube /Dynamitecomics

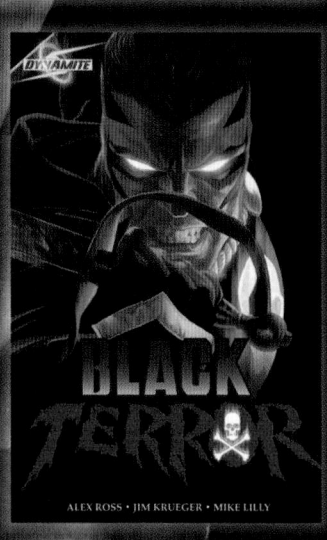

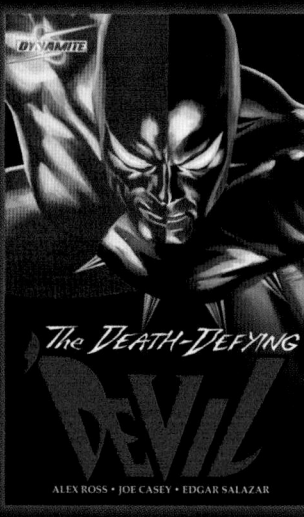

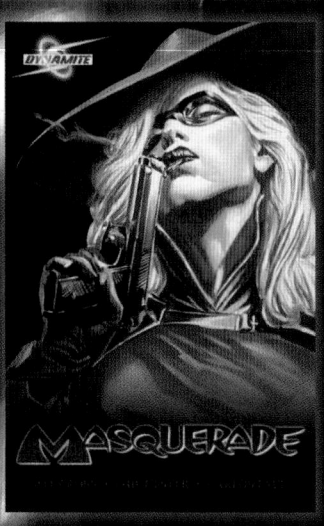

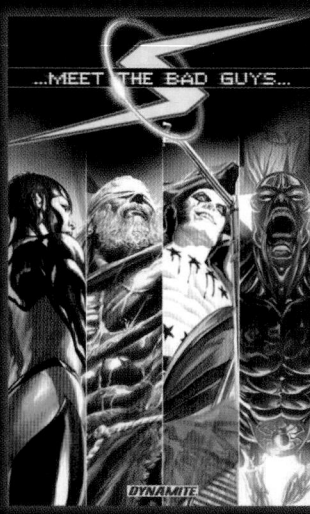